SECOND SIGHT

NOTES ON SOME MOVIES
1965–1970

BY

RICHARD SCHICKEL

SIMON AND SCHUSTER
NEW YORK

FIRST PRINTING

SBN 671–21122–6
Library of Congress Catalog Card Number: 71-179585
Designed by Irving Perkins
Manufactured in the United States of America
By American Book–Stratford Press, Inc., New York, N.Y.

These pieces owe much to many. Two managing editors, George Hunt and Ralph Graves, created and maintained the atmosphere of critical free speech that has made *Life* a joy for me over a half-decade. Dave Scherman, my immediate boss, Frank Kappler, his deputy, and Constance Tubbs, the review section's researcher, have, with their discreet but acute editorial pencils, saved me from uncounted sins of commission and omission. And, with their unfailing cheerfulness, support and friendship, they have made movie reviewing the one completely delightful experience of my writing career. Two copy editors, Joe Kastner and Chuck Elliott, have seen most of my stuff through the final stages of preparation for print, and they too have worked on it with uncommon sensitivity both for the prose itself and the writer's feelings. In getting the material ready for book publication I have, for the most part, let stand the changes these people suggested, because they have nearly always clarified my meanings. In a few instances I have restored cuts that were made solely—and regretfully—to fit the pieces into their original Procrustean bed. In a few other places I have corrected factual errors and recast sentences in the hope of making them read more gracefully. No changes in the substance of the pieces have been made.

They represent a little less than half the reviews I wrote for *Life* in the period specified by the subtitle. The effort has been to choose for reprinting those pieces that continue to have some significance for the writer—because they dealt with movies that have had a substantial influence on the medium or a lively afterlife in my mind or because, at least inferentially, they dealt with larger issues that still concern me. I have added postscripts to some of them in order to expand on some of the points there was not space or perspective to take up when the reviews first appeared. I am grateful to Michael Korda of Simon and Schuster for supplying a wisely objective view of the dangerously subjective process by which this book was put together. Finally, I hope no reader will be deluded into thinking that because I have acquiesced in—indeed, encouraged—the gathering together of these pieces in this more permanent form that I believe they constitute some sort of final word on the movies of this period. My hope is that this book will be seen as nothing more elaborate than one man's chronicle of some events that interested him during an interesting time in an interesting field of endeavor.

—R.S.

FOR
JILL
ERIKA
JESSICA
(*In order of
appearance*)

CONTENTS

9

INTRODUCTION

1.

"Why him?" the reader must surely ask himself sometimes. "Why me?" the critic (or reviewer, to employ the more modest term I prefer) even more surely asks himself late in certain insomniac evenings. A simple answer to these questions is available to the critic functioning in most arts. He who concerns himself with music or painting or literature has (if he's not a total charlatan) subjected himself to the disciplined acquisition of a large body of sometimes arcane information, the careful lifelong shaping and sharpening of a sophisticated and cosmopolitan taste, which process differentiates him from his readers and grants him the right to speak authoritatively. But movie critics? They deal with a distressingly familiar form, the history of which can still be encompassed by a single life span, a new and extremely accessible expressive form that fits few of the traditional definitions of art and which has, as yet, no great tradition to comfort and guide them. So far no one has succeeded in formally defining the body of information which, ideally, the would-be critic should encompass before setting up shop, no Ph.D. program he should try to survive before venturing his opinions. There are not even very many distinguished forebears against whose examples he can test himself and few enough contemporaries sufficiently wise to be worth engaging in a defining dialogue. As for scholarship, it is mostly a joke—

a thin mixture of pedantry and buff books and cheesy journalism, out of which one would be hard pressed to create a decent
reading list for a freshman survey course in movies. Worse,
from the point of view of the insecure critic, he keeps en-
countering mere children whose background in the art is nearly
as extensive as his own, whose opinions strike him as being
every bit as sensible as his own. And what of those older people
whose memories go back to the great days of the silent film and
who have ever since been quietly soaking up knowledge
through the effortless and pleasurable practice of regularly
attending movies and who can legitimately challenge him on
almost any aspect of his subject? Authority in almost every
other field is at least in part based on mystery, on the possession of information not generally available to the layman. But
the movies are the most public of phenomena—no mystery
about them. There are, indeed, plenty of people around who
are every bit as qualified as the critic is to comment on them in
public. Or so it seems.

Later I shall try to demonstrate that there is at least one
substantial difference between the professional and the amateur critic, but here at the beginning it seems fair to admit that
most of us who write regularly about the movies had our
professionalism foisted upon us, that very few of us consciously
and consistently sought to become what we are. Oh, the hope
was there flickering, but since there was no formal method of
preparing oneself to become a movie reviewer, and since there
was no clearly marked path toward attaining the goal and, until
recently, no very great interest among public or publishers for
much serious critical comment on film, no sensible man allowed the hope to take up much room in his thoughts. When I
look about me at a meeting of the National Society of Film
Critics, I see reformed (and unreformed) journalists, literary
critics, academics, editors, a sometime novelist or two, but
perhaps only one or two individuals who (I guess) long aspired
to membership in this peculiar trade association. With the vast
majority of us I suspect that the desire simply to write, to

express ourselves on some topic or other, preceded the desire to express ourselves specifically on movies.

So it was with me, anyway.

One would, of course, have to say that interest in the movies preceded, perhaps, even the ability to write a simple declarative sentence. By the time I was ten years old—long before I had any idea of becoming a writer when I grew up—they had become what they were to remain—one of the most enduring habits of my life. The movies—along with another enduring habit, that of reading almost anything my eye fell upon—were simply the most readily available stimuli for my imagination in the middle-class Middle Western suburb where I passed my pleasant, but not very venturesome, boyhood. I needed books and movies, used them really, because there were very few other cultural excitements readily and cheaply available in that snoozing time and place where most people did their best to keep the great world at a sanitary distance. They also offered, of course, escape from the intellectual, social and artistic constraints which the region placed on its offspring in those days. Why the movies appealed so strongly to me—except as another form of storytelling, an extension of the same mode as the boys' adventure books—I cannot say. Nor do I know why they continued to exert such a powerful hold on me as I grew older. Other interests—sports, photography, the theater, among others—came and went. But this one, along with reading, remained a constant that never wavered or diminished. I was, I think, lucky, for I have come to believe that serious involvement with any art must be established very early on as a habit, so that one in effect thinks about it unthinkingly, so that no act of will is required to engage with it.

Even so, such was the odor in which movies were then held that it never occurred to me that I might become, say, a movie maker or a movie critic. Such careers seemed impossibly exotic in the 1940s and 50s. Journalism, on the other hand, was not. One knew newspapermen, the craft was taught in the colleges (though I did not linger long in journalism school), it seemed a feasible—no, attractive—career. I had decided upon doing some form of it sometime before I enrolled in the University of Wisconsin. That institution, so nobly subversive of its region's collective conventional wisdom, taught me a little about political science and American history, and provided the opportunity to practice journalism on its quite professional student daily, where, among other things, I did a lot of smart-assed drama reviewing, which brought delegations from the Wisconsin Players to my office to plead for the impossible dream, "objective criticism." Moreover, the university supported a plethora of film series and societies, for one of which I wrote my first movie review—program notes for *Duck Soup*. I attended these showings of the classic films mainly to feed my still ravening habit and with no conscious thought of gaining a background for future critical practice. In the way of college students, however, the members of these groups were desperately, refreshingly serious about movies, and they did make an impression on me because they were the first people I'd ever met who discussed movies as art, not as "flicks." They conditioned me to at least entertain the possibility that "film" (as they insisted on calling it) was just as worthy of sober consideration as Senator Joseph McCarthy, the history of American labor, academic freedom and all the other matters that preoccupied my consciousness in those days.

And their example stayed with me. In the first few years in New York I allowed the Museum of Modern Art and the circuit of Greenwich Village revival houses to continue the unconsciously educative work that had begun in college. I still didn't see that this had much relevance to my journalistic career, and mostly, in a period that was sometimes lonely and frustrating, I continued to be grateful to the movies just for existing, for relieving the frustration and assuaging the loneliness for a few hours every now and then. By now I was working as a staff writer and editor on magazines and accepting all the outside work I could find. This mainly took the form of book reviewing, an activity I discovered I liked better than any other journalistic endeavor—perhaps because in the 1950s, before personal journalism was reinvented, book reviews were about the only place where the first person singular was actually encouraged. Later, when I became a free-lance writer, I continued reviewing books, and if someone had asked me in the early sixties where I thought (or hoped) I was going, I would have replied that I wanted to become a full-time writer of literary and social criticism. And, indeed, more and more of what I published in the magazines was of that character. Even the two books about movies that I had published by 1964 were, to my mind at least, social histories—not ventures in criticism or aesthetics. They represented pleasant methods of deploying the odd bits and pieces of information and opinion I had gathered in the sheltering darkness, but not, so far as I could then determine, turning points in my life. I still could not see that there was, despite a decade and more of growing interest in film-as-art among the middle-brow and intellectual communities, any wild desire among the publications for which I wrote (or might write) for movie reviewing by me or anyone else. There was "coverage" ranging from profiles of stars to consumer-guidance listings of current releases in the big-circulation magazines, there were occasional essays in the journals of opinion, but not much call for reviewers. Or so I believed.

Then, however, I did a long text piece (my first) for *Life* magazine, and about the time it was closing, Bayard Hooper, who had edited it, was put in charge of the magazine's new review section, and he rather casually asked me if I'd like to write about movies for him on an occasional basis. Just as casually, I agreed to try and in the spring and summer of that year did three reviews for him. Then I went away on vacation and didn't hear from anyone at *Life* until the fall. By that time Bayard had moved on to another assignment and had left his address book with Dave Scherman, who has remained the section's editor ever since. Dave called me up, asked me to review a novel and when that turned out all right, he, too, inquired if I'd like to do a movie now and then. "Why not," I said, and through the spring and summer of 1965 I was one of about a half-dozen people he regularly called on to handle this chore. The work was congenial, Dave was even more so, but I still couldn't imagine movies becoming the central metaphor of my writing. The pieces were nice and short and required neither interviewing nor reading to complete and so provided a pleasant change from the sort of reportorial and essayistic work I was used to doing. I was glad to do them and not displeased with the results and that was that. Then, in August 1965, I received a fan letter from Helen Deutsch, the screenwriter, in which she said that she liked my work better than that of the other reviewers and suggested I talk *Life* into letting me do the reviews on a more regular basis. I sent her note along to Dave, adding that I thought she had a sound idea here. He took the notion to Ralph Graves, now *Life*'s managing editor, but then the assistant M.E. with executive responsibility for the reviews as well as other sections. They had apparently already decided —for a variety of reasons, not the least of which were convenience and the establishment of continuity of viewpoint—that someone ought to undertake to do most of the movie reviews, and since I seemed to be available, interested and more or less qualified, they offered me my first contract in the fall of that year, and I have been *Life*'s principal movie critic ever since and, from 1968 on, its only one. Thus, the rather accidental making of a critic, 1933–1965.

2.

To say that in the beginning I was something of an innocent is an understatement. As I've suggested, we are all movie critics to some degree, especially in my generation, on which the movies had such a pervasive influence. Yet it seems to me that whatever we said about them was set in the context of a basic, easy affection for the movies, which neither older nor younger generations quite duplicate—the former being suspicious of them, the latter rather self-conscious in dealing with them. That movies carried the potential of art as it is traditionally defined I had no doubt as I began working for *Life*. That they rarely attained that stature I could observe. That these repeated failures seemed of slight consequence to me is an admission I cheerfully made, for it seemed to me that for a long time the best movies succeeded mainly by defining art in their own terms, and that these had not yet been successfully formalized as a usable critical theory (they still have not). In short, anarchy of a most stimulating sort reigned in movie criticism and the basic task of the reviewer was, in effect, to make up his terms as he went along. To take just one example: it was obvious to me that movies aspiring to be among the finer things often provided one's most dismal moments in the theater, while unpretentious little genre films—westerns and spy stories and what-have-you—offered delights that had proved nearly inexplicable to audiences and critics—excepting a few people like Manny Farber, whose efforts to comprehend these movies were herculean, if generally unappreciated. It seemed patronizing to dismiss them as "entertainments" or "real movie-movies." It seemed equally ridiculous to borrow the other arts, making a Don Siegel melodrama sound like a Mozart quartet or a Picasso painting. The art of criticism, Sainte-Beuve said, lay in "just characterization," and the movies seemed to me to present a very large challenge in that area.

At first I solved it by taking what seems to me now a rather dispassionate tone about movies. As of 1965 it seemed to me probable that most people did not expect and did not want a masterpiece every time they ventured out to a theater. What they wanted, what I wanted, and what we were getting, especially with the increased flow of foreign production, was a wide range of diversion. It seemed to me that the average quality of studio-made American movies had fallen off, that we were losing the knack for the kind of fast-moving action, adventure and comedy films that we had invented and on which the prosperity of the movie industry here was based, and that a Hollywood still (perhaps permanently) panicked by television, the loss of its theater chains and the inutility of the old factory production methods was unable to find consistently satisfying substitutes for the kind of films that had been its glory.

There was a certain irony in this, since the New Wave—so stimulating to so many who had "given up" on Hollywood —was acknowledging in its films and its criticism its debt to the benighted Baghdad, and insisting upon its central position in the development of a unique tradition of film art, thus granting the standard American "product" a status it had only rarely achieved among American critics and, indeed, among American movie makers themselves. So it seemed to me important to call attention to those few films that still demonstrated the old American virtues. And, it should go without saying, pointing out those few domestic films that were trying to grope their way, however haltingly, toward new subjects and styles. Essentially, I was quite conservative in my praise of these new venturings: the motives of the experimenters often seemed tainted by commercial desperation and by the lack of a sure sense of what they wanted to say about the world they were confronting. There was much violence, much sexual teasing, all sorts of zoomy camera work and jumpy editing, but in our commercial films, taken as a whole, no true expansion of vision. With independent productions, Hollywood had successfully established exquisite tax shelters for its leading stars, directors, producers, but no temple of art.

Sadly—since I so much wanted the American film to reassert itself—I had to concede that the truly memorable, truly influential films were coming from abroad. They not only often satisfied many of the aesthetic criteria we were used to applying to literary and graphic art, they also were expanding the consciousness (and the technical resources) of the film medium itself. So for a while I operated on a double standard, in effect judging American film against the standards of its history, and demanding more in the way of novelty and creative intensity from the new generation of artists that had emerged in Europe and, to a lesser extent, in Asia, mostly because, like everyone else, I expected more from them.

This was not, I think, a conscious decision on my part. It just seemed to work out that way as I began the process of defining myself as a reviewer through almost weekly practice of the craft. Moreover, I was trying quite consciously (if paradoxically) to be unself-conscious as I went about the job. I had always co-existed quite comfortably with the movies as a consumer, and I saw no reason not to continue to try to be easy with them as a reviewer. In fact, it seemed to me a very sensible way to conduct a weekly column in a space that left little room for instructive moral disgressions, extensive social criticism or speculation on the economic and industrial problems that were holding back the development of the American film. To be on the lookout for the rare work of art, to deflate the more common phenomena, films that substituted pretension and good intention for actual achievement, to try to pick and choose rather carefully among the genre films that still (as of 1965–66) composed the bulk of theatrical programming and to ignore (unless their offenses were particularly egregious) the routine films that never managed to transcend their origins as purely commercial ventures—these were my basic intentions.

The biggest strategic problem for me was posed by the foreign film. The New Yorker, living in the city that is port of entry for films made abroad, has a wide choice among them and could easily accustom himself to the novelty of movies that spoke in highly personal rather than industrial tones. But out across the country that was not true. There was not then, and there is not now, a really efficient system for distributing them. If they get bad notices in New York, where, because of the example of the theater, critics have a great deal of power over the box office, their grosses are poor. And if their grosses are poor, they are simply not booked elsewhere, except possibly years later in sixteen millimeter on film society programs. Thus, from the start it seemed (a) pointless to review the obviously hopeless cases among these films, because most of *Life*'s readers didn't stand the faintest chance of seeing them, but (b) very important to stress the virtues of the worthy films, even to the point of overselling them a little bit, in the hope that such notices might improve the take in the New York theaters and even, perhaps, create a demand for them elsewhere. Anything to get them truly national releases.

In part, the nature of what I was doing in *Life* dictated some of these attitudes and assumptions. I've mentioned the necessity for brevity which the available space imposed on me, the limits the distribution system imposes on the critic with a national audience. Most important, however, was—is—the fact that I was writing only forty to fifty columns a year, so that I could consider less than a quarter of all the films released in the United States, which meant that, in effect, a good deal of my reviewing was done by the simple process of selecting the films to actually write something about. Good or bad, when I committed space to a movie, I was implying that this was for some reason or another an important film, one I judged to be worth taking up the magazine's valuable space to discuss.

I won't pretend that subjective considerations didn't enter into these decisions. *Life* recently stood mute, for example, on two movies that most of its readers probably saw and certainly were interested in—*Airport* and *Love Story*. Journalistically, I made a mistake in not writing about these pictures, since anything that attracts such a sizable audience is at least phenomenologically interesting. But the fact is that both bored me insensate. I literally couldn't think of anything to say about them that was very original or interesting. I really don't know why the mass audience fell for them and, I discovered, I didn't really care. These things happen and I firmly believe there's nothing the critic can do about them. Polls tell us the majority of our citizens trust in God, General Motors, Richard Nixon and Marcus Welby, M.D. One is astonished—not least because one personally knows no one who holds to any, let alone all, of these beliefs. One feels depressed by such evidence that one is, without trying, alienated from the taste of his fellows. But it's too easy, too familiar, simply to exercise one's contempt for it, for them. If, as T. S. Eliot suggested, the task of the critic is basically to elucidate masterpieces and elevate taste, then the movie reviewer is in a difficult spot. There are, obviously, not that many masterpieces to elucidate, and the elevation of mass taste is not accomplished by repeatedly demonstrating one's sense of superiority to it. Better, I feel, to elucidate whenever possible the nonmasterpieces that are at least partially successful, better to save one's fire and ire for movies more profoundly despicable than *Airport* or *Love Story*.

As I began my job at *Life*, it seemed to me that a strategy not dissimilar to this had served James Agee well in his time, and his was the model that appealed to me, since he was the only literate man to have regularly reviewed movies for a fairly large audience for a fairly long time without apparent loss of intelligence and emotional stability and without becoming a cynic in the process. Agee never lost his capacity for momentary outrage, but it was not that, I think, that commended him to my generation of moviegoers. What we liked best about him was his generosity, his eagerness to find some silver threads among the dross. Best of all, his spirit was a necessary corrective to all those critics who could scarcely hide their contempt for movies. In particular, I thought of Dwight MacDonald, reviewing at *Esquire* in the early sixties. I recall him, quite literally, reviewing press releases instead of the movies they promoted, and though that was a cute (and tempting) trick, it seemed to me fundamentally irresponsible, as did his refusal to immerse himself in contemporary film. For comparison and analogy he was always reaching back to Griffith and Eisenstein—because, of course, he had to, given his self-imposed limits—and more often than not they seemed irrelevant to a reasonable consideration of the new films. Besides, his endlessly querulous tone struck me as tiresome over the long haul. My assumption was that by the mid-sixties absolutely everyone knew that Hollywood had long been afflicted by vulgarity, materialism, moral, intellectual and artistic crudity and all the other kinds of bad values. The miracle seemed to me, as it seemed to Agee, not that so much poor work emanated from the far coast, but that a fair amount of good stuff found its way through the system, and the important thing was to encourage those responsible, since one imagined them as lonely and embattled.

So, in the beginning, and also quite consciously, I came more often to praise than to blame. A couple of things W. H. Auden said in his great essay "Making, Knowing and Judging" influenced me greatly. Noting the really terrible demands great works impose on their auditor, he wrote that "there is something frivolous about spending every day with one. Masterpieces should be kept for the High Holidays of the spirit." And in heeding his strictures against becoming as a critic, a prig, a critic's critic, a romantic novelist or a maniac, I adapted to film his idea "that to be worth attacking a book must be worth reading"—that is, that a film must be the product of a truly exciting mind or talent gone wrong, there being no news in the fact that hacks go wrong and no great utility in attacking them . . . unless the critic wants to gain a quick, easy reputation as the fastest gun on Manhattan Island. Then, too, though acutely aware that reviews only occasionally have a very strong effect on a domestic film's progress, and that usually in the case of movies known by the awful phrase "art films," I do think a good critical reputation can help film artists to build coherent careers, perhaps free them somewhat from the tyranny of the industry's conventional wisdom, which holds that you're only as good as your last picture and that goodness is determined by the size of its grosses.

Beyond all that fiddle, it seemed to me that the most important thing the reviewer ought to attempt was to lead or moderate (in every sense of the word) a mutually informative and above all *rational* discussion between the groups that have quite contradictory interests in films—the audience, the creators, and the businessmen who finance and distribute movies. Such a discussion still seems to me a good idea. The trouble is that the longer I have practiced the reviewer's craft, the more it has come to seem purely an ideal and not accurately descriptive of what I'm actually doing, week-in, week-out.

3.

Earlier I said there is a difference between the critic and that member of the audience who is just as concerned and knowledgeable about the movies as he is. It is a much bigger difference than I at first realized, much bigger than the average reader, even the average producer, director or actor, is likely to realize. That difference is arrived at existentially. For the regular reviewer movies become, however he may fight against it, the central fact of his life, which in turn becomes a kind of trial by immersion in the stream of production. He is obliged to attend a great many more movies than the most devoted fan or the most dedicated movie maker is ever likely to see. More important, he must week after week organize a great tangled mass of thoughts and feelings, not only about the work immediately under consideration, but about how it fits into the traditions of the medium and into current tendencies of the art and/or commerce of film. He must try to see how it is influenced by (and how it might influence) the life and ideas of its historical moment. And then, finally, he must submit these thoughts and feelings to the discipline of writing about them readably, intelligently, persuasively (even, at times, wittily or passionately). He cannot escape into the night flinging behind him some muttered comment ("neat flick" or "rotten"). He may begin his task with no more than a feeling that can be summarized so briefly, but he must in the end rationalize it, transforming gut response into reasonable, civilized discourse.

Art—even semi-industrialized art—is born in the unconscious (or at least draws its greatest strength from that source) and so is criticism. And, like the artist, the critic must shape this irrational material rationally, so that it makes some kind of sense that others can apprehend. But the artist need not, should not, explicate everything; he is not, should not be, bound by the inflexible conventions of logic; he has time on his side, time for himself and his audience to come to some understanding of all he was trying to do when he sat down to work. On the other hand, the critic or reviewer is bound by logic, bound by the fact that as a rule his work has an afterlife that is likely to be nasty, brutish and short, bound above all by what I sometimes think of as the judicial imperative. By that I mean one is, finally, in the business of rendering just verdicts on difficult cases. Happily, one is not the only justice sitting in the case of a given movie, and one certainly has no hanging power. But even so, one must take into account all relevant precedents, yet allow for the novel argument as well as the sometimes convincing evidence drawn from all sorts of strange disciplines (economics, the sociology of group creation, that sort of thing). And like all judges, the reviewer wants to avoid being too frequently reversed on appeal—whether to the higher authority of history or to public opinion—even though he knows that judicial error is in some cases inevitable.

One doesn't want to stretch the judicial metaphor too far. And one certainly doesn't want to imply that the critic is some kind of lonely culture hero, patrolling the ramparts on the lookout for Philistine assaults. After all, the work is more often than not fascinating and even fun if you have the temperament for it. But the regular deadlines and the necessity of rendering verdicts in public—especially when one's deepest instincts often suggest the wisdom of silence or the need for more time for thought or some tone less authoritative than is customary—in time work a change on one. At least that's the way it happened with me.

To put it simply, after a couple of years as a reviewer it is impossible to be as relaxed about movies as I was at the beginning. One becomes much more acutely aware of the tricks and cons the movie industrialists (and some of those who pose as movie artists) try to pull. One becomes increasingly wary, increasingly cynical about film and begins occasionally to long for the uncomplicated love once felt for this medium, long for the days when the banality and silliness of most movies could be quite irresponsibly laughed off, long for the time when the brutality, stupidity, provincialism and insensitivity of "da industry" was the stuff of rather glamorous legend, not the material of one's daily speculations. What happens then, of course, is that the desire, finally, to protest in public the repeated abuses of talent, the trivialization of what might be great themes, the endless mediocrity with which a great medium is debased becomes overwhelming. At which point, and almost unconsciously, for good or ill (actually a little of both), the critic's old identification with the audience—which does not deeply care about such matters—ceases and, although he may not have actively or consciously sought to become one, though he may have no very good answer to the questions "Why him?" and "Why me?" the fact remains that he is that rather strange beast, a reviewer of movies, a critic of films— there isn't even a term for him that everyone can agree upon.

4.

Logically, one might suppose that as a reviewer moved away from his old home in the audience, as he more and more consciously defined himself as a critic, his basic tone would change. Before I sat down to make the selection of pieces for this book, I would have guessed that mine had. But it hasn't—not much anyway. The percentage of favorable notices has dropped fairly steadily, I think, but even so, there is a fair amount of positive thinking in the later pages. The difference is all subjective. Where once the reasonable tone came naturally to me, it is now the product of conscious effort, a discipline I impose upon myself largely because I have grown increasingly disturbed by the air of urgency, the intensity in the tone of the critical dialogue about movies. In the last few years many magazines and newspapers have upgraded and expanded their efforts in this once more or less neglected field. Radio and television stations now have critics (so-called) and several individuals have become multi-media celebrities by posing as critics. All of us, indeed, are better known to more people than critics and reviewers of the other arts—at least in part because the distributors, ever anxious for blurbs, plaster our names all over their ads whenever we happen to like some movie or other (and sometimes when we don't like it, by the clever use of ellipsis marks and exclamation points). If you have any integrity at all, this is bound to lead to a certain reserve in the way you measure out praise (any competent writer can avoid giving quotable lines to the ad men), and I think this has had a chastening effect on my prose, enthusiasm now being in large supply among reviewers who like to think of themselves as junior members of the celebrity system, their price of membership being to cry, "Masterpiece, masterpiece," once a week to the confusion of those who read only the ads, not the reviews from which their copy is culled.

There are, however, complexities to this issue of the critic-as-celebrity of more general importance than its effect on my own reviewing strategy. There is, to begin with, the fundamental irony that interest in the critical discussion about movies has risen precisely as interest in movies by the large audience has declined. John Simon's last collection of reviews was rather smugly entitled *Movies into Film*, and his introduction is a rather smug piece in uncritical praise of this development. The notion is that, with no need to seek the least common denominator, the movie maker may now reasonably aspire at all times to the status of artist. I would argue that, of course, that's a good thing for some people. The relatively limited audience for movies—less than one-fourth the size it was before television—can guarantee success for a relatively limited sort of art. Bergman, Truffaut, Godard—to name three disparate artists—have this in common, that it requires only small casts, short shooting schedules, severely limited technical means to achieve full realization of their visions. What critic who cares the slightest about movies can be anything but pleased by the fact that in today's world these men can function—as two or three decades ago they could not—because there is a caring audience that, if not huge, is at least big enough to return profits to the backers of their economically modest ventures and enable them to go on with their work. But great as I think all of them can be, the potential of movies (or film) is wider than their grasp. There is spectacle, for instance. There is the musical. There is the action film. And if these forms are routinely used, and often abused, their potential is unlimited. Indeed, these forms seem to me the ones in which the American film maker has most fully realized himself, most fully expressed a vision of the nation's historical experience. But these *movie* forms are expensive, they are in bad repute with the now almost exclusively middle-row audience, and they require the patronage of the lost mass audience if they are not to fail. So how can one be entirely pleased that that big audience is drifting away, that the medium is becoming more and more a thing for the cognoscenti, led by the critics, to natter about in overly intellectual terms? On the contrary, this seems to me a disaster for the medium. Truffaut, that gentlest and most loving modern master of movies, recently complained that "Whenever I go to the movies, all I see in the theater are almost empty rows; the few seats taken hold familiar habitués of the film library, students of the cinema, a few fellow directors, a few impassioned script girls and above all lots of assistant directors, actors and would-be actors. I realize Hollywood [he should have said the whole movie world] has been described as a city of bakers where all they make is bread, but what will happen when the bread itself will no longer be eaten except by those who bake it?"

That question seems to me unanswerable by the John Simons of the world. And it is not merely a question of this art becoming like all the other performing arts—that is, no longer self-supporting, and sustaining itself on handouts from wealthy patrons and the cultural bureaucrats of foundations and governments. The fact is that, as Truffaut also says, the glory of the movies is finally that the greatest films have always succeeded, in some near-magical way, in allowing "everyone in the audience [to use] the same means to follow the action and understand it." It was precisely from this fact that the creative energy—and our pleasure in and excitement over that energy—derived. To lose that—and we are in danger of losing it—is to reduce the scope of the art, to cut it off from its historic roots, to curtail its social function as a force that held a vast and various nation together by providing it with common metaphors through which races, classes, generations might communicate.

Against this trend, and mostly by implication, I have tried to stand in my reviews. In *Life* I have, I guess, potentially the biggest audience of any non-televised reviewer. So, as much as possible, I have tried to encourage the mass audience to test what seems to them exotic fare, to set aside their prejudices against subtitles, against the new conventions of shooting and editing, their endless and largely misplaced fear of moral subversion, their unspoken insistence that movies must remain "entertaining" in the same ways they used to be. In the process, I think I've changed considerably myself, having had, for example, no less than a conversion experience in the case of Bergman and having developed a tolerance for artistic failure (and partial success) that matches my former tolerance for failures (and partial successes) among the beloved genres of childhood. Indeed, I should say that I have become increasingly impatient with Hollywood's incessant whoring after the youth market, its endless romanticizing of childishly revolutionary attitudes, its indulgence of directors who insist on the right to make personal statements when they have not bothered to figure out just what it is they want to say, its pursuit of chic stylistic effects that are merely empty gestures. As I write, I am fascinated by directors who speak to us in terms of exemplary austerity—Bergman in *The Passion of*

Anna, Eric Rohmer in *My Night at Maud's*, Roberto Rossellini in *The Rise of Louis XIV*, Truffaut in *The Wild Child*. I think I see some rough correlation between what they have achieved through radical sophistication and what the American primitives achieved through their equally radical innocence—purity of image, clarity of characterization, ease and grace of movement through plots and against backgrounds which turn out to have an initially unsuspected ambiguity and richness.

Whether the connection between that which I used to love in movies and what I now love is real, or whether it exists only in my own mind, I don't know. For the fact is that I am also open to the baroque romanticism of Ken Russell, to the melodramatics of Malle and Chabrol, to the violent attempts of Sam Peckinpah to reclaim a western myth usable for our time, to John Cassavetes's near-maniacal pursuit of the completely true actor's gesture, to the simple sentiment that animated so much of the short-lived Czech film renaissance. All of which is a way of saying there has been such a substantial change in both the kinds of films we see and the kind of audience we have become in the few years since I started reviewing, that I have had to alter some of my reviewing strategy accordingly. The old clear line between the film that was art or at least consciously aspired to be art and the film which might unconsciously achieve that status through intensification or subtle variation on the generic stylizations has blurred. Today many films, including skin flicks, have the look of art, have adopted (and adapted) its currently fashionable manner. The cowboy-as-existential-hero has become a standing joke, but no less present for his absurdity and his occasional truthfulness. As to the audience, it is eager for the new and wants to think of itself as "with it." As a result, the defense of certain values has become difficult. Older people, for example, can often only see the nudity in an otherwise commendable film and dismiss it angrily. Younger people see similar nakedness in a bad film and take it to be an earnest of honesty. The same can be said of stylistic conventions, certain recurrent themes that preoccupy and also polarize us. In this confusion I have found myself reverting more and more often to Orwell's ultimate test of art: Is it or is it not the product of common human decency?—by which I always took him to mean: Does it deal with recognizable human beings, not sports of nature, freaks? Is the world in which they exist recognizable either as present reality or as a past or future that can be reasonably projected from our own knowledge and experience? Does it, in resolving issues and problems, do so in such a way that the integrity and the believability of the posited human personalities (not to mention reasonable political and social values) are maintained? Most important, do its creators understand that art is not a value-free enterprise, that a vision must not be sold out to achieve a fashionable look or a quick, cheap box-office success?

I cannot account for the reshaping of my tastes and my rising concern for the moral tone of movies in any but subjective terms. I find most critical theory—Arnheim, Kracauer, Eisenstein—very nearly unreadable and quite totally useless when one tries to employ it in evaluating a specific movie. Film is simply too various a medium to be successfully encompassed by any theory, no matter how hard it tries to account for the exceptions to its rules. Even Auteurism, more an ideology than a theory, but certainly the most discussed general approach to film in recent years, seems to me not to work out very well in critical practice. Its adherents often end up trying to explain away works of quality made by directors whose credentials as Auteurs are dubious, or constructing desperate rationales for works by certified members of their pantheon which common sense must tell them are dogs. This is not to say their work does not have its benign aspects. They have focused attention where it belongs, on the director as the key figure (though not, I think, the only significant one) in film creation and by so doing have given us a useful method of gaining a purchase on film history. Moreover, through their work they have rescued a great many deserving reputations and happily deflated a number that were quite overblown.

Still, I am not now, and am unlikely to become, an Auteur-ist. Strict adherence to any aesthetic theory—especially one that posits not merely the greatness of Howard Hawks but his infallibility as well—leads to limited and distorted responses to the work at hand.

The same may be said of the politicalized response to movies. With the horrid example of all those popular-front movies of the 1940s still fairly fresh in memory, I don't see how anyone can be pleased by the growing number of radical chic movies or by the welcome they receive in some quarters. My deepest impulse is to oppose the politicalization of all art, since it leads to tampering with the individual vision so that it may more conveniently fit some party line or other. It's not that I dislike films about politics. It's only that the ones that appeal to me are likely to explore the subject with a degree of ideological reserve and with an eye alert to the human drama going forward beneath the surface play of ideas. *La Guerre Est Finie* seems to me a splendid film, *The Best Man* a very amusing one, *The Revolutionary* a damn good try at examining the politicalized juvenile delinquent. What I despise is Agitprop—*Soldier Blue* and *Catch-22* as Mike Nichols realized it, *Oh! What a Lovely War* (on film) and *How I Won the War* and all the rest of the nonsense that may have its beginning in a commendable desire to do something about the state of the world but ends up as hysterical preachment to the already converted.

There is, I must add, especially in New York literary and intellectual circles, a degree of pressure to conformity with the new apocalyptic vision. It's fairly easy to resist, considering its sources—hack journalists latching on to attitudes which save them the trouble of actually thinking, editors and film makers and writers compensating for the fact that they went dry a few years ago (and trying to cover it up), the whole dismal crowd who embrace radical chic with the alacrity that they embrace new hair styles, hemlines and the rest.

Thus, one finds oneself defining a critical position reactively at least as often as one does positively. And just now I find myself reacting not only against theoretical debate and politicalization but against the general intensification of the critical discussion of movies. For those who still care about movies— now distinctly a minority in our society—movies have ceased to be a habit. They are now consequential cultural events, and what the reviewers and critics have to say is also newly consequential. More and more one finds critics responding to this interest by writing as if they were reporting an endless cultural crisis that is going badly for the forces of light. A literary gentleman observing this scene recently declared that on one of the rare occasions when his movie colleagues actually agreed on something it was as startling as a sudden inexplicable pause in a cat fight.

He's right. We squabble endlessly. Perhaps it's because the idea that what we have to say about movies actually matters to someone is so novel. Perhaps it's because we are alienated from audience and creators in a way that is not true of the literary critic, who shares certain basic assumptions about the nature of the art in question and the motives of the people who consume and create it, assumptions that civilize all concerned. I don't really know, I can only speculate about all this. But I am convinced that, on the evidence, the influence of the critics on the fate of a movie is erratic and unpredictable. There are simply too many movies that our accidentally combined praise could not help, others that an equally accidental concatenation of condemnation could not prevent from succeeding. Of course, there are a few movies we have helped to find an audience, a very few from which we have kept at least a few people. But the fact remains that power is meaningful only when it can be exercised predictably and efficiently, and that by this standard we are essentially powerless. Therefore, it seems to me our shrill discussions in print and in person are largely meaningless. Everyone is so proud and prickly that we can't even be said to have any influence on one another. And this being so, it seems to me that the best thing we can do—

and a thing we very rarely manage—is to set an example of civilized debate. This seems particularly important at a historical moment when in almost every area of life the emotional and the irrational are exalted, reason held at a discount.

5.

It comes to this: there is no dialectic at work in movies or movie reviewing. There is no such thing as "progress" in this or any other art, only change. For example, during the time I was writing the pieces contained in this book, we witnessed the consummation of a wish devoutly prayed by many—a great shrinkage in the power of the major studios. But, if anything, the art of film in America has regressed as a result of this change. The percentage of genuinely good and genuinely bad movies has remained pretty constant, but the middle ground, once crowded with decent, inoffensive entertainment, has shrunk. And the audience has shrunk with it. And it is fragmented in a dangerous way, having become, in fact, a multiplicity of small audiences, each of which is unwilling to sample the works that appeal to the others. This situation has reached a crisis point and it is, of course, the basis of the much discussed economic crisis of the movie business. I think that as I wrote these pieces I probably underestimated the extent of this phenomenon and that I should have paid more explicit attention to it, if only as an aid to readers trying to get their bearings in a subject where the forces of radical change are operating no less powerfully—and ambiguously—than they are elsewhere.

Still, it is always the object itself that most powerfully interests me, because it is the single work, the singular artist, that we have some hope of comprehending. There is no generalization without its exception, no trend without its countertrend, no way for a reviewer to respond properly to a movie without to some degree accepting the terms, innovative or conservative, in which it was created. The history of movies is replete with examples of films that, having accepted the conventions—commercial or otherwise—of their historical moment, transcend those conventions. One owes them consideration no less than one owes it to works that challenge currently received opinion. The task, finally, is to find excellence, not to write a week-by-week socioeconomic history of the movies. I can no more give an abstract definition of what I mean by excellence than I can abstractly define the responsibilities of the critic. That, too, is something I've worked out existentially, learning by doing. Looking through these pieces, now that the heat generated by the act of composing them has cooled, I have a few tentative conclusions to offer about what I've tried to do.

More than ever it seems to me that my opinions, or those of any other critic, are unprovable; that there is no single aesthetic standard to which we can all repair in comfort; that the reasonable tone I have strived for holds up pretty well and lends weight to those pieces where I have permitted my passions to play through; that my reluctance to join my critical colleagues in their quarrels and in their crusades for right thinking—that is, *their* subjective truth—about movies was also right.

For despite my inability to prove that I've ever affected the opinion of anyone but a stray reader or two; despite the certain knowledge that the movie business goes on its self-destructive way no matter how much good free advice I (and my colleagues) have given it; despite my dismay at discovering that reviewing movies involves a great deal more than just simply reviewing movies; despite my regret that movies—and their critics—have abandoned some of the innocence with which once they could afford to confront one another; despite my concern that movies are losing their grip on their old audience while discovering the new one is not nearly as good as it thinks it is; despite my belief that we sometimes take the success or failure of an important movie too seriously, reading into it too much cultural significance; despite all this, I still think reviewing movies is worthwhile work—especially in a magazine that reaches a large audience. For one thing, movies remain, to put it plainly, a wonderful subject, one which touches on almost every other subject and one which, despite the declining attendance figures, continues to exercise a peculiar fascination on huge numbers of people. Moreover, it is a subject which seems continually to open up as one plunges deeper into it. Best of all, it is a subject unburdened with a great critical tradition; there is no sense, as there is in literature, of great men, great minds peering disapprovingly over the reviewer's shoulder. Supposing we can defend ourselves against the dangers of elitism and academicism, the business of writing critically about film need never become sterile, constrained, the joyless playing of the illiterate specialist. It can be something for everyone to share at some fairly intelligent level.

This last is important to me. I firmly believe there is an organic relationship between democracy and criticism. As we know them, both are products of the Age of Reason, and there was initially a strong assumption that the former could not properly function if the latter did not. Therefore, since movies are such a widely interesting subject, the discussion of them seems as good a place as any for large numbers of people to habituate themselves to the conventions of critical discourse, a thing not widely practiced (and less widely understood and enjoyed) in modern mass democracies, where the debasement of language through politics, technocracy, bureaucracy and sheer sloth proceeds alarmingly.

That is an immodest hope, of course, the product of a belief in the value of my subject unabated by the passage of time and the accretion of experience that might have dulled it. I must say that as the violence of rhetoric has escalated in our society, I feel increasingly that those of us who attempt to maintain a reasonable tone, untouched by hysteria or despair, untinged by either revolutionary or repressive fervor, may be fighting a losing rear-guard action—whatever our subjects may be. Still, I'm not ready to concede that struggle, either within the metaphor that chose me as much as I chose it, or in general. Put it this way: let truth and error contend—but in the manner of a debate, not an alley brawl. Given my taste and temperament, I have very little choice in the matter. But given my subject, I have little choice but to believe in the inevitability of happy endings.

RICHARD SCHICKEL
March 1, 1971

DARLING

The first two movies of the English director John Schlesinger were unaccountably underrated when they were released in this country, though both *A Kind of Loving* and *Billy Liar* revealed a talent for subtle, biting social satire and, to my mind at least, were far superior to such flashy but essentially flabby offerings in the same genre as Fellini's *La Dolce Vita* and 8½. I hope that *Darling*, Schlesinger's latest, will finally establish him where he belongs—in the very first rank of the new directors.

Darling is the story of the worldly rise and inner collapse of Diana Scott, a London model, from her beginnings in the bra ads, upward through the new demimonde of the arts and communications (which produced Christine Keeler), to her final hollow triumph—a chic marriage to a rich minor Italian nobleman. Refreshingly, it is not a tale of innocence betrayed or of the first flowering of a bad seedling. It is instead a tragicomedy about the degree to which moral imagination fails us in the modern world—not by much, but just enough.

Diana's problem is that she is an ordinarily pretty, ordinarily intelligent, ordinarily decent person who would like to lead an extraordinary life, that is to say, one in which she is neither particularly bored nor particularly bad. She ends up both, because although she has just enough quality to know that something has gone wrong for her, she does not have quite enough to rise above her weaknesses and the world's failures. She imagines the right goals—those are always easy—but she can't imagine the proper practical steps to attain them—the hard part, as everyone sooner or later realizes.

All this sounds a little too finely tuned, a little too novelistic to make an effective movie. But there is genuine will-she-or-won't-she-make-it suspense in Diana's moral brinksmanship, thanks to a performance by Julie Christie that is pure gold. This is characterization such as one rarely sees. By turns willful and willing, greedy and contrite, intelligent and self-deceiving, innocent and teasing, funny and touching, Miss Christie gives us the agonies, the too-occasional pleasures of free young womanhood in a poignant, unsentimental and never hysterical fashion.

There is a performance almost as good from Dirk Bogarde as her first lover and only love, an integrity-ridden journalist who has the best chance to save her, but who is just a little too steady, a little too square to cope with her (another but different failure of moral imagination). Laurence Harvey again plays one of those ultramodern stinkers on which he practically holds a patent and he, too, is most effective as he helps Miss Christie take a giant step down the road to her peculiar hell.

But in the end, this is Schlesinger's picture—a rare work of bravura direction that for the most part resists the temptation to underline or otherwise call attention to its own skill. His talent, like Miss Christie's, is for wonderfully elaborate embroidery, deepening, enriching and further illuminating the basic line of his work. It's complex but never confusing, for the touch of his needle is near perfect.

I especially liked the hordes of bored, frightened, cruel, stupid, decayed faces—virtually Hogarthian caricatures—which he found and used, casually yet devastatingly, as living scenery. These, he seems to say, are the faces of our time and they are a shock and a revelation.

Then there are his set pieces. A charity gambling party, the opening of an art show, a man-in-the-street TV interview show, a ghastly suburban dinner party, ad men in meeting assembled to choose a new "Happiness Girl," Capri in season, shoplifting in Fortnum and Mason's, a mock newsreel of Diana's marriage to her prince—the emptiness of it caught in a few quick winks of a wicked and restless camera eye that never lingers on after an essence has been caught, the point made.

There is wit in this, and a cruel satirical edge. But more important, Schlesinger's range forces us to see that there is no essential difference between Diana's world and our own, indeed it could not exist without our acquiescent and envious curiosity. The moral sensibility of those men on the street, those newsreel watchers, is no better, no more capable of fine moral distinctions than hers. In short, Diana Scott is something of a modern everywoman and there are no easy morals to be drawn from her story, not even an easy tragedy. She does not at the end choose either reform or suicide. Schlesinger is too honest to indulge in such dramatics. She simply settles for what she has, the cold and loveless villa of her Italian prince, empty grandeur. The last we hear of her she is selling the story of her life to a fatuous ladies' magazine. What else can you do with goodness, with badness, that is only ordinary, appearances to the contrary notwithstanding?

8/27/65

Schlesinger made it to the "first rank" among directors, all right, but as is so often the case when a man gets the prestige— and the budgets—denied him at the beginning of his career, he has been a disappointment. Far from the Madding Crowd was beautiful, but empty. Midnight Cowboy was too easily moralistic. Sunday, Bloody Sunday, a well-acted, well-observed movie that was difficult to care about emotionally or intellectually. The careful ambiguity I found in his attitude toward Diana in Darling becomes simple sentimentalism; Joe and Ratso are innocents—and implicitly homosexual at that—done in by the cruel materialism of an unthinking world. They are viewed with a romanticism entirely missing from Darling—perhaps because of the implicit homosexual relationship between them. In any case, Schlesinger's interest in the grotesque is no longer balanced by a cleansing, objective wit. The man who earlier made moral tales for adults scored his greatest success with a fairy tale for adolescents, and one must wonder if he will dare in future to argue with success. Still, I'm not the least bit apologetic about this review of Darling. It remains for me a memorable movie, not least because its heroine remains for me an archetypal figure of our time.

THE LEATHER BOYS

Sidney J. Furie is an off-beat movie director. I mean that quite literally. The special quality of his previous release this year, *The Ipcress File,* resulted from its daringly slow rhythm, more gripping somehow than the jazzy pace that has lately become a convention of the spy genre. Now in *The Leather Boys* (forget about that awful title) he has employed a jumpy, jagged beat in his cutting that matches nicely the semi-improvisational style of his actors, as well as the restless, rootless quality of the adolescent lives he is examining. The film is sputtery, fitful, full of half-finished actions, half-fulfilled intentions. In short, it has a cinematic style all its own, as did *Ipcress.* It therefore conveys the quality of contemporary juvenile life far more effectively than does Hollywood's sensationalism disguised as realism. On the other hand, its unique rhythm is artfully achieved; it is not the product of technical ineptitude as it was in the recent ridiculously overpraised Canadian study of demi-delinquency, *Nobody Waved Good-bye.*

Though a motorcycle gang is the ostensible subject of the film, this is not *The Wild Ones* reset in England. The kids never once encounter a bobby. They are, indeed, less rebellious or anti-social than they are bored, seeking in aimless locomotion the illusion that they are going somewhere, anywhere, in a closed class-ridden society that must pretend either that they are dangerous aliens or that they don't exist as human beings at all.

The movie is about what happens when three of them seek reassurance, in the form of love, that they really do have value as individuals—at least to their peers. Reggie and Dot (Colin Campbell and Rita Tushingham) decide to marry. But the relationship quickly founders; they can play house, but they are not up to the more difficult demands of their roles as husband and wife. She's cute, but she has the heart of a slattern; he has a sweet temperament, but he would rather fool around with his motorcycle than make love to his bride.

He drifts back to the gang and innocently into friendship with a "mate" named Pete. As far as Reggie is concerned, this is just another boyish palship, comforting in the familiarity of its demands. What he does not realize is that cynical, raffish, yet oddly vulnerable Pete (wonderfully played by Dudley Sutton) is a homosexual biding his time, engaging in an oblique but deadly war with Dot for possession of Reggie.

Neither wins. On a long motorcycle race to Edinburgh, Reggie and Dot rediscover one another, but he waits too long to reclaim her, and when at last he does, he finds her in bed with another member of the gang. He attempts to run away to sea with Pete, who thereupon makes his homosexuality overt, forcing Reggie to turn away from the last intimacy available to him (by this time, even his beloved bike has been sold). The picture ends in desolation.

It's not much, really—a simple story of innocence ended, of youth betrayed and a bleak and probably hopeless adulthood begun. But it is very effective. The acting is good, although Miss Tushingham's studious lack of manner is rapidly becoming a mannerism; the scenes of working-class life, by now all too familiar in English films, are uncommonly sharp-edged; the set piece of the young couple's honeymoon in a combined motor court and playland is wonderfully awful, but with the temptation to step over into mood-breaking satire skirted for a change.

In general, Furie has kept his balance, neither sensationalizing nor sentimentalizing, trying always to see with his own fresh eye. Thus he has taken familiar material and created from it a whole that is, if not highly original, at least a good honest piece of English tweed—rough to the touch, made warm by solid craftsmanship and given life by the subtle weaving of disparate emotional threads. I think it will wear well.

12/10/65

Sidney Furie is a difficult case. The Leather Boys, an early film, was released here after the success of Ipcress and picked up some small change in the art houses. Whereupon Furie got himself into various messes—The Appaloosa, a Brando western very self-consciously shot; The Lawyer, a version of the Sam Shepard case, which was badly released by its distributor and indifferently received by critics, perhaps because of its shady origins, though I thought it was a good lively courtroom piece; Little Fauss and Big Halsy, a tough and funny look at Middle America's obsession with winning and losing games—in this case cheap motorcycle races—that aren't worth the candle. I think Furie remains a talented and uneven director with a taste for sharp dialogue and a wonderful feel for empty spaces and empty lives. He is, I fear, out of joint with the times—an unromantic man who insists on working themes the rest of the movie makers have conditioned us to expect to be romanticized. But in a day when it's almost impossible to find clean-cut hard-driving action sequences, he remains a director for whom I have an affection that is not entirely rational.

DOCTOR ZHIVAGO

The most important thing one carries away from David Lean's movie version of *Doctor Zhivago* is a series of visual impressions—of the vastness of the Russian landscape, of the hugeness and therefore the uncontrollability of the forces necessary to effect revolutionary change within such a landscape, of the puniness of man when he measures himself against this scale and, finally and most important, the nobility and the sadness of the luckless individual who would, contrary to Tolstoy's advice, set himself in opposition to the gigantic historical pressures generated in this almost immeasurable caldron.

The action of the film may be described very simply as the disillusionment—but not the souring—of Yuri Zhivago. One by one his hopes of preserving his identity as doctor, as poet, as family man, as unique individual are casually and wantonly destroyed by a revolution with which, ironically, he mildly sympathizes but in which he does not want to involve himself. Finally, and most cruelly, the one thing the revolution has given him—the opportunity to possess physically his great love, the magnificent Lara—is taken from him, too. He survives even this for a while but then dies, anonymously, of a heart attack in the street.

This fairly simple tale achieves its cinematic impact not through its construction, which is only adequate to its larger purposes; not through thronging spectacle, although one is always conscious of the distant rumble of historical thunder;

not through great performances by its actors, though there are several fine ones. It succeeds, in the last analysis, because of the perfection of its visualization by Lean. This is not a matter of isolated shots designed to overwhelm or of tricky rhythms designed to ensnare the unwary. Rather it is the product of great care in the construction of long sequences. One thinks of the deserters leaving the front in World War I meeting replacements going forward, mingling with them and then joining them in riot against their officers. Or the long oppressive journey of Zhivago and his family by cattle car across Russia, trying to escape the terrors of life in Sovietized Moscow. The contrast between their claustrophobic conditions and the empty expanses rolling away outside is the film's most vivid projection of their sense of loss and reduction. But there are others—Zhivago wandering alone through endless snowfields, trying to find his way home after his escape from the Forest Brotherhood. Or finally, and perhaps most memorable of all, Zhivago and Lara in their last refuge, a summerhouse in which all the floors and furnishings have been layered with ice and snow, the familiar converted into a grotesquely beautiful mockery of itself by unchecked natural forces.

In these, as in dozens of other realizations in his film, Lean, with careful, conscious artistry, has created the visual equivalent of the poetic, symbolic essence of Boris Pasternak's novel, a work often misunderstood, and therefore underrated, as old-fashioned idealism. Indeed, Lean's natural cinematic style, vivid and compelling in its imagery, is well matched with Pasternak's compressed and highly imagistic literary style. Despite the largeness of the canvasses on which he now works and the richness of his colors, Lean is a rather austere and conservative director, conventional in his camera work and editing techniques. Like Pasternak, he is able to get the most extraordinary resonances out of constructions that seem at first glance to be simple almost to the point of flatness.

He has received surprisingly harsh criticism from some reviewers, who apparently had hoped he would trump up some high-adventure sequences like those that enlivened his two Academy Award winners, *Lawrence of Arabia* and *The Bridge on the River Kwai*. But Lean simply refuses to inflate his material for idle effect. It is true that his principal characters do not confront the great historical events of the period directly, but to have done so would have been to falsify Pasternak, who was similarly reticent; there is, after all, nothing like Tolstoy's evocation of the Battle of Borodino in his book. The whole point is that in the revolutionary situation Pasternak's characters must all remain on the margin, doomed by Marxist historical science—not to mention the raw psychology of revolution—to the junk heap of history. It is artistically essential that they be unable to participate in, shape or even fully understand the events that are transforming their lives. The compassion one comes to feel for them is based on their stubborn humanity. They accept their fate, they try to keep going, they even manage to be perversely cheerful on occasion, though it is becoming increasingly clear to them that what they are undergoing is not just a passing storm but a total and irrevocable change in the climate.

The film's more severe critics also claim that, in an attempt to create a dramatic line strong enough to support the weight of their long film, Lean and his screenwriter, Robert Bolt, have overstressed and in the process sentimentalized the romance between Zhivago and Lara. In any event, it occupies proportionately more space in the film, and indeed, their characters are less charged with historical and religious symbolism than they are in the book. But as acted by Omar Sharif and Julie Christie, both bring to the relationship a painfully sensitive and intelligent awareness of the self and the other, their separate and shared guilts, the hopelessness of their situation. If this be soap, it is not the soft stuff of the soap opera but rather that of the surgery—harsh, astringent, purifying. That it cannot wash away the revolution is a measure of the historical event's terrible force. That individuals are compelled to scrub away at it is a measure of their absurdity, perhaps, but also of an emotional strength that in the end must transcend the accidents of history.

I thought Sharif overemphasized the saintly, passive side of Zhivago's nature at the expense of a certain conscious emotional coloration. But Julie Christie is remarkably good. Pasternak often uses images of the sea in referring to Lara, and Miss Christie, whose chief gift is an effortless naturalism, suggests the shifting moods of an ocean—inexplicably calm at times, unreasonably stormy at others, but with the implication of hidden depths always present.

Oddly enough, the film's most serious flaw has gone mostly unmarked. That is the disappearance, halfway through, of Pasha, Lara's first husband—wonderfully played by Tom Courtenay. A prerevolutionary political idealist, he is transformed, when given power, into Strelnikov, fanatic killer of all who oppose his ideas. He was intended by Pasternak to represent spiritual death, as Zhivago represents life. The author believed that neither man nor society can be forcibly remade, that their regeneration is a natural process "out of reach of our stupid theories." It is this knowledge that gives Zhivago the strength to accept and survive the blows he is dealt. It is lack of it that drives the politicalized and therefore dehumanized Pasha to despair and suicide. In the movie this happens offstage, and thus the careful moral balance of the novel, not to mention its dramatic high point, is destroyed.

Yet the film, as an experience capable of reaching out and enveloping the viewer, surmounts this. At once generous yet austere, huge but never out of human scale, gently unfolded yet full of power, it is work of serious, genuine art. That such a work could be created within the conventions of the commercial cinema is almost as miraculous as the fact that a novel celebrating the unconquerable individualist could come out of modern Russia.

1/21/66

This is the point at which most reviewers began scrambling off the Lean bandwagon, while I hung on until the next stop—the lamentable Ryan's Daughter. I'm willing to concede now that I might have been wrong, but I do dearly love long lush movies, and for all its slickness I thought this was an absorbing entertainment—if not quite the "authentic" art I said it was in the enthusiasm of the moment. I wish it were commercially feasible to make more such movies, and I worry that we are not developing the skills to carry forward the tradition of the screen spectacle. There has never been a perfect one, and that alone is sufficient reason to keep trying—especially since even the failures and the partial successes (like this one) can be such a welcome relief from the ordinary run of releases.

HARPER

We fade in on Lew Harper asleep. The alarm rings. He opens a bloodshot eye. We cut to the television set, which he apparently forgot to shut off the night before. It is broadcasting that perfect symbol of the early morning despair of urban America, a test pattern.

As Harper and the camera begin to roam around his lair, it is clear that things are not going very well for him. He is sleeping on a rollaway bed in his crummy office. He is out of coffee and must rescue yesterday's grounds from the garbage pail before he can kill the taste of last night's booze. He is a gum chewer, and his sports clothes are a trifle too sporty. It shortly becomes clear that his wife is divorcing him and that his sports car is all rusty. He also has a wise mouth and a conscience in working order.

You know him—he's our old friend, the private eye, first sketched in hard pencil by Dashiell Hammett, given romantic depth and color by Raymond Chandler and finally physically embodied in some of the best American films of the forties by Humphrey Bogart with assists from Dick Powell, Alan Ladd and quite a few others. He has been absent from the screen for a long time now, victim of the possibly erroneous belief that there is no strong market left for genre films of the sort that used to form the bulk of old-fashioned studio production. Such action films as we have lately received from Hollywood have mostly been satires of the classic style, occasionally amusing but more often fatally marred by a self-consciously campy spirit, the main function of which is to demonstrate that the film makers are sophisticated fellows who know better than to take their own nonsense seriously. One's ribs fairly ache from the nudgings of these characters as they emphasize this all too obvious point.

It is the lack of any such condescension that makes *Harper* such a genuinely enjoyable picture. It is based on a novel by Ross Macdonald, whom many consider the only logical successor to Hammett and Chandler; and screenwriter William Goldman, director Jack Smight and star Paul Newman play their film as straight as the novelist habitually does his books. Goldman's script is full of snap-crackle-pop dialogue regrettably missing from Macdonald's customary style, but the essentially simple plot (Harper is trying to find a kidnapped millionaire) retains Macdonald's customary Byzantine twists and turns around which nearly always lurks a grotesque and curious minor character. Smight has a good feel for the tawdry nouveau-gauche Southern California atmosphere and, more important, he gives us a good approximation of the pell-mell pace and bluntness of exposition one used to be able to count on in American films and which nowadays one receives mainly from French imitators of the old school. As for Newman, this is the kind of superficial role—plenty of action, wisecracks and manly sentiment—for which his superficial talent is ideally suited.

He is supported by a long list of names—some of them fading, some of them on the rise, some of them just hanging around as they have been for years. This currently fashionable device works in this case because the list has been carefully compiled and every name on it neatly slotted in a perfect part. The likes of Lauren Bacall, Julie Harris, Arthur Hill, Janet Leigh, Pamela Tiffin, Robert Wagner, Robert Webber and Shelley Winters actually appear, as a result, to be acting instead of behaving.

But the strengths of *Harper* are not merely nostalgic, technical or thespian. Its true merit lies in its peculiar moral vision.

The best private-eye fictions, in print and on the screen, have always disguised, beneath the hoopla of their plotting and the fantasies of their characterizations, a hard gleam of honesty about the everyday banality and corruption in which we live and to which we are inured and indifferent until something like *Harper* recalls it to our attention. Everywhere our weary hero goes, filth is sure to follow. At the top of society, at the bottom and in the middle it is all the same, and it is never fun or funny or glamorous in the James Bond vein. It is always petty, mean, mindless and degrading. There is no point in making a big deal, a sermon in a cesspool, about it all, and *Harper* doesn't. It merely sends us an unemotional memo on the way things too often are in our society, shrugs, cracks wise and weary. But in the prevailing conscienceless climate of American movie making, it is good to see a film with at least that much awareness of its social context, that much critical objectivity. One gets so tired of movies pandering to or feebly trying to satirize the very mood of affluent amorality on which, commercially, their success depends. *Harper* does neither, and within the limits of its form and the limits of the crude yet vital sensibilities of its makers, it emerges as a strong and solid movie.

4/1/66

Smight has gone soggy, Goldman has never risen above his ability to write good gags and, in memory, the picture gives off a somewhat more feverish and desperate air than I indicated. Still, it was the last private-eye piece one could actually sit through. So let it stand—as a tribute to the pleasures of yesteryear briefly and imperfectly recaptured.

KHARTOUM

One respects Sir Laurence Olivier for his great performances in the great roles, but what one truly loves him for is the uncondescending high spirits and exuberant inventiveness he brings to character parts in films that without his leavening presence would be the sheerest trash. The examples are endless—the self-proclaimed "Fox of the Balkans" opposite Marilyn Monroe in *The Prince and the Showgirl*, the homosexual general in *Spartacus*, the tough, cool detective in *Bunny Lake Is Missing* and, best of all, the cheap, feverish Archie Rice in *The Entertainer*, a definitive portrayal of the no-talent, no-luck inhabitant of the lower depths of show biz. In these parts one never feels the great actor is slumming or camping out. Rather, he is like a usually sober schoolboy on holiday, free to exercise his imagination untrammeled by rules, traditions and duties. Inside Sir Laurence there is, one feels, a James Mason who not only struggles to get out but must get out occasionally if the actor is to maintain the sharpest possible edge on his talent.

To Sir Laurence's list of unlikely triumphs one must now add *Khartoum*, an infuriatingly indifferent film on what should be a great movie subject. He plays the Mahdi, the religious fanatic who whirled out of the Sudanese desert in the 1880s, laid siege to Khartoum for 317 days while the British vacillated, and finally defeated his equally (though differently) fanatic opponent, the English soldier-mystic-masochist, General Charles "Chinese" Gordon, who commanded the rag-tag native garrison and attempted single-handedly to uphold his nation's Egyptian "interests" in the city where the White and Blue Niles converge.

For the occasion, Sir Laurence has bushed his brows, grown a handsome beard, plastered himself with dark brown makeup and got up a fine Wog accent that compares most favorably with Peter Sellers's efforts in that direction. The historical Mahdi had a gap between his upper front teeth (a good luck sign among his people) and Sir Laurence does, too; he even contrives to lisp whistlingly through it in moments of high stress. He also smiles a lot, especially when contemplating slaughter or when he is nervous about the strength of the forces his ambition compels him to challenge. This is, in short, a characterization of pure gorgeousness—comic yet sinister, ignorant yet shrewd, energetic yet made hesitant by superstitious respect for the mad magic of Gordon's ego. Since the movies began, a thousand actors have given us versions of the rebellious native chieftain, but it has remained for Sir Laurence to infuse that cliché with humanity and depth. In this historical portrait one gains new insights into the pride, cunning and weakness of those who preside over the nations newly emerging in our time.

Would that a similar sense of appositeness, or even a little bit of Sir Laurence's lively spirit, had overtaken the rest of the group responsible for this movie. Robert Ardrey's script is reasonably intelligent about causes and effects, reasonably accurate with historical facts (he only occasionally, and with cause, abuses his dramatist's license), but it lacks thrust and suspense. He never licks the fact that Khartoum was a static, virtually actionless siege, only briefly productive of large-scale movie heroics. Most of its real drama took place back in the cabinet room in London. He faithfully reports this, but it is nonsense to try to fill a Cinerama screen with it. Basil Dearden's direction is tentative and rather distant—as if he never found a way to involve himself with his material. There is no feeling, such as one had in *Lawrence of Arabia*, of the terror and loneliness of warfare in the desert. Nor is there any sense of just how oppressive it must have been to be cut off in Khartoum without communication, the food supply dwindling and the waters of the protecting Nile falling day by day. Yakima Canutt's action sequences frequently have some spectacular effects at their centers, but even they are dulled because around the edges of the giant screen one frequently spots extras dogging it or too obviously faking their fights.

Finally, as in almost every spectacular these days, there is the Charlton Heston problem. It really passes all understanding why his presence is regarded by producers as a requisite for this kind of film. If he can do anything as an actor, he can produce a quality of stiff-backed rectitude, suitable for playing Biblical patriarchs or the military mind in its simpler incarnations. But a complex Victorian like Gordon, a man of strange moods and violent contrasts, is utterly beyond him. Perhaps spurred by Sir Laurence's example, he rises creditably above himself in their two scenes of direct confrontation, but his standard hero, hewn out of slick, cool American granite, is simply wrong for the part and a disaster for a script that revolves completely around Gordon and his temperament.

One gets the feeling that everyone connected with *Khartoum* approached it seriously and with the highest intentions; they genuinely wanted to make a spectacular for adults. They were apparently so sobered by their ambitions that somehow the strange beauty and tragedy of this peculiar interlude in colonial history eluded them. Only Sir Laurence, full of weird and wayward life, suggests the true nature of the fascination the story of Khartoum can exert on one's historical imagination.

Unpublished

This is one of the two reviews I wrote during this five-year period which Life never published. It got bumped out of a couple of issues by stuff that seemed more pressing to the editors and, God knows, the movie was awful—not really worth anyone's time. But the little tribute to Sir Laurence is heartfelt —he remains my favorite movie actor—and I include it here just to get it on the record at last.

THE GOSPEL
ACCORDING TO
ST. MATTHEW

The Gospel According to St. Matthew is certainly the best life of Jesus ever placed on film and it is probably the finest religious film ever made as well. Indeed, it may come to rank, as the years add to our perspective, among the great movies of all time, regardless of subject.

It is a raw, crude, tremendously vital movie, bearing no resemblance whatsoever to the passionless plays Hollywood has inevitably created when it has turned to "the greatest story ever told" for material. *Matthew*'s director, Pier Paolo Pasolini, is, incredibly, an Italian Communist, who made his film in the barren hills of southern Italy, using amateur actors exclusively. Lacking funds, it was apparently easy for him to avoid the temptation to prove his piety by lavishing expensive adornment on his film. He has also been forced to scrimp on the accuracy of the historical trivia (sets, costumes, etc.) that Hollywood always takes such pride in. But necessity has here mothered a blessed lack of elaborate invention, a stark simplicity that has an emotional accuracy to be treasured far more than empty spectacle.

Pasolini has caught the dusty, brutal, ignorant, superstitious tone of daily life as it must have been in a particularly remote and poverty-stricken backwater of the Roman Empire. In so doing he has overturned all the conventions of Biblical visualization we have accepted without thinking since the Renaissance. Jesus trudges the roads of Judea neither haloed nor clad in white, but in a scratchy, dirty black robe. His beard is scraggly and much of the time he has about him the fevered air of a hungry, exhausted man driven by the knowledge that time is short and that there is much to do.

All of the "big scenes" are understated. The Slaughter of the Innocents is a patrol action by second-rate troops; Salome's Dance is the clumsy sexual offering of an eager but very inexperienced courtesan; the miracles are country-fair tricks designed to catch the rabble's attention; the Last Supper is a poor meal in a bad tavern; the Crucifixion itself is seen as the ignominious death the Romans intended it to be, and it is suffered by a sweating, frightened man who screams most horribly when the nails are driven in.

In short, this is, in the most literal meaning of the term, an iconoclastic picture which refuses to offer the comforting blandness of overfamiliar images, those conventions and stylizations with which we have distracted ourselves from the terrors, enigmas and strangenesses of a time and place far removed from our own. By forcing us to see with a fresh and unblinking eye, Pasolini also forces us to attend to the character and teaching of Jesus with renewed concentration. It is up to us to leap the historical gap between his time and ours, between his character as Matthew reported it and as we have softened and blurred it through the centuries. The universal truth of his message is still there, but we must work to find it.

For this Jesus turns out to differ almost completely from the sweet-tempered liberal reformer the modern Sunday school texts and popularizers inherited largely from nineteenth-century reinterpretations like Renan's *Life of Jesus*. Matthew's Messiah—and Pasolini's—is a much more difficult character than that. He is a radical and like most of the breed he is angry, rigid, often petulant and egocentric. He is, as we sometimes forget, very much the son of man as well as the son of God. The sermons, parables and homilies are spat forth as bristling challenges to the conventional wisdom of his day and the only gentleness he allows himself is with children. To their parents he offers "not peace but a sword," warning those who would follow him that his teachings are bound to set brother against brother, son against father.

Because Pasolini places Jesus so firmly in the context of his time, because he refuses to smooth the rough edges off his character, there is an intellectual and dramatic excitement to this film that I have never felt in any treatment of its subject in any medium. Thus, the great confrontation between Jesus and the elders of the temple is not just an excuse for him to mouth some interesting thoughts but is instead a bitter, biting, brilliant duel between the establishment and a challenger it is quite right to fear. There is a similar tension in his talks with the disciples and in his meetings with ordinary people. Because these scenes are so firmly grounded in reality, Pasolini is able to abandon realistic staging entirely at times, focusing close up on the Messiah speaking the great texts directly to us. The end result of all this is not the simple shock of recognition that is the most we have come to expect from retellings of the "greatest story," but the shock of a new awareness, a new understanding that is infinitely more exciting.

Partly this is due to the ferociously intense performance of a young Spanish student named Enrique Jrazoqui as Christ. Partly it is due to the radically simplified cinematic techniques of the director, who has rejected the fashionable trickeries of the new cinema and gone back to the classic camera placement, the straightforward editing, the harsh contrasty lighting one associates with the visual style of D. W. Griffith. But mostly it is due to the fact that Pasolini has chipped away the encrustations of time and given us the story as it was written in the first place. It may shock some pious people who prefer traditionalism to the truth of art, conventionalized pageantry to the passion of an artist caught up in his own unique vision. It will certainly disturb those who prefer not to contemplate the social implications of the Gospel. That it requires a Communist director to remind us of them may be taken as an irony or as renewed proof that God works in mysterious ways his wonders to perform. What is important is that the film exists and that no one, whatever his faith or lack of faith, can fail to be touched by its grim and glorious sense of the life and the times of a Jesus who is here truly, agonizingly, a living Christ.

3/11/66

Gush, gush, gush. I think I was in love with the idea of atheist me responding positively to a religious subject. Still, I suppose it is at least the best "religioso" (to borrow a word) I've ever seen, though, considering the competition, that's not very high praise. As for Pasolini, he's devoted himself since to homosexual fantasies of truly stupefying wretchedness. Still, movies are an accidental art, and we must concede bad directors their occasional—and amazing—successes.

DEAR JOHN

There is going to be a certain amount of foolish controversy over *Dear John,* which is the official Swedish contender for the Academy Award as this year's best foreign film. Partly—but only partly—this is because the movie is what they call astonishingly frank about the physiology of human sexual union and remarkably uninhibited and specific in its recording of the way lovers talk and touch and think when they have just discovered one another. But, after all, we live in an age when every other film claims to be "adult" about these matters, and a small percentage of them actually are. If the frankness of *Dear John* were only a matter of an occasionally bared breast or a few lines of blunt dialogue, I don't think it would at this late date stir much censorious interest. What will agitate the prurient and, if the usual custom prevails, give the movie the notoriety it deserves but for the wrong reason, is its unique tone, which is both direct and casual.

By this I mean that it does not take any of the three currently acceptable cinematic attitudes toward sex. It does not have the earnestly clinical manner of a college course in marriage and the family. Nor does it adopt the style of those middle-aged ladies who don't mind a risqué story if it's cute. Nor, finally, does it make of sex a heavy-breathing tragedy in which lovingly detailed transgressions are suitably, if cursorily, punished in the final reel.

Rather, Lars Magnus Lindgren, who wrote and directed

Dear John, has attempted something infinitely more difficult, which is to show us with unusual fidelity how ordinary people ordinarily experience the pleasures and difficulties of loving. This sounds like a fairly commonplace task, but it is not until one witnesses a success like *Dear John* that one is struck by how rarely one actually finds in our love fictions language and incident and behavior that are anything like the stuff of real life.

Lindgren's basic story could not be simpler. Two lonely people, the captain of a small freighter and a cafe waitress, meet when he berths his ship in her small town for a weekend. They are naturally attracted to one another, but each has good reason to be wary of love; he is a cuckold, she has a child fathered by a lover who has abandoned her. Through a long day, during which they take the child for an outing, they test one another hopefully but carefully, and each finds the other a decent, if wounded, human being. Each wants to make love with the other, but through clumsiness, through failures to understand the cues and clues each is ambiguously transmitting, they almost fail. When at last they do embrace it is in an ecstasy of passions too long denied, lonelinesses too long accepted. Most of the story is told in the form of flashbacks from their bed—brief, allusive, sometimes repeated for emphasis—as they try to express their joy, explain themselves and add historical and psychological substance to their brief physical intimacy, hoping thereby to transform it into something more lasting.

The film only sounds conventional in the retelling. What gives it special depth and dimension are two factors, the first artistic, the second intellectual. The two principals, Jarl Kulle and Christina Schollin, are wonderfully attractive people and sensitive, naturalistic actors. There is a fine comic edge to his portrayal of the vain yet vulnerable male on the prowl; her portrayal of a woman learning to trust a man again is illuminated by sudden flashes of old fears, and she can be heartbreakingly beautiful in those moments. Lindgren's artistry matches theirs. He has a gift for selecting the perfect detail—a gesture, a symbol, a memory—and placing it before us with deft allusiveness. Not a scene, a speech, a shot is held too long on screen. The lovers, for example, are naked together in bed for at least a quarter of the film, but one never has the feeling that the camera is lingering lasciviously or turning away too quickly in embarrassment.

Lindgren has a sound intellectual reason for emphasizing the physical aspects of love. In the basic paradox he is examining he sees the physical as an equal partner to the poetic. Love, he says, may be sublime in its transports, but it begins in animal grapplings. Men may make poetry out of the experience, but it is also in their nature to make bawdy jokes about it. If Lindgren did not show us the earthy side of this paradox, the lyricism would lose its force.

What his film makes inescapable is the belief that love at its fullest is neither a wholly profane nor a wholly spiritual experience. If it is to last—as this time it does—it must be a complex intertwining of both moods. That his film so touchingly and joyously dramatizes this point proves Lindgren's artistic and intellectual maturity.

3/18/66

The controversy alluded to in the lead never developed. Carefully released, Dear John was cheerfully and widely accepted by audiences as a decently romantic film that of inner necessity dealt with some of the explicit details of how a particular man and a particular woman coupled. What did develop, over the years I've been reviewing, is an endless, feckless debate over the general subject of pornography and the movies. True to my libertarian instincts, I've insisted that the long-sought freedom of the screen should not be lightly discarded because, so quickly following its establishment, stag movies—and that's precisely what they are—have profitably gone public. Unfortunately, there is a tendency to lump together all movies dealing with sex—the good ones and the horrible ones—in the bourgeois brain. This is especially true among people who go very little to the movies. Indeed, so crazily up-tight has the middle-class audience become that it has really ceased to think about this subject at all. Fear of sexual exploitation has become an excuse not to go to any movies except those guaranteed to be whiter than white. And yet there are sensible remedies. For one thing, no respectable reviewer ever bothers to review skin flicks. For another, no major movie company distributes them. Therefore, if there is critical silence about a film and if the ads for it do not contain a familiar trademark, the wary customer will avoid it. On the other hand, a glance at even brief reviews of films being released under respectable auspices should serve to warn him of what he may expect in the theater. Prior ignorance is no longer an excuse for subsequent outrage. About the hard-core pornography, which generally plays grind houses in the decaying downtowns of our big cities, I must confess I don't worry. The customers appear to be mainly lonely middle-aged males and there is probably some social benefit to be gained by gathering them together under one roof to indulge their sexual tensions voyeuristically. At least they aren't wandering around trying accidentally-on-purpose to rub against girls in crowded subway trains. As for the adolescents who occasionally join them there in the anonymous dark, I doubt anyone can make a movie as steamy as the fantasies typical of that particular age of man. Of course, I couldn't agree more that the proliferation of all kinds of pornography has in recent years lowered the general tone of life in the United States. But then, so have a lot of other things, including the level of our political discourse. I hate and despise the general shoddiness of our culture, but I still want us to be able to see the Dear Johns when they come along, and censorship still seems to me more debilitating to society than a proliferation of skin flicks.

JOHN F. KENNEDY:
YEARS OF LIGHTNING,
DAY OF DRUMS

John F. Kennedy: Years of Lightning, Day of Drums is the much publicized documentary of the late President's years in office which the United States Information Agency produced for overseas distribution and which so impressed official Washington that Congress was easily persuaded to pass a special resolution exempting it from the prohibition against domestic release of USIA material. Proceeds from its commercial run here will go to the Kennedy Center for the Performing Arts in Washington. Given the intrinsic interest of the film's subject and the quality of the advance word on it, these will undoubtedly be high. But by any reasonable standard of documentary art, the quality of the film is low—disturbingly so.

The movie was written and directed by Bruce Herschensohn, who also contributed a musical score full of sobbing violins and slushy choral effects. From the opening moments, when bold credits in forced perspective announce the flabby title by gliding through the frame to disappear in a glowering cloud bank, it is obvious that Mr. Herschensohn's sense of style is borrowed from the less exalted reaches of Hollywood and that it could not be less appropriate to a film about Mr. Kennedy.

The narration is orotund, portentous, pretentious and thus at obvious odds with the preferred prose style of Mr. Kennedy, which tended toward the aphoristic and the understated. Similarly, the film's organization is confused and mushy, while the

66

organization of its subject's life and career was nothing if not cool and well calculated.

In fact, the movie is composed of two separate and distinct parts. The first is a fairly straightforward record of the "day of drums," that is, to put it in plain English, of the state funeral of John F. Kennedy. This is not especially distinguished as film art, but it is inescapably affecting, stirring again the most terrible memories. Woven through this footage is what amounts to a second film, a compilation of film clips designed to recapture the "years of lightning." There is something basically cheap about this attempt to transfer the primal emotions of the Kennedy funeral to the political realm, where they are not only in poor taste but work against the attempt to gain a sober, rational perspective on the late President's policies and personality.

Not that Mr. Herschensohn demonstrates any capacity for even rudimentary political analysis. He has adopted the arbitrary conceit that there were "six faces" to the New Frontier (why not a dozen or a hundred or better yet, why not try to find its single most representative aspect?). These he lists as the Peace Corps, the Alliance for Progress, the fight for civil rights, the exploration of space, the pursuit of peace, the strengthening of our military posture. On its surface the list is a peculiar mixture of specific legislative goals and policies so general and agreeable that they might in fairness be claimed by any world power including, ironically, our enemies when they are trying to put their best feet forward.

But even as he pretends to examine these matters, Mr. Herschensohn speaks with forked tongue. The Bay of Pigs fiasco is dismissed in a half-sentence of narration, which is perhaps understandable if foolish; but Mr. Kennedy's best moments— the Cuban missile crisis, the Nuclear Test Ban Treaty among them—are given scarcely more attention. Instead, Herschensohn caters endlessly to the gang in the back row of the mud huts, showing endless sequences of the President abroad, surrounded and cheered by mindless mobs—not the atmosphere in which he was at his best or his most comfortable or, indeed, most importantly engaged in shaping the life of our times. Missing entirely from the film is any sense of the man's presence and personality, which in the last analysis was the true source of his appeal and of his impact on our history. Where, one wonders, is the man who was so wonderfully quick and sharp at the press conferences? Where, more important, is the man who could so artfully and forcefully articulate for ourselves and the world our old, best dreams and sometimes even bring to light yearnings we had almost forgotten? Mr. Herschensohn has, very simply, an unerring eye and ear for Mr. Kennedy's lesser moments, plus a taste for emotionality that at this moment is precisely what the Kennedy legend does not need.

It would be easy to dismiss the banalities and ineptitudes of this movie as the inevitable failures of government-supported propaganda. Its producer was, after all, a bureaucracy, and bureaucracies would always prefer to burble about the "six faces" of policy than come to grips with individuals—even Presidents—in human terms. They are also fearful of truth—it might offend opinion abroad (where the movie's primary audience is) or at home (where Congress worries about our image and also controls budgets). The temptation in these circumstances is always to make the unexceptionably unexceptional film, to stay as close as possible to a least-common-denominator style of expression, the only offense of which is aesthetic.

But one wonders . . . Some of the great documentaries of all time have been created under government auspices and for propaganda purposes. One thinks of *The Land* and *The River* and *The Plow That Broke the Plains* from the Depression years, *Fighting Lady* and *San Pietro* from the war years—all films that said something valuable about our country and our spirit. One even recalls artistically effective films underwritten by dictatorships as reprehensible as Stalin's Russia and Hitler's Germany. Good film artists have a way of driving out indifferent and even evil government policy—when they remain true to the dictates of their art. It is precisely this that Mr. Herschensohn does not do as he panders to what he imagines to be the demands of his employers and his potential audience. The result is a film as completely sold out as any Hollywood hack work. One leaves it insulted, as one always is by compromised art, and, remembering its original intention, just a trifle ashamed of the tone this nation takes when it tries to address the world.

4/15/66

This seems as good a place as any to say a few words about the question of pressure. For the most part, it takes a very modest form. There is a phone call from a press agent, bearing the glad tidings that Director X has long been an admirer of one's reviews, that by a happy coincidence he will be in town next week and would so much like to have lunch. It nearly always happens that there is a further odd coincidence: Director X is about to release his latest movie. And so, haltingly, modestly, the luncheon conversation turns to the new work and to the artist's attempt to enlist you on his side against the cruel distributors who are, inevitably, mishandling his delicate little bloom. Often enough he is right—they are, indeed, sending the thing right down the drain by putting it in the wrong theaters or dumping it in multiple release. These conversations are harmless enough, and occasionally, they produce some useful information about intentions, problems, etc. For the most part, however, they are just a waste of time—pleasant or unpleasant depending on the personality seated across the table. Once or twice there have been modest attempts to suborn the witness—usually by expressing interest in the reviewer's unsuspected gift as a screenwriter. Generally, however, directors are aware that critics, whatever their other faults, are not for sale—certainly not for the price of a lunch.

Occasionally, however, a bad review escalates the inevitable tension between creator and critic into open warfare—the opening shot of which is always a letter to the editor proposing that a more "objective" critic be engaged to reconsider the masterpiece that has been irrevocably damaged by the reviewer's insensitive and uncomprehending notice. The pleasant practice at Life has been for the editor to send these over to me to answer as I see fit, which has led to some gratifyingly splenetic correspondence. However, no one in the industry has gone to the lengths to which the director of the Kennedy documentary went. He called not just for a re-review but for my ouster first for this piece, then, a second time, for the letter I drafted in response to that proposal. In five years no one else ever pressed his outrage to such lengths, and it has always amused me that this most vicious attempt to redress a grievance came not from a representative of crass commercialism, but from a man engaged in what appeared to be an idealistic enterprise. There is a moral in there somewhere.

SHAKESPEARE WALLAH

Shakespeare Wallah is a slow, sweet, sometimes sad, sometimes funny film that very gently, very quietly, very politely asks for your attention and then, once it has obtained it, proceeds to envelop you in a rare and special atmosphere with a subtle artfulness that lingers long in memory.

Though its surface has a deceptively simple quality, the human issues examined by the movie are complex and, in the best sense, ambiguous. "Wallah" means peddler or small-time operator in Hindi, and James Buckingham is surely that. Owner, manager and leading man of a tacky but genteel troupe of Shakespearean players endlessly touring the Indian provinces, he is a man trapped in an old dream. With his wife he came out to the subcontinent in the last days of the British Raj, vaguely, idealistically hoping to offer cultural uplift to the masses, meanwhile providing their rulers with a little touch of the amenities they left behind. Now almost two decades have passed, very few Englishmen are left in India and the natives are made exceedingly restless by an evening with the Bard. If Buckingham had any sense he would pack it in.

But there is no place to go. It is too late for him to resume his career in England, and besides he and his wife find their dusty road comfortably rutted. Then, too, he has a teen-age daughter, Lizzie, who is the company's ingénue and who knows no other life. Finally, there are the others who have cast their lot with him—a very old English character actor named

Robbie, the Indian technicians and small-part players. What would happen to them if he quit?

Yet even as he proceeds, the evidence of the decay of the old Anglo-Indian culture that was his chief support grows more and more forceful. The keeper of an English boardinghouse confides that she is closing up and going home, an English-style school that has always been good for several performances now has no time in its schedule for Shakespeare, the English club where the company once found such a warm welcome is now run down and almost deserted. Sometimes there is not enough money to pay salaries, and one day on the road old Robbie's heart simply gives out.

But what finally rends the fraying fabric of this existence is Lizzie's affair with a young Indian playboy she meets in her travels. In his way he is as dreamy as the Buckinghams. The lover of an Indian film star, he vaguely aspires to become a movie director. Meantime, he is drifting along, decent but indecisive, hoping something will happen to give *him* direction. He very nearly finds it in his love for Lizzie, but caste and weakness of character will out, and he can no more make this commitment than the Buckinghams can abandon theirs. The best they can do is send their daughter back to England to recover from the affair and perhaps find a more meaningful life than theirs. They, however, will continue on—brave, absurd, touching—until undoubtedly they too expire somewhere on the road to nowhere.

Clearly this is fragile, wispy stuff, requiring delicacy and precision in its handling. It could easily have been sentimentalized or romanticized by a heavy hand. A diffident director, conversely, might have made it seem terribly distant and minor. But James Ivory, a young American with only one feature to his credit, is a deft and thoughtful worker. He has a wonderful feel for the Indian landscape and a sure eye for the detail that tells more than any script can about a place or a character or a society in transition. Moreover, he has the courage and taste to unfold his story at a studied pace, forcing no conclusions on the viewer but allowing him to observe—no, absorb—these people with clear-eyed yet sympathetic objectivity. The result is a tone that resembles that of Chekhov, who also found in a decaying society the universal truths about the sadness of self-absorption, the tragicomedy of indecisiveness.

Ivory and his scriptwriter, R. Prawer Jhabvala, are wonderfully served by their actors. The Buckinghams are played by the Kendals, whose own experiences as strolling players in India closely parallel those of the people they portray. On the evidence of this film, there is no need for them to hide away in the forgotten outposts of a lost empire any longer. They are most gifted people, and Felicity Kendal, who plays Lizzie, is more than that; she appears to have a depth and spirit not usually found in ingénues. They are ably abetted by Shashi Kapoor as Sanju, the playboy, and by Madhur Jaffrey, who has some of the film's strongest moments as his petulantly foolish mistress.

Shakespeare Wallah is not a film about the clash of cultures but rather about the haunting reverberations that linger in the air long after such a clash. It is, therefore, utterly unique in its subject matter. That its humanity, its intelligence and its imagery match its novelty is an incalculable added boon, making it a film everyone who cares about the movies should see.

4/29/66

MORGAN!

Morgan! is a supposedly comic film about a young artist in rebellion against our dehumanizing modern society. It contains a couple of nice performances (by David Warner in the title role and by the lovely Vanessa Redgrave as his estranged wife), some familiar but still pleasantly farcical turns, and evidence of competent but by no means electrifying—or original—cinematic skill on the part of its director, Karel Reisz (who did *Saturday Night and Sunday Morning*).

But frankly, it is one of those movies that ran through my mind like an undistinguished popular song—fashionable and forgettable and hardly worth the effort of praise or blame. Upon its release, however, what to my wondering eyes should appear but a set of astonishingly superheated reviews—very nearly the best of the season. It appears that all unknowing I was in the presence of a rare orchestration of comedic genius and social awareness as I nodded through *Morgan!* Indeed, such is the enthusiasm of the initial critical response to the picture that I find it almost more interesting than the object under analysis. What *did* they see in it?

Safe pseudo-seriousness, I think. *Morgan!* offers us the attitudes of revolt without ever posing a genuine threat to our conventional comforts or wisdom. We tolerate this non-hero in his moments of rebellion as we might tolerate a two-year-old child in his. The issues are obviously serious enough to him, but since he is neither smart enough nor strong enough to coerce us into action, it is easier to ignore him or, perhaps, pat him on the head and say, "There, there," without giving him another thought. If he gets really troublesome, you can always give him a spanking.

That's pretty much what happens to Morgan. His principal preoccupation is to win back his divorced wife before she marries an intensely bourgeois art dealer. To accomplish this he lays siege to her house, alternately pleading with her and nagging at her, rather like my daughter when she has her mind set on an ice cream cone. Occasionally he becomes charmingly destructive—placing a small bomb under her bed or wiring a sound system to startle her and her lover in tender moments. Once he even invades the art dealer's office with intent to kill, only to meekly surrender one weapon after another to his cool rival. Even his attempt to kidnap the lady and spirit her away to a woodland idyll fizzles like a kid's first attempt to run away from home. It's all a tantrum in a teapot, pathetically easy to turn aside.

Well, all right. A lot of revolutionaries are a little weak in the technical skills of their trade, but they at least provide some intellectual stimulus for the rest of us. So perhaps the secret of *Morgan*'s success with the critics lies in its ideas? Nope, all Morgan offers his wife as an alternative to sensible prosperity is the opportunity of joining him in going literally ape.

His fantasy life revolves entirely around the hairy primates. They are the only subjects of his paintings; his most prized possession is a stuffed gorilla, and in crisis his thoughts turn to imaginings of how he would handle things if London were a real rather than a metaphorical jungle. In his final flip he dons a monkey suit and breaks up his wife's second wedding as if he were King Kong.

There is a certain amount of visual humor in all this, though it lacks the delightful, careless anarchy of Richard Lester's Beatle films, which were clearly Mr. Reisz's models. One can even sympathize with Morgan's situation a little bit. At one time or another all of us have wanted to run through the streets in a mad reversion to childhood. The trouble is that such behavior solves nothing, either personally or socially. It is not even effective as protest; it is merely self-indulgence. And I'm getting tired of these film and fictional heroes who exist only to illustrate the fact that life is capable of driving us crazy. We *know* that—the trick lies in avoiding this all too predictable fate.

In my opinion, Morgan's wife is quite right to divorce him and quite right to call the cops when his attentions grow excessive. He is, in fact, as intrusive in his addled way as the conditions that he is protesting, and on balance I should say her right to privacy is at least as valuable as his right to self-expression, which amounts, in any case, to nothing more than a series of monkey imitations.

How the protest movement in English films and drama has declined! From the awakening abrasiveness of the straight-talking angry young men to the inarticulate gruntings of a would-be ape man in less than a decade. If that's progress, I'm a monkey's uncle.

5/6/66

God, what a dopey movie! But if we seek the historical roots of Hollywood's infatuation with the youth market, we might well look to the surprising commercial success of this movie. In any event, it had all the qualities that have since become so dismally familiar—the subject's belief in his own superior innocence and insight, his paranoid certainty that the adult world was a vast conspiracy to rob him of same, the doomed impracticality of his revolutionary techniques, the self-conscious craziness of the film's style. We were on the road to all the post-Graduates without knowing it.

KANCHENJUNGHA

Satyajit Ray, the noted Indian director, is up to his usual lack of tricks in his latest film, *Kanchenjungha*. Once again he has dared to make a movie of such stately pace and conventionality of imagery that it—and the audience—always teeters on the brink of boredom. Once again his characters are fictional familiars—archetypes in danger of becoming stereotypes. Once again his story is little more than a cliché. And once again, by a magic that is peculiarly his own, he forces us to attend his deliberately difficult work closely and to care, perhaps more than common sense would dictate, about its outcome.

It is afternoon in Darjeeling, "queen of the hill stations," whither the Choudhuris, a wealthy family from Calcutta, have repaired for vacation. It is their last day at the resort, a run-down remnant of the British Raj, and constant mists have prevented them from seeing its principal sight, the mountain of the title, which is the third highest in the world. The family itself is also enveloped by psychological mists. Father is a benevolent despot, director of five companies, inordinately proud of a British title which symbolizes his devotion to a social order he understood better than he does the new India, of which his children are the restive representatives. His son is a wastrel, his eldest daughter is unhappily married to the man her father chose for her, his younger daughter is attempting to fend off the prematurely middle-aged engineer Daddy approves for her. Their mother has been reduced to suffering silence quietly, and her brother, obviously supported by the patriarch, watches birds.

Into this stiflingly non-communicative atmosphere a young man intrudes. He needs a job, and his uncle, who once served the family as a tutor, arranges a meeting with the elder Choudhuri. Indeed, he has several encounters with him and his family in the course of their afternoon's promenade through Darjeeling. He finally rejects Choudhuri's aid, but by the end of the afternoon his shy and poetic nature has commended itself to the daughter as an alternative to the paternally approved engineer, while his spirit in rejecting her father's job offer has demonstrated the practicality of revolt. By the time the sun begins to set, it is clear—to all but him—that Mr. Choudhuri's grip on his family has been broken. In the final scene the mists clear and Kanchenjungha suddenly becomes visible. Preoccupied, Choudhuri fails to notice it.

Some sketchy subplots underpin this central situation, but they are no more thrill-packed than the major premise. The Darjeeling setting is interesting, but Ray, who is no pictorialist, handles it routinely. The technical quality of the film is distractingly poor. What, then, is so fascinating about it?

I cannot fully answer that question, since I know the picture did its most forceful work on me below the conscious level, but I suspect it has to do with Ray's patient, insistent probing for the meanings of gestures and glances and silences, his search for the psychic realities that lie beneath conversational conventions and banalities. All these small matters carry a weight in this film that is far heavier than normal, and as we strain forward to catch their true meanings we are, almost against our wills, caught up in the mysteries, the psychopathology if you will, of everyday life. Almost imperceptibly the gentle flow of this film draws us beneath the surface of an ordinary situation, involving very ordinary people, and reveals unsuspected depths, material for speculation that lingers in the mind long after the film has ended.

In an era when most directors are exploiting the visual possibilities of their medium to the utmost, Ray, filming in a crude and even antique style, is perhaps the most daring of them all. He has deliberately cut himself off from all the gaudy gimmicks now available to help the director over the thin and through the rough spots of a script. By also avoiding the more traditional attention-grabbing devices—glamorized settings, décor, costumes, scenes highly charged with overt action and emotion —he has set himself extraordinarily narrow limits within which to work. His films are too "uncinematic" for the purists, too lacking in sensation to appeal much to the wide audience. Essentially, he is like a novelist of sensibility compelling us, through his sensitivity to nuance and the purity and economy of his art, to observe with him the small telling details that reveal the ways people relate—and fail to relate—to one another. Such artists are rarely popular, but they are valuable, reminding us that there are strengths in limitations, truths in subtleties.

Mr. Ray's Darjeeling brew is neither brisk enough nor bracing enough to be everyone's cup of tea. I doubt that many contemporary film makers will attempt to imitate it, and, indeed, I am not sure I would care to become a regular imbiber of such potions. But I am glad Mr. Ray continues to experiment with them, for on occasion they leave one with a curiously refreshing, oddly lingering aftertaste.

8/12/66

It's movies like this that profoundly frustrate the reviewer. It never to my knowledge played outside New York in thirty-five-millimeter theatrical release. (The same may be said of Ray's subsequent The Big City *and Ivory's* The Guru, *though the latter had the benefit—if that's the word I want—of release by a major company, Twentieth Century-Fox.) It is the fate of quietly excellent films like this that betrays the shallowness of* the new audience's alleged devotion to the alleged "central art form of our time." The fact is that they, no less than the old mass audience, basically seek sensation and basically won't be bothered with films that speak softly in a cultivated tone and in a traditional style of the small matters that are the quintessence of our shared existence on this planet.

ALFIE

You may hate yourself for it in the morning, but I think you are going to enjoy *Alfie* very much. It is an exuberant movie on a savage subject—the contemporary anti-hero, a coward, ne'er-do-well and mighty fornicator, a man who uses people—mainly women—and when he is finished with them throws them away like Kleenex. The trick that writer Bill Naughton (adapting his own play) and director Lewis Gilbert have brought off is to show you this all too familiar modern character whole, without blurring sentiment or crowd-pleasing dishonesty, and make you like both him and the process of discovering all the twists and turns of his disconcerting personality.

Several factors contribute to their unlikely achievement. There is the sheer joy they seem to find in the business of making a movie. They don't indulge in a lot of fashionable camera and editing tricks, but there is a zing in the language, a zip in the pace which give the film the sort of life that technique alone can never impart. The principal novelty devices—old-fashioned theatrical asides, interrupting the action and delivered directly to the camera—are no annoyance here; indeed, they function perfectly to draw us into Alfie's conspiracy to expose and thus undermine the conventional moral wisdom. Along with him we joyfully discover that we are all brothers in our moral incapacity.

Then there is the pleasure of watching Michael Caine, late of *The Ipcress File,* make something wonderful out of the title role. His is a portrait in which the hard bright primary colors of his basic characterization are blended and shaded into the most subtle designs. Somehow he manages to engage our sympathies without ever once asking for them outright. Finally, and most important to its success, this is the first in the long, honorable tradition of English working-class films that does not blame its protagonist's stunted growth on the sociology or politics of postwar Britain. Alfie is not a poor Midlands lad trying to cut his way up through the unfeeling establishment. On the contrary, he is content with life on the lower rungs of the ladder—so long as he can indulge his penchant for petty graft. Nor does he appear to be particularly afflicted by the new life of swinging London, an atmosphere that in recent fictions seems mainly to engender tedious demonstrations of the rebellious rootlessness of the young and equally tedious (and ostentatious) searches for true values on the part of one or more frightfully sensitive leading characters.

Alfie never searches for anything more complicated than a new bird. He remains, exactly as he describes himself in the first reel, a man whose only article of faith is a belief that love in any form makes you vulnerable and in the end is bound to lead to unsupportable disappointments and rejections and is therefore to be avoided at all costs. The film is, then, on the simplest level simply a string of anecdotes demonstrating Alfie's skill at getting what he wants without giving anything.

Prominent among the many women he tricks into succumbing to his very special charm are a homebody who becomes his common-law wife and bears him a son, a fancy woman, a masochistic beatnik, even the wife of the man who shares his room in a TB sanitorium. Indeed, if the film has a fault, it lies in the overabundance of evidence it lays before us to demonstrate the deadliness of Alfie's aim. But this has its uses, for it shows us how widespread and desperate is the need to love, for surely no one would fall for Alfie's ersatz product if the real thing were more readily available.

But there is more to *Alfie* than that unexceptionable point.

At the end of all this his sometime victims are given the opportunity to turn on him when he needs them. Not viciously or even very dramatically, merely as casually as he left them when it appeared they were about to make unreasonable demands on him, distractedly, offhandedly. The irony is that by now he has learned from some of his experiences—the lost love of the son he loved without even knowing it at the time, the terrors of an abortion that is the wages of his adventure with his roommate's wife—that he was wrong, that worse than the dangers of love is its total absence. As he wanders away from the camera, his last aside cast aside, he knows—and we know—that he has condemned himself to the worst sort of exile, outside the circle of warmth and light which only love can create.

It's a simple message, but it is delivered with respect for the small truths of modern life as most of us live it, and with an awareness that Alfie is not the product of a special time and place but is, instead, a timeless character all of us emulate some of the time and some of us emulate all of the time. That he has been placed before us on the screen in a style that blends sympathy, savagery and satire in such satisfyingly lifelike proportions is a small, gaudy but at heart authentic boon. Michael Caine's Alfie is somebody you are going to carry around with you in your mind for a long time, as you did Laurence Harvey's Joe Lampton or Julie Christie's Darling.

9/2/66

A MAN AND
A WOMAN

There seems to be a trend in recent European films to involve children in the plots of mature movies about mature love affairs. In *Dear John* the heroine is the mother of a young daughter, and one of the film's most touching sequences deals with their trip to a zoo accompanied by the man who eventually becomes the mother's lover. In *Le Bonheur* the rather innocent philanderer is the father of two small children, and his affection for them is an important element in his psychology and therefore in the outcome of the story. Now, in *A Man and a Woman*, the lovers, a widow and a widower, are brought together by the fact that their children attend the same school. (One rainy visitors' day the man offers the woman a lift home after she has missed the last train back to Paris.)

The presence of the children in these films serves, I think, as an earnest of innocent intent on the part of the producers, proving that they are after something more than the sensationalism of frankly photographed "adult" love scenes. But they have a deeper, more aesthetically significant function as well. The kids lend to the movies not only an air of poignantly heightened realism but some human substance to the moral and psychological debate of the adults over the advisability of physically consummating their affair. After all, the children must be considered, and that consideration allows us to see more than we otherwise might of the lovers' sensibilities in action.

This business could easily become yet another in the rapidly expanding list of the clichés of the new cinema, but for me it so far is not. *A Man and a Woman* is not so earthily attractive as *Dear John*, not so intellectually intriguing as *Le Bonheur*, but it does have an appealing texture all its own. It is perfectly possible to summarize its plot cynically as boy meets girl, etc., but that does not do justice to director-writer Claude Lelouch's skill in first particularizing the characters and incidents of his story and then lightly, uninsistently transforming them into universally intelligible symbols. As such they show how hurt and vulnerable people grope toward a mastery of their troubled pasts and thereby learn to accept the possibility that the future could be no more than a repetition of it.

The meaning of the movie, however, lies not on its plot lines but between them, and in particular within the character of the woman. Played with marvelously subtle femininity by Anouk Aimée, she is, without being fully aware of the fact, attracted to danger-prone men. Her first husband was a movie stunt man killed in the line of duty; her would-be lover here is a racing car driver (whom Jean-Louis Trintignant does with a fine, thoughtful boyishness). Her blend of wariness and longing, her sudden bursts of open affection, her equally sudden fears and withdrawals give the film its basic, off-beat emotional rhythm, its suspense and surprise.

Lelouch provided both underscoring and contrast for her moods with evocatively photographed scenes like the first meal the adults share with their children, their first boat-and-beach outing together, quick flashbacks to the woman's idyllic first marriage that are full of rue, humor and joy remembered. He is equally good when he takes his camera to the man's world, catching the tense loneliness of an early-morning test run at the track, the gritty-eyed grime-in-the-joints exhaustion of the drivers in a long road race. Finally, the tactful yet chilling sequence when the woman tries to give herself to her new lover but finds his presence blotted out by an anthology of the happiest moments of her first marriage—a scene that could easily have been sentimentalized, vulgarized or otherwise spoiled by directorial ineptness—becomes a moment of touching and terrible truth in Lelouch's hands.

Superficially, and perhaps even quite deeply, A Man and a Woman is only an old-fashioned romance deceptively done up in the modern movie manner (in the end, boy does get girl, and through the age-old method of persistently applied patience, at that). But in this instance style lends real substance to the end product. It is more than a means of capturing the many moods of a difficult affair, it actually tends to draw you deeper than usual into the couple's struggle to understand themselves, each other and their developing relationship. As if to emphasize the changeability of the relationship he is presenting, Lelouch shifts without apparent pattern from black and white to color film throughout the picture. It is a device that could be annoying, but like everything else in this film it reinforces the feeling that here is a director who respects truth and is bringing all his skills to bear on presenting all of it— right down to his own small shifts of perception and inner feelings about his subject. Lelouch will undoubtedly tackle larger, more original subjects than he has here, but A Man and a Woman cannot be dismissed as merely a small promise of things to come; it is a lovingly wrought and lovely thing in its own right.

9/9/66

THE FORTUNE COOKIE

There is nothing sweet about *The Fortune Cookie*—the image it leaves with you has nothing to do with desserts, Chinese or otherwise. It is, instead, a jackhammer of a film savagely applied to those concrete areas of the human spirit where cupidity and stupidity have been so long entrenched. It has all the defects of a power tool—it is crude and noisy and nerve-wracking. But it has a virtue that cancels out these faults; it is a bitterly, often excruciatingly, funny movie.

Directing from a script he co-authored with his faithful screenwriter companion I. A. L. Diamond, Billy Wilder has returned to the kind of relentless hard-eyed social and moral observation that has marked his best work from *Double Indemnity* through *Sunset Boulevard* to *The Apartment*. His story is of a sidelines TV cameraman (Jack Lemmon) who is bowled over and slightly hurt by a hard-running member of the Cleveland Browns and who is persuaded by his shyster brother-in-law (Walter Matthau) to fake more serious injuries in order to bring a huge phony damage suit against everyone even remotely connected with the accident.

Hoping the dough will help him win back the divorced wife he despises even as he lusts after her, Lemmon reluctantly plays along, and before the poor schlemiel returns to his honest senses, we are treated by Wilder and his co-workers to a short course in the common venality of our times that is unparalleled in recent Hollywood history. At the top of his form, Wilder never tries to woo the audience's consent to his sardonic vision of man; he simply overpowers its resistance with an endless salvo of first-class one-line gags, the prodigal introduction of grotesquely distorted comic characters, as if he were some latter-day Ben Jonson. He mounts the whole gaudy high-pressure display against a background that seems to include every monstrous mistake ever made in the arts of architecture, home furnishing and dress. I would never claim that Wilder's is a total or even balanced vision of our world. But the landscape he presents is familiar enough to make one uncomfortably aware of the fact that there is an irreducible minimum of dreadfulness in any human society and that its contemporary manifestations are very much as he presents them.

The message inside *The Fortune Cookie* is that when so many of us so cheerfully enter the vast unspoken conspiracy to commit minor frauds on the expense account or steal a few pencils from the office supply cabinet, then the climate is also right for grander larcenies like the one that forms the film's central situation. This, of course, leads to escalated defensive measures on the part of the beleaguered victims, who must resort to private eyes, hidden cameras and bugging devices to protect their interests. In combat at this level there is, finally, neither right nor wrong. The only product is that querulously low level of moral discourse that makes daily living such a joy these days. Wherever Wilder's camera wanders, it emphasizes this point. In little throwaway scenes he discovers one character cheating another in a locker-room game of odds and evens, still another carrying around with him in a paper bag the precious banana peel on which he slipped and which he believes will bring him untold riches when he brings the negligence suit of his dreams against someone, anyone. In short, the disease is everywhere, the totality of its infectiousness is the heart of Wilder's hilarious and pathetic one-joke view of man.

Technically, Lemmon does a superb job in the main role, but the fact is that he just naturally exudes too much intelligence to be totally believable as the easily led TV cameraman.

The picture really belongs to Matthau, who is rapidly becoming the W. C. Fields of the 1960s. Like the Old Master, he is all our petty paranoias, all our paltry dreams of avarice, all our sly, bullying, cynical and changeling instincts rolled into one whey-faced lump. Like Fields, he can change tactics in the wink of an eye, but his basic distrust and dislike of humanity, derived from an all too clear knowledge of his blighted inner self, is as constant as the evening star. In short, he is a joy to behold. So is Judi West as Lemmon's wife, infusing a standard tart part with a wistful, only half-expressed desire to be better. And Ron Rich neatly catches the inarticulate simplicity of the athlete who runs over Lemmon and turns out—naturally enough, in the upside-down Wilder world—to be the only completely decent person in the picture, and then is almost destroyed by the ambiguities of the gray area over which Matthau reigns.

One could wish that Wilder would learn that half as loud and half as fast can sometimes be twice as funny and that he would pursue the logic of his peculiar vision all the way to the end, instead of tacking on falsely cheerful resolutions. Still, he is just about the only American director of comedy who finds his material not in manufactured "situations" but in the artful exaggerations of all too recognizable human and social traits. His is a cold rather than a warm comic spirit, and therefore not to everyone's taste. But if you can stand the chill, I think you'll find—at least in this picture—plenty of truth in what he has to say.

11/18/66

Here's a curious sandwich—tough, chewy Alfie, bitter, crusty The Fortune Cookie and in between a soft, mild cheese spread called A Man and a Woman. How defend such a strange taste? Well, Caine and Matthau each gave performances that transcended the inherent values of their roles, and one might note in passing that one of the basic problems with the brave new movie world is its inability to consistently find good parts for such fundamentally appealing actors. It's been mostly downhill for both of them ever since—and I think under the old studio contract system both would now be firmly established stars instead of one-shot successes flailing around trying to find suitable material. As for A Man and a Woman, Lelouch diminished and did not grow as I thought he might. But the picture remains for me a pleasant memory—its romanticism felt, not fabricated, by the director; its honest sentiment providing a refreshing contrast to most of the work in that vein that we've had in recent years.

BLOW☀UP

The photographer (played with superb authority by David
Hemmings) is preparing a book of his more sordid and violent
pictures but seeks an image more peaceful than the rest as a
conclusion of it. One day, killing time, he wanders into a small
park and there discovers a young woman (Vanessa Redgrave)
and an older man disporting themselves in the more innocent
attitudes of love. Their mood is precisely the one he seeks to
capture on film, and he stalks them like a hunter, snapping
away at their happiness. At last the clickings of his shutter
alarm the girl, and she confronts him, demanding restoration of
her privacy and surrender of the exposed film. He refuses and
she (and perhaps a confederate?) follows him to his studio,
where she offers herself to him in a simple exchange for the
photos—an act which quickly grows complicated as genuine, if
transitory, desire unexpectedly arises.

The incident is the most important one in the long chain of
circumstances out of which Michelangelo Antonioni has expertly fashioned the fuse that finally ignites his *Blow-Up*,
which seems to me one of the finest, most intelligent, least
hysterical expositions of the modern existential agony we have
yet had on film. The most obvious of its many endlessly dis-
cussible implications—that we are so submerged in sensation
and its pursuit that we cannot feel genuine emotion any
more—is hardly novel. But the cool specificity of Antonioni's
imagery (it always reminds me of Henri Cartier-Bresson's great

still photography), his effortless, wonderfully intelligent control of his medium, the feeling he conveys of knowing precisely what he wants to say, and the sense that his perfection of style grows organically out of this awareness, not out of a desire to show off cinematic technique—these are indeed novelties in a day when febrile frenzy is often mistaken for mature motion picture art.

Also novel is the plot that develops out of the encounter between "Jane" and "Thomas" (symbolically charged names to readers of *Lady Chatterley's Lover*). Her offer turns out to be only a tease, the film he hands her is not the film she wants. He then proceeds to develop and print the real stuff, and, casually studying the results, he discovers that his supposedly peaceful scene is anything but. Lurking in the shadows is a man with a gun.

Now he begins to work feverishly over his photos. In an exhausting, beautifully orchestrated study of the futility of seeking the hidden meanings of life through purely technological means, he blows up this and that tiny section of each picture to enormous proportions, but learns only enough to tantalize him further, never enough to resolve the curiosity that has been accidentally transformed from casual professional voyeurism into a consuming passion for the truth. In the end, both audience and anti-hero are left despairingly constructing alternative equally acceptable theories as to what actually happened in the park—one of which is that he may have imagined the whole murderous part of the incident.

But if the central symbolic mystery—like that of the disappearance of the girl in Antonioni's earlier *L'Avventura*—remains insoluble, the quality of daily life as it is experienced by his characters has that brilliant hard-edged clarity that we most often associate with the dream state. In particular, the contrast between the almost sexual passion the photographer works up when doing fashion work and the essentially trivial and vapid nature of his subject is a superbly realized comment on the values of our time, as well as a remarkably realistic study of the mood of such sessions and of a style of conducting them that is quite common.

There are other sequences almost as good: the encounter between Thomas and Jane, where she strips to the waist in an act of bravado, then spends the rest of her time trying to keep herself covered without actually putting her blouse back on, is a strangely poignant vision of the perils of trying to be a free and modern spirit when your heart isn't in it. The photographer's emptily lustful assault on a pair of teeny-boppers who have been begging him to take their pictures is an equally vivid study of the peculiar demands that must be satisfied when sexual freedom becomes a categorical imperative. As for such set pieces as a riot in a discotheque and a visit to a pot party, they, too, are done with an unblinking rightness, a canny selectivity of details that are truly stunning.

Antonioni may be summed up, I should think, as one of the few sober artists attending the long hallucinogenic party that a significant portion of our culture has been staging for the past decade. He has hung around long enough not to be shocked by anything that happens, and he is too intelligent to be tricked into making any easy moral judgments on the events he witnesses. In the last analysis, he is a great realist, laying before us in the most limpid imaginable style nothing more than a simple record of what he has seen and heard and felt about the scene before him. That he sees at the motivating center of our noisy desperation an existential mystery of the most profound sort—and has no pat answer for it either—is further evidence of the personal restraint, the lack of self-indulgence, the emotional control with which he—uniquely among the great new directors—tempers and informs all his excursions to the heart of our contemporary darkness.

1/20/67

One crude, convenient way of dividing critics and the movie-going public is into the Fellini Camp and the Antonioni Camp. In the end we all commit for one or the other. I'm in the latter. I like his textures and his silences and his sly use of mystery stories to metaphorically discuss the larger mysteries of life. Blow-Up has, of course, suffered a decline in reputation with the passage of time, and there were always critics like Pauline Kael who thought it was wildly overrated—though her arguments were never couched in persuasive logic. Anyway, it is a historic movie moment, and it is one of the few movies that continue to burn as vividly in memory as they did on the screen. Its imagery for me is unforgettable—perhaps because, unlike Fellini's imagery, it is the product of conscious, careful thought instead of being ladled up in great gobs from the unconscious. Moreover, his characteristic weary tone wears better than Fellini's hysteria. At least it strikes me as being a truer measure of and response to our peculiar time-spirit.

LA GUERRE EST FINIE

La Guerre Est Finie is an exciting movie on two counts. It is, I think, the most successful representation on film we have had so far of the archetypal political drama of our time, in which a man's psychological need to make ideological commitments wars with the disillusionment such commitments must inevitably bring. It is also the first truly well proportioned—and therefore the first truly satisfying—feature we have had from director Alain Resnais.

Resnais's best-known previous efforts, *Hiroshima, Mon Amour* and *Last Year at Marienbad,* were famously stimulating as visual experiences, but both were curiously empty as human experiences. The latter was deliberately—and infuriatingly—so, while the former failed largely because the director never found a way to make an ordinarily neurotic love story match in significance the terrible historical moment he was trying obliquely to illuminate—the dropping of the Bomb. But in *La Guerre Est Finie,* story, style and symbols are much more carefully balanced, Jorge Semprun's script is a model of intelligent character and thematic development, and Resnais, faced with the challenge of exploring a plot that is densely packed instead of wide-ranging, responds by digging deeply and carefully into his material. The result is an energetic, ironic and mature exploration of the sensibility of an aging revolutionary in an aging century.

Diego (Yves Montand) is a Spaniard who has devoted his

life to fanning such few Communist embers as continue to
faintly glow in his native land, but as we meet him it is clear
that he has few illusions about the possibility of getting a real
fire going. It is also clear, as he slips back across the border to
France, where he is based, that the police are mounting a major
drive against his comrades in Spain. Objective circumstances,
not to mention the ache in his bones, tell him that "*la guerre
est finie.*"

And about time. Revolutionary ardor has cooled into habit,
he has begun to see his cellmates for the fantasists a quarter-
century of exile has made them and his own posture as a professional revolutionary as an absurdity. Unfortunately, withdrawal for him is not as easy as it should be. There is, to begin
with, his commitment to commitment to consider. Could he
live without a cause? Is he, indeed, evaluating the prospects of
this one correctly? Isn't it possible that his desire to settle down
with his beautiful, devoted and totally apolitical mistress
(Ingrid Thulin) is clouding his judgment?

Around and around the ambiguities whirl, and around and
around Paris he travels, pursued by memories and possibilities
which we see in almost subliminal flashes. His fellow revolutionaries, who haven't run a risk (or a border) in years, assure
him that it is theoretically impossible for the movement to be
collapsing in Spain and insist on going ahead with their
treasured scheme for a general strike, infuriating him by deny-
ing the evidence of his own senses because it does not match
their preconceptions. An encounter with a group of younger
revolutionaries, who assure him that his life is a mockery
because his tactics these many years have been wrong, further
confuses him. Yet in the end he goes back to Spain, an act
which draws Miss Thulin into peril and which almost certainly
means his own entrapment. But go he must—not out of any
lingering allegiance to antique grand designs, but out of loyalty
to the friends of a wasted lifetime and to the memory of the
man he thought he was.

In this role Yves Montand gives a performance in which

rage, weariness, self-pity and self-humor quietly and constantly war with each other, and as he plays simply, surely, incisively with each mood, he does as intriguing a piece of screen acting as you are ever likely to see. Miss Thulin is, in her way, his equal, giving us a perfect vision of mature sensuality, and their scenes together are small masterpieces of professionalism.

La Guerre Est Finie is, in effect, a *Man's Fate* for the 1960s—a muted, thoughtful, truthful film about the way time betrays all revolutions and about the absurd, desperate, ennobling expedients men must take in order to escape the destruction of the self that is so often the by-product of that betrayal. The Franco government has objected to the film for obvious reasons, but in fact it quite transcends specific political realities and is a judiciously composed metaphor that says something essential about the human condition—not merely the Spanish one. This is a very important film, yet also a graceful and stylish one.

3/10/67

YOU'RE A BIG BOY NOW

One feels duty bound to try to like *You're a Big Boy Now*, for it is the kind of experimental venture Hollywood should undertake much more often than it does. In this case, a very young man, twenty-seven-year-old Francis Ford Coppola, was given carte blanche by the producers to write and direct a determinedly free-wheeling, putatively personal filmic statement somewhat in the manner some of the younger European directors have achieved. A number of well-knowns (Julie Harris, Geraldine Page, Elizabeth Hartman, Rip Torn) were somehow persuaded to appear in support of such comparative unknowns as Peter Kastner, Karen Black and Tony Bill in this enterprising enterprise. The City of New York joined in the fun by permitting more than usually extensive shooting in its streets and even allowing cameras to intrude for the first time into its normally decorous public library.

Unfortunately, the result of all these good intentions is a movie that is probably eligible for federal relief as a disaster area. This is principally because while everyone was busy turning each other on, no one remembered to ask Mr. Coppola if, in fact, he actually had a personal statement to make or a personal style in which to make it. He does not. His story is a compendium of clichés partially disguised in fancy dress, and his style is an anthology of what used to be new among the avant-garde pussycats—tricks and gimmicks that have now been so thoroughly absorbed into film language that you can see them any night on the television commercials.

The story may be brushed off very briefly. An unformed, vaguely rebellious young man named Bernard seeks to shake off a domineering mother and father, find love and generally grow up. To this end he involves himself not with the nice willing girl who keeps throwing herself at him but with a sado-masochistic Off Broadway actress who also dances in a cage at a mixed-media discotheque. After many merrily sick mishaps he finally shakes free of all the bad people who have been clutching at him and ends up with the nice girl after all.

To give this mess movement, Mr. Coppola relies very heavily on shots of people running through the streets. One time they are chasing a balloon, another time they are chasing a dog, yet a third time they are chasing Bernard, who has absconded with one of the treasures from the library's rare-book room, over which his father presides. Sometimes people run around for no reason at all—they just run, run, run to demonstrate what free spirits some of the younger characters would be if the world were not so much with them. What they are running from or through or (in misguided moments) to are lots of crazy shots of the garish and vulgar sights of the Broadway area, of that discotheque and of the nightmarish lair Miss Hartman (as the beloved sicky) is made to inhabit and where, of course, Bernard suffers a dreadful sexual failure (it shouldn't really bother him—Don Juan himself would have been put off by the room's décor and her manner). All of this symbolizes decadence, while Bernard symbolizes healthy life, and the message of the contrast between him and his surroundings comes through loud, clear and repeatedly. Bad values, bad values—our Bernard has been growing up absurd, in his own little way is fighting a society that would rob him of his youthful innocence but replace it with nothing of value.

For the sake of argument let us concede that this viewpoint may have some validity if not, any more, much news value. The trouble is that it is only an abstraction, the merest and indeed the most conventional starting point for the true comic spirit to work from. What an artist would do is particularize it in terms of characters and situations which might give us a new, or at least arresting, vision of the ancient seriocomic battle of the generations. Instead, Mr. Coppola gives us only grossly exaggerated caricatures acting out the clichés of a psychological casebook, against backgrounds containing only the most conventionalized symbols of evil and innocence, joy and anguish.

About the only good he accomplishes is providing Elizabeth Hartman with a chance to burst forth from the gray-mouse roles in which she has previously been seen. Her performance combines simpering and savagery in a mercurial yet carefully controlled characterization of neurotic hysteria à la mode. If anything, she is too strong and artful for her surroundings, and the harsh light of her work spilling over on the rest of the film intensifies one's sense of dismay with its juvenility.

Mr. Coppola is a young man standing in front of a distorting mirror, trying on both the old and new intellectual clothing of his culture while trying out at the same time the imperfectly observed manners and gestures of the adult world. Somehow he has managed to convince himself that the occasionally bizarre combinations that sometimes result from this activity are, taken together, a creative act and not just self-indulgence.

It makes one very tired, as self-admiring brattiness always does. Worse, it makes one fearful. If the film is by some mischance a success, the imitations of it are going to form the most unbearable cycle since the Gidget pictures. But if, on the other hand, it achieves the failure it intrinsically deserves, will other young men be so quickly given the chance Mr. Coppola has blown? I hope so, for a transfusion of young blood is the only cure for the bad case of tired blood currently afflicting Hollywood. A single mistake should not be held against what is fundamentally a sensible course of therapy.

3/24/67

This is, I think, an example of critical overkill. The picture sank without a ripple. And in any case, one should probably take toward first features an attitude similar to that taken toward first novels—"benign neglect," to borrow a phrase. On the other hand this, along with my notice of Morgan!, betrays one of my strongest critical biases. I was prematurely anti–youth cult—mostly on aesthetic grounds. In this period a standard style evolved to express a rather standard youthful world view, and it seemed unhelpful in explicating the real problems of growing up absurd or enlisting a genuine sympathy with them. Curiously, the pictures that actually achieved what I would guess everyone wanted—sober communication across the generational lines—fared no better with the public (See p. 105: The Family Way) than these more obvious attempts to shock the bourgeoisie into awareness of the revolt beginning to simmer in the adolescent subculture. Indeed, films like You're a Big Boy Now succeeded only in helping close everyone's mind to the subject—and to better films about it. Probably I should have not allowed my outrage to get the better of me here, should have adopted an attitude of exemplary patience and thus, in a small way, made a contribution to rational discussion of an issue that had already evoked too much cheap outrage.

THE WAR GAME

The film begins with a portentous BBC voice filling us in on the details of yet another eyeball-to-eyeball confrontation between East and West, and as the voice runs on we see that familiar modern symbol of impending doom, the black-clad, helmeted and goggled motorcyclist, wheel through the streets of a Kentish town and up to the municipal building, where he delivers dispatches of an obviously unpleasant nature. With admirable economy we learn that this time the government regards the crisis as rather more dangerous than usual. They are, indeed, beginning to evacuate the most populated and strategic areas of Britain in an attempt to protect at least some of the people from a nuclear exchange that has passed suddenly from the realm of the possible to that of the probable.

Scenes of confusion follow: householders are summarily informed that they are legally obliged to take in at least eight refugees or face the confiscation of their homes; police begin to pass out civil defense pamphlets—too little and too late; profiteering on bomb-shelter materials begins; the confused and alienated evacuees begin to arrive and their welcome is not exactly in the Christian spirit. *The War Game* has begun— only it is not a game any more, it is reality.

At this point the viewer, benumbed by two decades of grim reportage and vivid warnings about the horrors of atomic war, may well suffer a perfectly understandable desire to become a refugee himself—from another exposure to the radiation of the overfamiliar. I think, though, that the impulse should be blocked, because this brief (forty-seven minutes) flatly stated no-nonsense semi-documentary, which Peter Watkins originally wrote and directed for BBC television and which, after its success at the New York Film Festival, is now having a theatrical release here, has a cumulative emotional and educational effect that is quite overwhelming and which everyone probably ought to force himself to experience. After all the scare stories, here is one that really scares, precisely because it stylistically underplays a theme that could scarcely be overplayed, but often is anyway.

It is not science fiction. Each physical and psychological effect of an atomic attack which it reports is one that has already been experienced somewhere—at Hiroshima or Nagasaki or after the fire bomb raids on Dresden, Germany—within living memory. Everything that happens to the anonymous non-professional actors has happened to someone, somewhere in our time. There is no speculation about what the effects of our more sophisticated new generation of atomic weapons might be. Obviously they would be worse; obviously what we already know is bad enough and ought to have a suitably cautionary influence on the more eager cold warriors.

But the point here is not preachment. *The War Game* is neither a pacifist document nor propaganda for better civil defense. The task Watkins has assumed is best described as one of jogging and vivifying our memories. At least that is how his film affected me. It is so easy when one is preoccupied with the basic facts of life to push aside—or just plain forget—not only all the words one has read about World War III but all the facts one has perforce absorbed while living through the Atomic Age. Even such knowledge as one has managed to keep in the forefront of consciousness tends to be conveniently abstract. What Watkins does is force us to get down to cases—human cases. He makes us look at the people being whirled into the draft of a firestorm like so many leaves, at the bulldozers stacking the bodies, at the firing squads putting the hopelessly maimed out of their misery, at a child who in his innocence looked up at the fireball and who now stands sightless in a garden weeping in pain and confusion.

He even makes us attend the less spectacular, if no less devastating, aftereffects of atomic exchange—food riots and martial law, a man trying to protect his family from his knowledge that all of them have a form of leukemia and are going to die in a few months, the dead eyes and toneless voices of people who have entered into a lifetime state of shock because they cannot possibly comprehend the sights they have been forced to witness and who, in this condition, will be expected to rebuild a world in which the absurd has passed from its status as a polite literary term to that of being the chief condition of life.

There are a few lapses in the film—the fictional pretext for an atomic attack seems hokey; and in his zeal to point up the contrast between the reality of atomic attack and the bland terms in which we usually discuss the possibility, Watkins has probably been unfair to those people in government and out who have made it their thankless task to give us a realistic idea of just how bad it might be. Even so, the film is a work of truth if not necessarily a work of art as we ordinarily define that term. There is truth in the stumbling authenticity of the amateur actors, truth in the grainy newsreel-like photography and, most of all, truth in the terror we feel as we watch—and which pursues us outside into the quiet normalcy of the street. Watkins poses no answers, specific or general, to the dilemmas of life in the Age of Cold War. He merely reminds us—as someone should every once in a while—just exactly what the consequences of the War Game can be. They are, unfortunately, a reality. The imagined scenes Mr. Watkins shows us form a reality as forceful as any we can actually see or touch, and perhaps all of us should attempt to work them into our Cold War calculations more prominently than we do. After all, the War Game is, finally, the only game in town.

4/7/67

THE FAMILY WAY

The ability of the polluted atmosphere of England's industrial north country to nurture and sustain intelligent cinematic life is nothing less than amazing. Entering the theater to see something like *The Family Way*, you can be forgiven for thinking that you may scream if you see one more shot of a crude and honest workingman crudely and honestly dousing his overcooked meat pie with HP sauce and talking with his mouth full while seated at an oilcloth-covered kitchen table. But I think by the time you leave this latest product of a genre that by all rights should be played out at this late date, you will probably be conceding that somehow it is still a viable one—at least in the right hands.

The Family Way is a middle-ground sort of picture—not as flashy stylistically as *This Sporting Life* or *Saturday Night and Sunday Morning*, not as satirically daring as *Billy Liar* or as corrosive as *Room at the Top* or *A Kind of Loving*, which it is quite like in theme. It is, in fact, most accurately described as a comedy-drama, which is an unfortunately wishy-washy term for a strong film. In manner it is more like the people who are its subjects than any of the movies I've just named—bluntly honest, lustily lively, somewhat narrow in outlook, but strangely gentle and sympathetic when the occasion arises. In short, it has the common virtues of common humanity, or at least the ones we like to impute to it.

The story is unelaborate. A young man (Hywel Bennett)

who works as a movie theater projectionist marries a local lass (Hayley Mills), but the honeymoon they were counting on to supply the aloneness their courtship lacked is canceled when the travel agent who was arranging it absconds with their funds. They are forced to make their first marital adjustments in the cramped quarters he shares with his family, the patriarch of which is domineering and difficult John Mills, with whom the boy has never gotten on in the best of circumstances.

The result, of course, is shame for the boy—and sexual disaster. He is excessively sensitive—especially to the thinness of the wall separating the bridal chamber from the parental one— and she is excessively inexperienced, foredooming all her innocent efforts to salvage the situation. Before long their secret is out—he is observed sneaking into the local marriage counselor's office—and then, with the gossips gossiping, their families joining in the fumbling search for a solution, the boy is forced to defend his honor, and his wife's, in a brawl, which gives you an idea of the nature of their troubles but none of their extent.

That comedy—and sweet, unsniggering comedy at that—is drawn from this situation is a tribute to producer-directors Roy and John Boulting, who handle the film with firm, sure hands, and to Bill Naughton, who adapted the film from a play of his that had a short run on Broadway. Their trick, which is no trick at all until you try it, is always to let the characters play it straight, always to let their situations run true. No one and nothing is forced to strained double duty as overt symbol or conscious comment on the times. Neither are the demands of farce or intense satire imposed on the film; the actors are required only to be, not to mean. And so they get angry, baffled, sentimental, awkward, stupid and wise in constantly changing, very human patterns, thereby creating so much sympathy and so much empathy that the laughter they generate (which is very much the purpose of the exercise) seems almost an unconscious by-product of their efforts, not something they are desperate to achieve.

There is not a weak spot in the cast, and there are some very strong ones. Hayley Mills is now grown up enough to play a modest skin scene, but more important, she is grown up enough to play a young woman facing her first set of adult problems with charm and wit and never falter into the cuteness of the virginal cliché. Hywel Bennett is extraordinarily good as her husband, just boyishly beautiful and indecisive enough to make you wonder about him, just possibly strong enough to make it to manhood if everybody will give him the chance— and a little trusting help.

As for John Mills, this marvelous actor, so often relegated to the lower reaches of the all-star-cast listing, so often mentioned merely in passing by critics, deserves at last a paragraph all to himself. His range through dozens of pictures has been truly astonishing, and here he is at his very best, playing a man actually willing himself to vulgarity and insensitivity rather than admit to a softness his culture has convinced him is unmanning and unmanly. It's a lovely piece of work and the contrast between his solution to the masculine identity problem and that of his son, who is much more honest about it, is the soul of the picture, the thing which definitively lifts it out of the ordinary run.

We have had a great many plays and novels and movies about the gap between generations, but few as carefully honest in their handling of it as *The Family Way*. We have read and seen much about rebellious youth, but few works that deal with the problems of the kids who are forced to stick with the world they never made and try to find within it a viable way of life. Despite the publicity the rebels always receive, this is the choice most people make, and in lesser hands it usually becomes nothing but the stuff of soap opera. It takes a certain intelligence to find genuine drama within the common lot, a certain sensitivity to make something of it as consistently arresting, touching and funny as *The Family Way*.

5/5/67

TWO FOR THE ROAD

It is possible to describe *Two for the Road* as just another Audrey Hepburn picture. You know—a romantic comedy in which the beautiful and charming star is dressed in beautiful and charming clothes, photographed against a series of beautiful and charming backgrounds and placed in a succession of beautiful and charming situations which lead ultimately to her passage from the innocence of girlhood to the maturity of womanhood, an event which in her films is always funny and touching, gay and sad and, naturally, beautiful and charming. It is a ritual sufficient unto itself for those of us who are, without quite knowing all the reasons for it, her devoted admirers. All those who fall into this category are hereby advised that they may safely and enjoyably partake of their customary vicarious pleasure in Miss Hepburn's new film.

But it is unfair to damn *Two for the Road* with merely cultish praise. In point of fact, it is considerably more than a mere vehicle and it is possible, just barely possible, that it could come to be regarded as something of a turning point for the upper-class commercial movie. To begin with, director Stanley Donen and writer Frederic Raphael (who also wrote *Darling*) have sensibly noted that girls don't instantly become women just because they are sexually awakened (overnight, as it were). The process takes considerably longer than that in real life, and so they extend their examination of it through the young married stage and the young motherhood stage and on into that dangerously restless period when it appears that the growing children and the successful husband no longer seem to need her.

The metaphor they have chosen for this purpose is apt and obvious from the title. It is travel, in particular travel by car from the north of France to the south at holiday time. It is on these lovely roads that Miss Hepburn, traveling with a busload of schoolgirls, meets her future mate, an angrily ambitious architectural student who is hitchhiking from one historically important interesting building to the next and who is played with appealing and confused ferocity by Albert Finney. It is to these roads they return each summer, and the manner in which they do gives the clue to how things are going for them, while their adventures thereon provide the film's highest moments of comedy.

There is, for example, that commonplace of newly married life, the underfinanced vacation when everything goes wrong—the car breaks down, they are forced to stay in a hotel they can't afford and they must resort to desperate strategies to save face and money. Then there's the ghastly trip with another young couple, who spoil everything with itineraries, budgets and the worst offspring with whom anyone ever had to share a back seat. And, of course, there's the first excursion with their own child, with the threat of a tantrum at every turning and the chasm of parental hysteria always yawning at road's edge. Finally, there's the sullen journey of two people who have just discovered that they know each other all too well and are trying to keep all the little angers such knowledge brings from balling into one great big hate.

There is the truth of small universalities in these incidents, a kind of truth one does not always find in Miss Hepburn's films, and she has responded with just the right variations on her usual screen self. It is more than a matter of trading in her Givenchy gowns for clothes in the mod mode. Instead, she makes us see really with considerable clarity what that girl she has always played would be like five and ten years later. It is a well-observed, enthusiastic and properly self-delighted piece of acting.

But the most hopeful thing of all is Donen's direction, and it is worth risking a moment of serious consideration. The advantage the movies have always had over the stage is their ability to move freely, instantly, through the fourth dimension—time. The basic experiment undertaken by the modern screen artists —Bergman, Resnais, Antonioni and the rest—has been to radically extend this freedom. Their basic technique has been to break time into smaller and smaller fragments, the better to fling them at us in the random free-associational manner of our own unconscious minds. In the process they have created nothing less than a new film style which has up to now been frightening to American producers, however much the directors they finance have been attracted to it. The result has been a stylistic stiffness, a dull conventionality of realization that grows increasingly annoying to eyes that have, in effect, been retrained and sharpened by the new stimuli available at the so-called art houses.

It is infinitely to the credit of Mr. Donen and his backers that they were willing to attempt this new manner in an expensive film that cannot succeed without the backing of a mass audience. Fusing times past with time present, joyfully jumping around in his couple's history as the spirit moves him, Mr. Donen has abandoned all the conventions customarily employed to warn us that a flashback is coming. He simply throws the whole jumble of incident and anecdote on the screen and invites us to join in the fun as, in effect, Hepburn and Finney keep meeting their older, younger, different selves on the road. There is no sacrifice in clarity in these odd, sudden juxtapositions and there is much gain in surprise, suspense and humor. Mr. Donen has always been one of the truly stylish directors of light comedy, but here he has surpassed himself and in the process made it clear that the commercial film maker no longer has to be bound by the traditions of the past. In the work of the new men there are techniques which can revitalize the old genres and which, if they are intelligently employed, can only enhance the pleasures we have traditionally found in those genres.

This was a graceful, tasteful movie with a tough little core of truth to it, and thus it failed to please either romantics or realists, being neither altogether in one mode nor the other. Indeed, I should think the film that tries to suggest that on a day-to-day basis our moods fluctuate quite wildly, and somewhat inexplicably, does not fare very well with critics or with the audience. We like our movie makers to take a firm line toward life and stick to it, quite possibly because it makes summarizing their films in a sentence or two so much simpler. This is especially the case with directors like Donen, who are quick and slick by repute and therefore suspect when they turn unexpectedly serious—or half-serious—on us. For me at least, the movie's trickiness, stylistically and psychologically, was very appealing: not least because courtship and marriage are, in fact, tricky enterprises. Which is a way of saying that, finally, it referred us to life more than it did to other movies.

THE HUNT

The Hunt is a small, hot, tight, brutal film about the dirty tricks that prolonged intimacy, in a couple of its varieties, can play on men. In addition to its intrinsic merits it has a special interest as one of the few Spanish films to be exported to the United States in recent years. As such, it tends to confirm the cultural cliché that the Spanish mind is uniquely obsessed with blood and death, which means that it will powerfully attract some people and powerfully repel others—just as the bullfights do. Despite this fact, the work of thirty-year-old writer-director Carlos Saura must be judged a success within its own terms.

The story is quite simple. Three middle-aged men who fought together with the Falangists in the civil war come together again for a day's rabbit hunting at the incredibly barren site of one of their old military engagements. One of them, Paco, is very strong, the kind of man who seems to be able not only to survive any disaster but to profit from it. Another, Luis, is very weak, addicted to drink and defeat, silence and science fiction. A third, José, is a confused aristocrat who cannot manage either his life or his business sensibly. He has arranged the hunt in the hope of gaining a desperately needed loan from the prospering Paco. With them they have brought a young man, Paco's cousin, who has never hunted before and whose innocence about the sport is matched by his innocence about the history the others share, serving as an effective contrast to the drama they cannot help but act out.

As the hunt begins, everyone is more than a little edgy. The

112

older men know each other so well that they know in advance
just how they are going to fail one another. Their main hope
for getting through the day appears to be discretion and a
vague feeling that perhaps somehow they still have the capacity
to surprise each other with decency. This, of course, is the price
of one kind of intimacy—that of presences and memories and
mutual testings covering so many years and situations that
there is nothing left to learn about your fellows. One knows
exactly how to defend oneself against the others and exactly
how to trespass against them in the most hurtful ways. The
pressures generated by this kind of intimacy are only intensified
by the physical intimacy of the hunt. In this dusty landscape of
rocks and mountains and sparse, scrubby vegetation there is
nothing to distract, nothing to think about but the subjects
they already despise—themselves. The hunting itself is only a
momentary diversion, more a matter of slaughter than of skill,
and an event that tends to produce metaphors that cut uncomfortably close to their own problems. When the heat of the day
forces them to seek the shelter of a protective awning they have
erected, they are naturally driven still closer together and into a
condition of idleness, which produces a very unpleasant
luncheon atmosphere and an extremely restless siesta. By the
time they are ready for the afternoon's onslaught against the
rabbits, this time using ferrets, it is clear that the smallest
psychological miscalculation could cause them to turn their
weapons from game to the more interesting human targets that
present themselves. That temptation has already been toyed
with by one of them, and so the question—and the suspense—
becomes a matter of seeing if they can block that impulse.

The conclusion which Saura puts to this tension, though
certainly a possibility, seems to me not entirely justified by
what he has previously shown of his characters and their
imperfections. There is a forced quality about it that over-
burdens the dramatic structure on which it is placed, and it is
out of key with the patient, steady winding of tensions which
he so subtly accomplishes in the first three-quarters of his film.

Whatever doubts this conclusion raises, however, must be put aside in the light of his achievements. In strikingly simple black and white photography he somehow catches the dry, terrible heat of this terrible day so that you can almost feel it burning your own flesh. He controls his actors with the same sure hand, releasing their passions and checking them, releasing them and checking them, in bursts of emotion that reveal the underlying tensions without dissipating them prematurely. The puniness of these men and their concerns, when placed against the awesome desolation of the land, forms, in his visualization, a vivid visual irony which is especially destructive of the absurd masculine pride they take in their ability to kill animals that are in every sense of the word dumb.

There is also a marvelous sequence when the men, unable to relate happily to one another, take their guns out of their cases and demonstrate a love they are incapable of showing any animate thing. Not a word is spoken, but the combination of gentleness and mastery with which they handle and caress these graceful deadly instruments as they anticipate the pleasure of their use can only be described as a variety of sexual experience.

There is no gainsaying that the basic power of the film derives from the unblinking manner in which it records the brutality and bloodiness of the hunt. I would not say it is unnecessarily or unnaturally specific in this matter, given its larger purposes. It is merely truthful to a dreadful degree. But that was enough to make me want very much to avert my eyes from the screen on several occasions. It is entirely possible that those under no professional obligation to keep watching will want to follow through on that instinct, or even perhaps excuse themselves entirely from *The Hunt*. For those with the stomach for it, however, the film offers raw experience transformed by rough unself-conscious poetry into the kind of artistic statement that stays with you—even when you'd prefer to forget it.

5/19/67

WELCOME TO
HARD TIMES

Hard Times is an odd name for a town. But apt, for the place consists of one short muddy street with a half-dozen shanties straggling along it. There is no law here, and such life as it harbors centers in its depressing saloon, to which, one filthy night, the stranger, "the man from Bodie" (Aldo Ray), makes his way.

He speaks not a word. But he drinks. And he takes a woman, stripping her in public before carrying her off upstairs, where she is heard screaming and screaming before she is finally killed. Though she is a prostitute, she has a lover—which gives you an idea of the quality of life here—and when he tries to rescue her, he is killed, too. Now the bar's habitués send for Will Blue (Henry Fonda), who is by default the town's leading citizen, and he reluctantly makes a plan to rid Hard Times of its violent intruder. It involves asking *his* prostitute girl friend (Janice Rule) to distract the murderer so Blue can sneak a shot at him. She does, but he fumbles his play, and though she is not killed, she is subjected to the same kind of brutality that was visited on her friend. And Blue does nothing about it. He may not be a full-scale coward, but he certainly tends to value self-preservation over the Quixotic gesture.

The man from Bodie, still silent, sets fire to the town and rides off, and it is immediately clear from these first couple of reels that *Welcome to Hard Times* is a decidedly unusual example of its genre. Clearly, Ray's character is so far from the ordinary run of the type that he cannot be described merely as a "bad guy." He may, in fact, be the first out-and-out sexual psychopath ever to ride the range. And the setting for his depredations far exceeds in squalor anything we are accustomed to in the western, and is incomparable to anything since the great mining camp sequences of *Ride the High Country* some five years ago. Finally, one feels that the film's other principal characterizations penetrate close to the reality of life as it may actually have been in the historical frontier town.

Very simply, the film forces one to admit that in all probability the codes of rough chivalry and justice, the clean lines between good and evil, strength and weakness, which we have come to expect in our western were rarely, if ever, present in the thrilling days of yesteryear. The inhabitants of those hostile times were, alas, rather more like the citizens of Hard Times than we like to admit, which is to say that they were alienated from one another and lacking more than a rudimentary spirit of community. Clinging to a hostile environment by the slenderest of roots, they were probably at once panicky and morally dulled by boredom and by constant exposure to a climate where violence was a commonplace and evil a banality.

Moreover, writer-director Burt Kennedy also forces us to come to grips with a central figure—subtly played by Fonda—who is as close to being an anti-hero as you are ever likely to see in serious western garb. It is true that the substance of the film deals with his efforts to save Hard Times when everyone else is willing to abandon its charred ruins, and it is also true that he becomes somewhat more appealing as his character expands with his task.

But it must be understood that he undertakes the job only because he knows there is no place lower for him to sink than Hard Times, that if he cannot make this rotten town live he will be unable to find any place *worse* to try the luck of his flawed character. He does not basically change in the process of nursing the place back to a semblance of health. He willingly accepts an unmanning relationship with the vengeful girl whom he sacrificed to the man from Bodie, and, far from facing up to Ray's return in a manly fashion, he again confronts him with a trick and a desperate prayer. He is a westerner practicing not a code of honor but modern survival ethics.

He and his deromanticized environment may be a bit hard to take for those who insist on purity of convention in the western form. Certainly the violence of the film, though infrequent, is far too savage for exposure to childish or squeamish eyes, even though one can truthfully say, as one rarely can these days, that it is aesthetically justified.

Finally, one must fault Kennedy for a far too leisurely development of his theme. The gap between the opening burst of action and the final one lacks accent and punctuation. A certain amount of boredom is essential to his vision, but there is too much of a dull thing here. The subsidiary people he hopes will provide color in his gray landscape—the girls of a traveling bordello and their semi-comic owner, a retarded gunman, a weird Indian, an orphan in search of a father figure—vary from the strained to the clichéd, but mostly work against the originality for which he is striving.

Even so, he is a courageous man, risking far more than most directors who attempt westerns ever do. His work is not just a tinkering with a tradition-encrusted form but a serious attempt to extend the range of its possibilities. It may be imperfect, but it is well worth the attention of anyone who cares about such matters.

5/26/67

The temptation after presenting reviews of The Hunt *and* Welcome to Hard Times *back to back is to add a few hundred more words to the million or so that have lately been addressed to the subject of screen violence.* The Hunt, *however, is so clearly the work of a serious artist that it probably requires no* defense—although it surely deserved more of an audience than it found in the United States. Hard Times is a trickier proposition. In a laundered version it got to television faster than any other feature I know of—so dismal was its critical and popular reception in the theatrical release (to my knowledge, only Andrew Sarris shared my enthusiasm for it). But it was an early attempt to reclaim the western experience as relevant rather than nostalgic screen material in our historical moment. It followed Ride the High Country, to be sure, but it preceded The Wild Bunch, and if Burt Kennedy has never equaled Sam Peckinpah's artistry and his deep feeling for the region, if there is evidence of commercial calculation (or miscalculation, as it turned out) throughout the film, there is also evidence of serious intent as well. As to violence on the screen in general, it almost never disturbs me, and, in fact, I can think of no male critics it disturbs in the way it does Miss Kael and Miss Crist. I think men have some need—not shared by women—to discharge violent emotions vicariously, and I think we've been conditioned to expect movies to aid us in this respect—no questions asked. No doubt the imperative imposed upon us by civilized life to keep these emotions under control deepens our need for shoot 'em ups; no doubt this atavism is discouraging to idealists; no doubt, either, that the clean, quick bursts of action that characterized American films of the thirties and forties—so totally lacking in sado-masochistic overtones—were aesthetically preferable to the slavering style of more recent movies. But who can deny that there are sexual overtones to violence and that movie makers should probably take those into account—at least occasionally? In Hard Times I thought this was intelligently and interestingly done. Could be I was wrong or, more likely, that this is such a highly personal response that one can speak about it in only the most highly subjective terms, and should make that fact very clear in the review itself.

DIVORCE
AMERICAN STYLE

Divorce American Style is a rarity among comedies American style in that it actually has something truthful to say about the way we live now and says it with a savagery of tone that runs completely counter to the warm, babbling, socially meaningless flow of our comic movie mainstream. If you are looking for the sort of chuckly little situation comedy usually associated with stars like Dick Van Dyke and Debbie Reynolds, you may find the film a bit disconcerting at first. But if you believe that an occasional plunge into a cold needle-sharp spray of wit has a therapeutic effect, I think you may find this picture uncommonly refreshing.

It is mid-marriage time, and the Harmons (Van Dyke and Miss Reynolds) find their life together has become one long low back pain—not unbearable, but not much fun either. Marriage counseling of the professional and the over-the-back-fence varieties proves to be equally unanalgesic and before you know it, he's moved out and she's called her lawyer. So far, so routine, though the awful banality of their squabbles indicates that scriptwriter Norman Lear has observed marriage à la mode with an eye more observant and an ear more sensitive than most, while director Bud Yorkin has choreographed a door-banging, drawer-slamming non-verbal fight that is as intricate as a Chinese puzzle.

The film does not get down to cases, however, until man,

woman and their lawyers start divvying up the community property. She gets the house, he gets the mortgage; she gets the car, he gets the payments on it; and so on, until Van Dyke begins to get the point of this exercise in legalized larceny and cries, "She gets the stock in the uranium mine, and I get the shaft."

Enter—shambling—one Nelson Downes (Jason Robards), hairy and harried, a frightful vision of the penury that is to come when the law has finished with poor Harmon. So disastrous was Downes's settlement that he cannot afford even a two-bit shave and a haircut. He drives a rusting hulk of a car, he limps horribly because the operation he needs on his leg is beyond his now-ridiculous means, and he has taken to hanging around public places looking for someone to marry his ex-wife and thus lift the alimony burden from shoulders you can hear creaking.

Alas, Harmon is absolutely the wrong man for his purposes. So, of course, the former Mrs. Downes (Jean Simmons) falls in love with him. Which means that all must now try to find a mate for the former Mrs. Harmon so he can be relieved of *his* alimony. They come up with a pip—a mother-fixated used-car salesman (Van Johnson) of surpassing smarminess—and for a moment it looks as if we are about to witness something truly unprecedented, a comedy that actually leaves its principals worse off than when it began.

Unfortunately for truth, but perhaps fortunately for our already jangled expectations, Lear and Yorkin cop out and tack an ambiguously happy ending on the film. You can't complain too much, however, for they have by this time made their point—that there is something wrong with a legal system that intervenes in a situation where normally the guilt is equally divided to punish excessively only one of the errant parties. That they dare to make jokes about it seems a minor miracle of courage. That they are often such good, gutty jokes is an astonishment.

I particularly liked the way in which Harmon is divested of his goods and chattels in a series of casual asides as the lawyers attend to the really serious business of comparing country clubs and setting up a golf date. It is a perfect gem of comic writing. It is matched on the sight-gag level by the cautionary scene in which squads of children from just one couple's string of marriages and remarriages are sorted out on a suburban front lawn and handed around to natural and step-parents whose visitation hours have accidentally coincided one sunny Saturday. It is hilarious—and it is also poignant.

The performances match the script's best moments and, indeed, easily compensate for its occasional lapses into vulgarity, its more frequent signs of strain. Miss Reynolds finally acts her age, and she has never been better than she is as the housewife who can't stand to see the magic fading from her marriage. Van Dyke proves again that he is less self-conscious as a comic actor lost in a role than he is as a straight comedian lost in himself. As for Robards, his natural gift for the grotesque gesture here shines as it has not previously had the opportunity to do in a movie career that has been a very mixed blessing.

But the best thing about *Divorce* is what it says about divorce. It animates those depressing statistics and proves that what was once a scandal—or at least an anomaly—is now firmly established as a way of life. By holding up to an unsparing, unblinking satirical light the almost universal customs that have grown up around this most peculiar of institutions, the film suggests that it is time to make it into a psychologically less desperate, more humane thing. The cliché is that divorce is hard on the children. The truth is that it is even harder on the parents and that the kind of spiritual contortions *Divorce American Style* so expertly captures is no good for anyone, be he participant, innocent underage bystander, or just a member of a society which tolerates such absurd goings on.

6/23/67

I overpraised this movie. Usually there is no time for me to see films twice, but because I thought my wife might enjoy it and we were on vacation and this drive-in down the road was playing it . . . Anyway, it seemed pretty thin the second time around. What was good—notably Jason Robards's performance—was still good, but the banalities I had originally overlooked loomed distressingly large now. The thing is, I'm always looking for American movies that reflect what seems to me the most common experience in our daily lives—namely plain ordinary middle-class desperation—and there were a few passages in *Divorce* that got that quality just right. I was apparently so delighted (and amazed) that I chose to overlook a lot of material that was merely slick and comfortable. No great harm done, I suppose, since the movie at worst was not unbearable, but I'm still looking for the film that accurately reflects the sadness (no, it's not quite a tragedy) of a class just a little too dumb and numb to rule a great nation or even to raise a family properly.

IN THE HEAT
OF THE NIGHT

Murder has been done. The man who was going to build a nice new electronics plant in Sparta, Mississippi, and thereby rescue the little town's dying economy lies dead in the street, and everyone, especially the man's widow and the mayor, are telling Police Chief Bill Gillespie that he had better find the killer fast if he expects to keep his job. The trouble is that Gillespie, though zealous and even cunning in his crude way, lacks both the skills and the temperament of a detective, and he scarcely knows how to begin on the case, let alone end it. What he needs, though he won't admit it, is some expert.

Enter, under protest, Virgil Tibbs, who has been passing through. In ordinary circumstances Virgil would be the answer to any police chief's prayers. He's cool, smart, highly trained and the leading homicide investigator on the Philadelphia police force. There's only one thing wrong with him—he is a Negro, and this is the deep, deep South. To make matters worse, Virgil is just as uppity as he can be, which means that though Sparta literally will not be able to live without him— the widow says she'll pack up her husband's factory if Tibbs is not forthwith employed on the case—it can scarcely bring itself to live with him either.

Obviously the makers of *In the Heat of the Night*, based on a novel by John Ball, have a good gimmick going for them, one so intrinsically intriguing that little more than its statement alone would have been enough to hook and hold our attention.

Greatly to their credit and without getting preachy, they manage to transcend their cute premise and make a sound, serious and altogether excellent film that is quite possibly the best we have had from the United States this year. For what develops out of the confrontation between an urbane Northern Negro and a crude Southern cop is not merely a good whodunit or a demonstration that races can work together but a drama of two deeply etched characters in conflict.

As played by the admirable Sidney Poitier, detective Tibbs is by no means a completely likable or easily apprehended hero. He stays on in Sparta not out of any abstract obligation to justice but because he has an irresistible opportunity to demonstrate his superiority to the hated crackers. So intense is that desire that for a time he devotes himself to a vain attempt to pin the rap on the most thoroughly nasty of his hosts. Finally, when his irritating manner has warmed local temper to the lynching point, he gives us a quick glimpse of the fear that he has been trying all along to master and which is undoubtedly the chief motive of his brazen behavior. In short, he is a difficult character, and the natural temptation to make him a repository of superhuman virtue has been sternly repressed by Poitier, screenwriter Sterling Silliphant and director Norman Jewison.

Rod Steiger's brilliant portrayal of Gillespie is shaded with similar care. He could so easily have been turned into a clownish caricature of the rube lawman. Instead, for all his scratching and shambling, he is a man learning and changing in a tense situation and under the impact of Tibbs's exasperating skill in their shared profession. The performance begins in contemptuous suspicion of the proud, carefully controlled Negro, expands through grudging interest in a specimen very strange to his eyes and ends in understanding both the forces that drive him and the weaknesses that pluck at him. It is a wonderful piece of acting—humorous, shrewd and strong without being domineering or self-admiring.

But then, almost everything about this movie is good—the

sharply drawn minor characters, the careful plotting, the wonderful rightness of each setting, mood and dialogue. Most admirable of all is the way everyone avoids oversimplifications. Poitier and Steiger may eventually come to respect one another, even to find a certain amusement in one another's company. But they do not suddenly become brothers under the skin, put down their old prejudices and vow to be better men. They have gained only a little more knowledge of themselves and of each other, perhaps a capacity to work with the strangers of the future on a slightly less suspicious basis. Intimacy greater than that is specifically rejected The policemen part as they met—warily. It is not exactly a resounding resolution, but it is a true one and therefore very suitable to a truthful little film.

7/28/67

Looking back, I see that most of the truth in this movie was in Steiger's performance and in Haskell Wexler's really masterful camera work, which definitively captured the look of the American small town today—neon and false fronts over decay. Again the wish that our movies might truly capture the texture of our common life fathered a review perhaps more enthusiastic than the film deserved. On the other hand, it had an honest energy, by which I mean that once we accepted an improbable basic premise, characters and situations unfolded in an unforced and logical manner. There was none of that feverish jerking around of people and events through which false life is imparted to most of our genre pieces today. So if it wasn't the best American film of the year, as I said it was, it was at least an honorable and craftsmanlike little movie in which at least a couple of the craftsmen quite transcended the natural limits of their material. Considering the way things have been going, that's rather good going.

THE BIG CITY

It is always a trifle embarrassing to set down in unadorned outline the story of one of Satyajit Ray's films, for in that form they generally seem too small, too simple to support the criticial enthusiasm they generate.

Take, for example, *The Big City*. It is nothing more than the tale of a poor family struggling to maintain its tenuous foothold on one of the lower rungs of the Indian middle class. A young man with a college degree, a small supply of English catch phrases, and bad teeth works as a minor and underpaid executive in a new bank so obviously unprepossessing that only the more ignorant inhabitants of an underdeveloped country would entrust their rupees to its raffish care. He has a shy and lovely wife, a child, a teen-age sister and two elderly parents whom local custom and common humanity dictate that he try to support.

It is all too much for him, and so his wife hesitantly decides to go to work for an aggressively hustling entrepreneur, demonstrating and selling from door to door a comically awkward patented knitting machine, which is not exactly the first thing an Indian housewife needs. At first glance the job could not seem more inappropriate to her retiring nature, but in her modest way she is a gritty girl, and before long she becomes a star saleswoman. Which is a good thing, because her husband's bank fails and he is unable to find another job. In the end she also gets fired—for speaking up in behalf of an Anglo-Indian salesgirl victimized by their prejudiced and fatuous employer. The last shot of the film is of man and wife setting forth together down a twilit street, jobless but perversely encouraged because their skill at survival has grown under adversity.

You see, it all seems rather banal. But it is perfectly wonderful when you see it unfold at Mr. Ray's customary unforced pace in his customary unfancy style. The real substance of his films lies between their plot lines, in the interaction of his almost Chekhovian characters. In *The Big City* there is a deep conflict between the young people and the young man's father, a retired schoolteacher who is going blind and despises his inability to contribute to the family economy but refuses to speak to his daughter-in-law when she offends tradition by going to work. Then, too, there are some terribly touching scenes between the young wife, exquisitely played by Madhabi Mukherjee, and her child. The boy cannot understand why his mother must leave him each morning and she, full of guilt, tries desperately to buy back his favor with presents, which only confuses both of them further; he is temporarily cheered but not permanently eased by receiving them; her conscience is momentarily eased but not cheered by giving them.

It is, however, in the related processes of Miss Mukherjee's discovery of the world outside her sheltered home and of the strengths inside her sheltered self that the film is most subtle and alive. Her husband is nearly destroyed psychologically by his bank's failure—his sense of worth was drawn too much from his hard-won position, not enough from pride in his own unique self. Similarly flawed is the Anglo-Indian girl whose job Miss Mukherjee tries to save. She affects Western makeup and dress and a breezy style obviously borrowed from American movies. But under stress the mannerisms can't save her and she is pathetically vulnerable. Finally, there is the boss, who has borrowed not only all that is dreadful in the Western commercial style—its pompous smugness, its value of ends over means, its arrogant belief in materialism—but the whole-souled selfishness that underlies it. There is comedy in all these attempts to assume false modern identities, but there is a sadness and an occasional savagery in them, too.

At various moments we expect Miss Mukherjee to fall into one of the traps these people exemplify—the self-pity of her husband, the hysteria of her friend, the insensitivity of her employer. Instead, we witness the unfolding of one of those rare personalities who are able to function within a strange and dehumanizing environment without becoming alienated or less human themselves. Quite the contrary, the world stimulates her, drawing out her latent intelligence, humor, sense of justice and decently competitive instincts, without ever dominating her or changing her in any significant way. In short, it affords her exactly the sort of test she has always needed to become her own best self.

I imagine that Mr. Ray sees the emergence of this character under trial as symbolic of India itself, emerging into the modern world after the long personality-crushing ordeal of colonialism, and I imagine, too, that he is urging upon his nation a course similar to that which his heroine pursues—neither clinging blindly to the past (like her unseeing father-in-law) nor clutching unthinkingly at the future as the other characters around her do. Rather, he seems to say, try to blend the forces of tradition with the forces of change thoughtfully, testingly, without panic or excessive passion. In such a way might a wholly new character—strong, supple, subtle—emerge in a wholly new world.

I have no wish, however, to imply that Mr. Ray is heavy or particularly dogged in pursuit of messages, symbolic or otherwise. He is, instead, a careful, ironic and always very specific observer of human character, patiently building his films out of the small gestures, inflections and silences of ordinary life, finding in its pains, problems and victories the stuff of an extraordinary art.

8/18/67

THE WHISPERERS

It is an odd, simple fact: the most memorable movie performances by actresses in the last two years have been by elderly
women—Ida Kaminska in *The Shop on Main Street,* Sylvie in
The Shameless Old Lady and now Dame Edith Evans in *The
Whisperers.*

One naturally admires in their work the shrewd display of
those varied skills that an artist can perfect only over long years
of intelligent practice, but there is more to their successes than
mere craftsmanship. One also sees and celebrates in these
artists the miracle of intactness. Their performances are informed by the accumulated experiences and observations of a
lifetime, and they are animated by the kind of courage which
comes only when the cruder considerations of vanity are no
longer relevant to the performer. In short, they have forgotten
nothing and they are afraid of nothing and so, paradoxically,
the pulse of life jumps in their portrayals as it does not—perhaps cannot—in those of younger women who have less to give
and more to lose.

Of the three grand old ladies, it seems to me that Dame
Edith has undertaken in *The Whisperers* the most difficult
assignment, partly because the film, based on the Robert
Nicolson novel, is less carefully shaped, mostly because the
physical and psychological circumstances of the character that
director Bryan Forbes asks her to portray are the most desperately reduced. Miss Kaminska, after all, had her shop and the
familiar life of the small town where she had lived all her life

to sustain her; Sylvie's nature was given as fundamentally out-
going and curious, capable of being diverted and stimulated by
the process of discovering the strange new world that had
grown up around her while she was not looking. In contrast,
Dame Edith's character is almost completely out of touch with
reality. She is paranoid, convinced that a nameless evil conspiracy lurks around her plotting her destruction. When she is
not preoccupied by these imaginary threats, she loses herself in
reveries about the departed grace and elegance of an earlier life
that is, alas, equally a figment of her lonely imagination.

One can scarcely blame her for withdrawing so completely
into a world of her own, for the external reality she confronts is
totally depressing. She lives in a tumbledown tenement in one
of those slums that English film makers have an almost obsessive gift for visualizing in virtually palpable, invariably ghastly
terms. For diversion she has only the newspapers she filches
from trash cans, an occasional bowl of soup and a hymn-sing at
an evangelical mission, a corner of the public library where,
when the guards aren't looking, she can warm her feet on a
steam pipe. Her routine is varied only by trips to collect her
pension at the National Assistance office, where a kindly welfare worker humors her as much as time will allow, and by
visits to the police station, where the desk sergeant assures her
that her complaints about the great conspiracy are under in-
vestigation.

We are, in the film's first half, allowed no relief from its
quiet but insistent commentary on the callousness with which
a youth-oriented production-minded society treats citizens who
suffer the inevitable misfortune of becoming both old and
unproductive. Neither sentiment nor comedy is allowed to
color the flat gray statement of hopelessness that Mr. Forbes,
who also wrote the screenplay, and Dame Edith are intent upon
making. By the middle of the film they have succeeded in
making the befuddled, gallant old woman of the Nicolson
novel into something far more meaningful than a simple study
in character or sociology. She becomes instead, like Miss

Kaminska's small-town shopkeeper and Sylvie's suddenly self-assertive widow, a symbol of the alienation all of us must feel as we try to face, alone and afraid, the brutal and irrational forces of a world too big, too cold, too busy for the individual to comprehend, let alone master.

Once this point is reached, however, Dame Edith is less well served by her script than her predecessors were. A rather melodramatic plot suddenly begins to develop intrusively. A ne'er-do-well son hides stolen money in her flat, she discovers it, flashes it around and is robbed, after which she is left to die. Instead, she contracts pneumonia and while she is recovering from it, the welfare people trace her husband, who has long ago deserted her, and persuade him to return to her. Fate, however, presents him with an opportunity for ill-gotten gain and he quickly decamps, leaving her precisely as we found her at the beginning.

These alarums and excursions afford, to be sure, dramatic sustenance of a kind, as well as an opportunity to bring on the admirable Eric Portman as the husband. They also provide an opportunity to observe that careless meddling in the delicate web of fantasies by which some people maintain their grip on life is often worse than leaving them alone. They do, however, seem awfully heavy and excessively action-packed for the essentially simple structure of the film to support. It does not break under the strain, but it does get quite badly bent.

This does not, however, distract Dame Edith from following the line of her character to its logical end. Indeed, some of her most brilliant work is done in the scenes where, in a silent agony of approach and withdrawal, she attempts to adjust to the sudden presence of her husband in her life. Flawed though it is by careless dramatic license, The Whisperers remains an exciting and an exacting tour de force for a greatly gifted actress. And in its best moments it presents us with unforgettable images of the loneliness of the life of our times.

9/8/67

THE THIEF
OF PARIS

The time is the last decade of the nineteenth century, the place is Paris. The spirit of the age—at least among the prospering and dominant middle class—is one of sublime confidence in its wisdom, values and destiny. As Georges Randal (Jean-Paul Belmondo) approaches manhood, he sees no reason not to share in that spirit. An orphan, he has been raised in the smug, snug home of his ponderously respectable, respectably wealthy uncle. The atmosphere has always been a little constricting, a trifle hypocritical, but there have always been compensations as well. For one thing, his uncle is managing his inherited fortune, and Georges imagines that upon attaining his majority he, too, will be a wealthy man. For another, his childhood companionship with his uncle's daughter, the winsome Charlotte, has slowly and sweetly ripened into love, and there appears to be no insuperable obstacle to their marriage.

Then one day Georges returns from military service to discover that his uncle has converted and appropriated his legacy and that Charlotte is about to make a dismal but socially advantageous marriage. His former confidence is now a mockery, his world a small shattered ruin at his feet. On the night of Charlotte's engagement party he therefore indulges in a casual, careless, childlike act of revenge—stealing the jewel collection that is the basis of the fortune into which she is supposed to marry.

Up to this point *The Thief of Paris* resembles one of those crowded, rambling, moralistic and somewhat sentimental popular novels which the Victorian age produced almost as unthinkingly as it did its optimism. Do not be misled. The plot is no more than a convenience, and the lovingly detailed atmosphere customarily used in films merely to invoke period charm here provides an ironically contrasting, artistically profitable background against which director and co-writer Louis Malle coolly goes about his principal business, which is exploring the formation of a thoroughly modern absurdist sensibility.

Georges, you see, gains something more than a morally, psychologically and monetarily rewarding revenge from his first unthinking exercise in criminality. He discovers that he has been harboring, all unsuspecting, a temperament remarkably suited to a life underground. Fortuitously taken in hand by the criminal establishment, he quickly acquires all the technical skills needed to rise to the top of his new profession, where he can now satisfy what he has come to recognize as a passion for danger and for mastery over it, over himself and over the class that once wronged him and which lives in fear of the "criminal class" with which he is associated circumstantially but never in his own loner's mind.

Georges quickly learns that everyone is to some degree criminally inclined, for it is axiomatic that a burglar planning and executing a job gains the most intimate knowledge of the minds and lives of his victims. But he refuses to politicalize his skill by placing it in the service of anarchist revolutionaries. He will not sully its purity by opening it to simple social interpretation. In the end he regains his own fortune as well as his uncle's and even wins Charlotte back. Surely now he is satisfied, and he will accede to her request for an early retirement. But no—that would place a too simple psychological interpretation on his life. His misshapen honor, his sense of what he must do to remain true to himself in a world where everyone plays themselves false, intervenes. He can no more quit than he can sell out.

In the film's last sequence we see him emerge from a mansion he has just burgled and, staggering under the weight of his latest acquisitions, catch a train to make good his escape and get on to the next job. And the next. Georges has become a dark, almost parodistic, artist figure, with the destructive act substituted for the creative act as the vital center of his being. He will pursue his chosen metaphor (or did it choose him?) until it kills him—as he knows it inevitably will—and even though he has long since made his point with it. Meaning for him lies only in action, not in goals, and one cannot help but respond to his gallantry in basing a dangerous life on a proposition that may be generally debatable but which is for him the only indisputable existential truth.

So simple a summary of *The Thief* does not really do it justice. There is, for instance, the excellence of Belmondo's performance to consider; after a run of indifferent films it is a pleasure to see his devilish uncalculated cool employed in a worthy project. It has never been exhibited to better advantage than it is here, peeping out from behind the big droopy mustache he so effectively affects. Director Malle gets similarly sound performances from the rest of his large ensemble, and, abandoning the tendency toward spectacular stylistic gestures that marred his earlier work, he is here a precise, self-effacing and devastatingly accurate observer of character and of underworld and upperworld society.

The Thief, then, is not to be comprehended simply as a crime movie, though with its multiplicity of bold thefts and suspenseful escapes it was to me—unlike some of my colleagues—completely satisfying on that level. Rather, it is a film that in a quiet, reasonable, logical voice persuades us that life itself is a crime movie and that all of us are actors in it. It is in the contrast between the anarchical menace of this message and the offhand tone in which it is delivered that the great lingering strength of *The Thief* lies. Other movies have, of course, said much the same thing about life, but few have been so calmly, unhysterically acceptant of all the upside-down, inside-out implications of the philosophy it advances.

9/22/67

Just one brief note: The Thief of Paris *is my favorite unrecognized film of the past five years. I don't usually like Malle's work, but I think this is a brilliant movie and one which deserves a full-scale revival as some kind of a masterpiece.*

THE EXTERMINATING
ANGEL

Black being the preferred color in so much of the artistic community these days, I think everyone should go see Luis Buñuel's latest film, *The Exterminating Angel,* as soon as possible. It is not the darkest film the great Spanish exile ever made and therefore it is not the most powerful (that honor belongs jointly to *Los Olvidados* and *Viridiana*), but it still demonstrates very satisfactorily just how black the blackness can be when it is applied by a master, one who is trying to show us the color of his own innermost spirit and not merely trying to follow the latest fashion.

Buñuel's situation is absurdly simple and simply absurd. A group of wealthy Mexicans repair one night after the opera to one of their homes for a late and elegant supper. From the start things do not go very well. For reasons as mysterious to them as to their employers most of the help decide to walk off the job just as the guests are being ushered to table. Then one of the remaining waiters takes a spectacular tumble as he enters the dining room bearing the *pièce de résistance,* an exotic Maltese dish, and makes a very messy splash with it. Somehow the toffs survive this disaster, though the hostess is forced to cancel a mysterious entertainment involving some sheep and a trained bear. Up to this point she could regard the party as one of those unfortunate affairs that just didn't come off despite her best efforts.

But gradually what had been merely a hostess's bad dream starts turning into a nightmare. None of the guests, despite their boredom and the lateness of the hour, can bring themselves to leave. There's no discussion of this; the men simply loosen their ties and shrug out of their tail coats, the women kick off their shoes and draw their wraps more tightly around their bare shoulders and everyone settles down in sundry undignified postures for a little nap. Comes the dawn, as they used to say, and still no one can bring himself to leave. And so it goes, day after day, week after week.

There is no explanation for the nameless dread they suddenly feel for the world outside their self-created prison or for the ennui that combines with it to immobilize them. The little problems of survival—food, water, the disposal of waste—are solved in various grotesque ways, a man dies, a pair of lovers commit suicide, the rest either fall ill or fall to bickering. And still they wait, as if for Godot.

They are just preparing to kill their host to propitiate whatever god may be causing their affliction when, as suddenly as it came upon them, the spell lifts and they can at last emerge into daylight. This does not mean that Buñuel is quite finished with his allegorical horror show. The survivors, along with friends and relatives, gather in a church to offer a mass of thanksgiving for their deliverance. When the service is over, damned (and that's the right word in this context) if anyone can bring himself to leave the church, and it looks as if the whole experience is about to be repeated on an even grander scale.

Meaning? It is a disservice to Buñuel, an old hand at blending surrealist imagery with leftist social protest, to force an excessively rigid interpretation on his film. He obviously intends the little group of self-imprisoned to represent a cross section of decadent bourgeois society. The absence of a priest from their number—and the failure of the church in the final sequence to provide an adequate refuge—suggests a comment

on the failure of faith. The pathetic ineffectuality of the
rationalists present suggests a comment on the failure of men
to find a viable alternative to religion. The brute animalism
with which most of the assemblage react to the crisis suggests a
comment on the timeless, incurable evil of fallen man.

I don't think, however, that sweeping interpretations of
Buñuel's meanings are required here. Even when he is murky
he is fascinating. There is rich and savage satire in the dialogue
he provides for his characters, both before disaster, when he is
giving us a spectacularly forced perspective on common social
usages, and afterwards, when he is delightedly showing us the
spiritual contortions of people under pressure. He has always
had a special gift for making us see and feel (and almost smell)
the horrors with which we know life abounds but which we so
devoutly prefer to avoid discussing. That, no matter what addi-
tional meanings you read into it, is once again his business in
The Exterminating Angel.

Yet despite the fact that it will enhance his reputation as a
puzzling and/or shocking film maker, one does not feel that his
main objective is ever merely to puzzle or to shock. He is, I
think, a man possessed by the desire to communicate a private
vision of the world's hellishness, hoping, perhaps, that if he can
discharge it openly he will gain respite from his torments. It is
this sense of the man, the artist at work, which humanizes even
his most grotesque images and situations and makes them somehow bearable—especially in a day when many commercial
directors are finding it profitable to administer cheap thrills and
even cheaper enigmas to their audience. There is, in short, a
purity and integrity in Buñuel's work which puts me in mind of
another great Spanish artist—Goya. He also dealt in the horror
and degradation of life; he, too, placed his dreadful existential
vision in the context of a mysterious and inexplicable universe.
And he, too, made of all this a purging and perversely trium-
phant art, at once comic, tragic and worthy of our closest attention.

10/6/67

I want to take back part of the lead. I've since seen Viridiana and Los Olvidados again, and I now believe The Exterminating Angel must take precedence over them in the Buñuel canon. It is austere and—as I neglected to say—very funny if one appreciates the Spanish sense of humor. More important, it haunts the memory as few films do. There is also a somewhat apologetic tone to the piece—as if I expected my readers probably couldn't take the movie. Maybe they couldn't, or wouldn't, but it has the effect, as I read it now, of patronizing a director I regard as one of the true masters of the medium. Not, I'm afraid, a very good performance on my part.

BONNIE AND CLYDE

Controversy sometimes picks the strangest places to settle down and make trouble. Take, for instance, a stylish but seriously flawed movie called *Bonnie and Clyde*. As you probably know, it is a heavily fictionalized recounting of the gaudy rise and speedy demise of Bonnie Parker and Clyde Barrow, small-town, small-time bank robbers who simultaneously terrorized and titillated the dustbowl country for several years during the Great Depression of the 1930s. The film must be judged an interestingly failed attempt to transform and transcend the customs of the gangster genre which, despite its faults, is probably more worth the serious viewer's attention than the majority of American films.

What it is not worthy of is the terribly intense praise and damnation that have been visited upon it by critics and audiences. One reviewer, for instance, has issued three separate and distinct attacks on the film—for historical inaccuracy, excessive violence, moral turpitude and, I guess, bad breath—in an almost unprecedented display of critical overkill. He has been answered by colleagues and readers in terms as outraged as if he had failed to respond to some latter-day Sistine Chapel. Really!

There is much in *Bonnie and Clyde* which one can legitimately praise. Director Arthur Penn has caught, without seeming to strain, the aridity and emptiness of the countryside through which Bonnie, Clyde and the rest of their addled and

unbright mob rattled at dangerous speeds in a succession of
comically antique stolen cars to pull their undistinguished jobs,
and in the process he has created an arresting visual equivalent
of their blank, bleak inner lives. The script by Robert Benton
and David Newman emphasizes to good effect the fact that the
robbers were at least as interested in their press clippings as
they were in the monetary rewards of the depradations. Everyone concerned keeps the violence which attended their activities casual, unthinking, childlike. Though this has proved disconcerting to some observers, I think it is aesthetically correct,
for it carries none of the sadistic (and therefore sexual)
overtones usually present in mass-media representations of
violence.

What emerges from these good aspects of the film is a
comment on the quality of some American lives. Bonnie and
Clyde are the products of the rootlessness and aimlessness of
morally and intellectually ill-educated youth responding to the
problem of growing up absurd in a period of historical transition (the parallel between the middle 1930s and the middle
1960s obviously never being far from the minds of the movie's
creators). They, like so many youths today, seek and fail to find
fulfillment in momentary thrills and momentary notoriety; and
by stressing the ordinariness of the landscape and society that
nurtured them, by making them comical rubes instead of
glamorous jet-setters, the writers and directors often manage to
hit us more stingingly where we live than others who have attempted to make an essentially similar—indeed, familiar—
message.

What, then, is responsible for the vague feeling of dissatis-
faction with which the film leaves one? Partly it is the thump-
ing emphasis on period costume, décor and music. It is all
awfully cute and cutely awful, and it surely enhances the
movie's appeal to those who seek only idle entertainment when
they venture forth to the local Bijou. But it irreparably dulls
the film's cutting edge; what might have been a purgingly

savage satire on a watershed period in American life all too often degenerates into an arch, trivializing attempt to get us to giggle along with the gang.

And then there is the acting. There are three marvelous supporting performances—by baby-faced, baby-fat Michael J. Pollard as the group's simpleton driver-mechanic, by Gene Hackman as Clyde's heartily All-American brother, who would probably have been happier peddling dubious insurance policies, and by Estelle Parsons as his hysterically blithering bride. They are all gifted character actors capable of abandoning themselves totally in their roles and imparting to them an energy and a richness of imagination that simply compel the suspension of disbelief. The trouble arises in the title roles, essayed by Faye Dunaway and Warren Beatty. They must receive A's for effort; they seem honestly to be trying to give us that combination of basic moronism and class ignorance that probably created the vicious vacuity of the historical Bonnie and Clyde. But, alas, they are movie stars, or at least demi-stars. They have their futures to think about, their public, real or potential, to serve. And so they are careful to indicate at all times that they are merely play-acting—just kidding, folks. See, underneath these funny clothes and makeup and mannerisms are the pretty, reasonably intelligent, reasonably glamorous people we hope you will come to love and admire and reward with your future patronage. Thus, at its very heart, at the place where it must be strongest, *Bonnie and Clyde* is at its weakest, its least authentic.

In the last analysis, then, the film fails not for lack of good (if hardly original or brilliant) intentions, but because those who carried the greatest weight of responsibility for it lacked the will and the nerve to follow their instincts and their intentions the final few steps of the way to fulfillment. What might have been a breakthrough of sorts for the American screen falls back in confusion at the final barriers to self-realization.

10/13/67

Wrong. Or at least partly wrong. The film was, indeed, a break-through. Its makers sensed far better than I the basic shift in the basic mood of its basically youthful audience. They turned these two-bit mobsters into romantic outlaws—misunderstood, inarticulate, but sympathetic to other underdogs and irritants to authority (for which read "the establishment"). By so doing, they created the first of the new cult films for the kids and helped establish the now infamous "youth market." And that, friends, was not merely "a breakthrough of sorts," it was the major commercial discovery of the past five years, the largest single determinant of American film content in the late sixties and early seventies. But by now, having sat through all the stuff designed to capitalize on the pioneering work of Bonnie and Clyde, I have come to look back on it with real affection. At least it contained some self-satirizing elements, at least it told its story in a highly stylized ballad form, thus distancing its material so that no one—except an adolescent—could mistake it for reality. Indeed, it did so in such a clever way that the whole intense debate among critics and customers proceeded almost without reference to its romanticization of youthful emotions. It was, of course, Bosley Crowther who thrice attacked the film and thereby hastened the end of his long career as the New York Times movie critic—but he attacked it, as noted, for its violence, which even at the time was not excessive but merely disturbingly pretty and casually amoral in its handling by writers and director. Pauline Kael was Bonnie and Clyde's great defender, and she did note that "our experience as we watch it has some connection with the way we reacted to movies in childhood: with how we came to love them and feel they were ours—not an art we learned over the years to appreciate but simply and immediately ours." But even this perceptive lady apparently saw no better than the rest of us how directly the film plugged into youth's new, or at least newly intense, image of itself as a band of outsiders entitled to embrace (or at least applaud) even illegal methods in attacking the corrupt, corrupting social order ruled by old men and institutions. What I'm saying is simply that Crowther, given his age, had every right to feel discomfited by this film but erred in identifying the source of his discomfort; that those who rose in righteous indignation at his attacks sensed that the issue between them and Crowther was generational rather than aesthetic; and that it is perhaps understandable, given the fact I am of a middle generation, that I found myself taking a middle position on this film. Still, distressing as some of the results of its success have been, I wish that I had set down a feeling I had as I watched the film but then suppressed when I wrote about it—which was that for all its flaws it had a freshness, an exuberance of spirit, that was terrifically refreshing in the context of that moment in our screen history. In short, I should have hopped off the fence and, as they say, "gone with the feeling." But then, as Robert Warshow so memorably put it, "A man watches a movie, and the critic must acknowledge that he is that man." Which is a way of saying, among other things, that we are prisoners of our selves and sometimes must remain so even in moments when intelligence and instinct inform us that we should not be.

POINT BLANK

There is a scene in *Point Blank* that microcosmically summarizes the main things wrong with American movies at the moment. Lee Marvin has taken on the Syndicate, attempting to regain from it the loot of a robbery he regards as rightfully his. In the course of his vengeful misadventurings he is set upon in a mixed-media nightclub by a pair of thugs. Much cinematic fancywork ensues; the sound track wails weirdly, colored lights flash on and off, strange images tumble dizzily about in the background until the brawl—and the sequence—ends with Marvin delivering a brutal, explicitly photographed blow to his last assailant's groin.

There it is—that blend of gratuitous violence with gratuitous artiness that is increasingly the hallmark of a Hollywood trying desperately to catch up with a shift in the sensibility and the stylistic preference of its competitors abroad and its audience at home. No one should object to the effort. To rub the standard studio gloss off the standard studio product so it corresponds a little more closely to the texture of ordinary life is perhaps the first order of business if American film makers seriously want to be taken seriously. But what goes on in *Point Blank*, and in dozens of movies like it, is exactly the opposite of this reformation, is merely a substitution of a new slickness for the old.

In outline, *Point Blank* is a completely familiar tale of a good-bad man's revenge complicated by a dramatically satisfactory number of betrayals, mysteries and affairs of the heart.

Straightforwardly set forth it would be unworthy of extended critical comment but possibly worthy of attention some restless night when the need for escape is powerful. As the film stands, however, it irritates—even offends—more often than it entertains.

Director John Boorman has crammed his film with deliberately obscurantist sound, camera and editing effects. One of the most typical and annoying of these, and one much in favor with the young crowd, is the repetition through flashbacks of action already observed and comprehended. Thus, in case you missed it, you get a chance to see Mr. Marvin's cheap shot below the belt a second wonderful time, and you are treated to innumerable re-viewings of the events—by no means difficult to understand—that motivate his pursuit of vengeance. Yes, the human mind does return obsessively to its shaping memories; no, it is not necessary for the artful storyteller to go along on all these trips.

Why, then, do Mr. Boorman and his gang of screenwriters insist on doing so? Why, at the same time, is the camera set up and the film edited so that trivial detail and connective tissue are momentarily concealed? At first one hopes it is merely an attempt to build conventional suspense in an unconventional way, to upset our expectations of the usual. But that is not the case. All this breathless effort results in no more than a series of minor annoyances. In effect, Boorman has placed a pillar in front of every seat in the theater, forcing us to strain for meanings that soon turn out to have been perfectly unambiguous and not worth our effort.

Paradoxically, however, they are not the least bit coy when it comes time—as it so frequently does—for sex and/or violence. It is almost impossible to count the number of assaults and murders in *Point Blank*, but one is sufficiently typical to warrant some discussion. Marvin persuades a seemingly nice girl (Angie Dickinson) to divert one of his enemies with the offer of herself so that he can sneak up behind the punk and murder him. It is, of course, the oldest ploy, and the girl registers a modicum of disgust at it; but with that aimless amorality that characterizes all present, she carries it through. Now Mr. Boorman's camera abandons its previous mood of elliptical discretion and plunges forward to make a detailed record of the squirmings and shudderings of loveless love, including the convulsive separation of the pair when Marvin yanks them apart for the kill. The sequence concludes with a lingering shot of the bad man's naked body hurtling to its doom, buttocks gleaming, after a fight on the edge of his penthouse.

All right, we live in violent times and it is aesthetically correct for our films to reflect that violence. We live in a time when sex without love is not unknown, and if it is proper for the ladies' magazines to discuss it, I don't see why films should not. I will even admit that I received some kind of unelevated, unelevating kick out of the blunt juxtaposition of sex and death in this scene, some kind of titillation out of catching a glimpse of Angie Dickinson naked. And yet *Point Blank* is to me a shocking film, as indeed are a great many commercial movies these days. This is less a question of what they say than of what they refuse to say. Quite simply, what is missing from these films is feeling, a sense that their makers are involved with the larger meaning and the ultimate fate of their characters—a sense that they are not merely exploiting them the better to exploit us. I don't care what the nature of this feeling is—compassionate, tragic, even comic—but I do know that when it is absent no amount of artful cinematography can compensate for it.

One leaves a blank, pointless movie like *Point Blank* feeling cheapened by it and, yes, by the adolescent fantasies it awakens and caters to as one sits alone in the darkness with it. Surely it will win this year's sweaty palm award—hands down. But that the long fight to liberate the screen from its restrictive taboos should result in a plethora of films like this saddens and infuriates. Adult movies should awaken adult responses, not return us to the primitive emotional landscape of childhood.

10/20/67

"I contradict myself? Very well, I contradict myself." But it is right to place this piece in fairly close proximity to the one on Welcome to Hard Times, *for it indicates exactly how subjective is our judgment on the question of violence. I can't really say why Hard Times was acceptable to me and Point Blank was not. I think possibly the answer lies in the pretentiousness of the latter film, which wrapped itself in the flag of art (or artiness while the former was simply and directly what it was. No doubt, too, the fact that Kennedy's film was historically distanced disarmed me, as did its discretion in keeping its sadistic treatment of women off-screen. Very middle-class, very hypocritical of me, I'm sure. But however firmly one tries to draw the line between acceptable and unacceptable violence, the pen is bound to waver sometimes. It may even be, as this review suggests, that I was, in fact, more sexually excited by Point Blank than I was by Hard Times and that part of its tone arises out of a certain shame at this weakness. Try as one will to be rational, the irrational element in this business of passing critical judgments does arise and one can't always keep it out. Mea culpa.*

COOL HAND LUKE

What one remembers best—and most gratefully—about *Cool Hand Luke* is its vision of the American landscape, a vision compounded of a sensitivity to the ways its face and mood change from month to month, even from hour to hour, and of an intensity of realization (thanks largely to Conrad Hall's color photography) that makes the dews of dawn and the heat of noon and the cool of twilight almost palpable on your flesh.

I suppose in itself this is not remarkable. The one consistent artistic distinction of the American commercial film throughout its history has been its marvelous ability to convey what Vladimir Nabokov called the heartbreaking beauty of our "lyrical, epic, tragic but never Arcadian American wilds." No matter what absurdities of plot, characterization and meaning have taken place in this setting, our films have generally at least remained true to the unique spirit of the land that forms their backgrounds. What is curious about *Cool Hand Luke* is how this fidelity works to falsify—I think unintentionally—the meaning it is trying honestly to pursue.

It is a prison movie, specifically one of that now extremely rare species that deals with life on a Southern "chain gang" (perhaps a misnomer, since chains are apparently used only as punishment for infractions of institutional discipline). At this late date there is no point in making another exposé of this system and none is intended by the film's writers or its director, Stuart Rosenberg. But the prison atmosphere is used as Schofield Barracks was used in *From Here to Eternity*—merely as a forcing chamber in which to expose the workings of a determinedly non-conformist character caught in an atmosphere where the only choice lies between conformity and death. The difference between Paul Newman's Luke of the Cool Hands and the late Montgomery Clift's Robert E. Lee Prewitt is largely one of emphasis. Both are at bottom rather stupid, but Prewitt as he was originally written by James Jones and played by Clift had a weird motivated sensitivity, an oddly arresting frailty that gave his eventual destruction by the System a note of genuine tragedy. Luke, on the other (cool) hand, is a cheerful, hearty and frequently comic figure who mindlessly torments (and is therefore mindlessly tormented by) the prison "bosses" (guards), less as a matter of principle than out of an unexamined habit of high spirits.

So there is, then, a certain irony in his ultimate destruction—no one really meant things to go that far—and a certain dramatic validity in the string of absurd fights, escapes, punishments and manhood-proving escapades that form the film's substance. But somehow, despite all the good scenes and a number of technically competent performances, the film as a whole does not come off.

There is a lack of genuine development in the characters involved in the story's central combat. Luke and the bosses remain throughout precisely as they were given in the beginning; no one ever seems to learn anything from their repeated —and finally repetitious—conflicts. There is none of that groping toward an understanding of self and world that was the excuse for and the pleasure of not only Clift's but everyone else's performance in *Eternity*.

Then there is the terrible problem posed by the film's greatest virtue—its sheer physical beauty. The stark black and white photography employed by director Fred Zinnemann in *Eternity* emphasized, indeed symbolized, the bleakness and menace of the system Prewitt was forced by conscience to oppose.

It must be admitted that the loveliness of the rural backgrounds against which Newman and his fellow cons move and work does occasionally suggest the irony of men so near and yet so far from freedom. And it also suggests the film maker's wish to transform Luke into the archetypal American optimist and activist remaining true to himself even in a setting where optimism is hardly a suitable virtue. A coda, suggesting that in the minds of the men still imprisoned Luke has become in death a life-giving mythic figure, carries out still further this rationale. But more often than not, all that beauty just keeps suggesting the notion that prison camp is really a rest camp, that the men are, after all, getting plenty of sleep, food and healthy outdoor exercise, and that despite the occasional unpleasantries of the guards there are worse ways of paying one's debt to society. And so the movie's potential strength is constantly undercut by its visual style.

In defense of a film made with more than usual care as to details and with obvious seriousness of purpose, it must be observed that none of the above comes from a conscious attempt to ape the customary Hollywood desire to glamorize the unglamorizable. The flaws of *Cool Hand Luke* are not the flaws of total cynics but of reasonably serious men who set out to make a serious film and made some honest mistakes. You may well respond generously to these flaws since the intention behind them is so manifestly honorable. Surely you will find in several scenes, both comic and melodramatic, richness enough to reward your attendance. What you will not feel, on balance, are the satisfactions of true art observed.

11/3/67

CLOSELY WATCHED TRAINS

Closely Watched Trains is a film much simpler to enthuse about than it is to catch the flavor of on the printed page, so let's get the easy part out of the way quickly. This work, by a twenty-nine-year-old director named Jiri Menzel, is quite the best product of the celebrated renaissance of the Czech cinema that we have seen in this country so far, and it is also the best movie I have seen this year.

But the nature of the experience the film offers cannot be summarized nearly so neatly as one's response to it. When I say that it is mostly about the sadly comic attempts of a gawky, jug-eared, inarticulately sensitive adolescent to enter upon manhood, which he imagines to be simply a matter of losing his virginity, and when I add that he finally achieves this goal in the classic manner of such stories, through the understanding kindness of an older woman, I fear your silent, knowing withdrawal in the face of the clichés that have launched a thousand indifferent films and novels. One must look between the plot lines to discover the film's special distinction and delight.

The young man's misadventures occur for the most part in a provincial railroad station during the German occupation of Czechoslovakia during World War Two. He is employed there as a trainee, a job that, unfortunately for him, fortunately for us, leaves him plenty of time to observe and misunderstand the life around him and to observe and only half understand the life churning about in his own psyche. The station itself is observed in marvelous detail by Menzel's ever questing camera. Its antique equipment and furnishings—including the most uncongenial sofa on which anyone ever attempted a seduction—perfectly symbolize the unyielding outlines and the drab coloration of the adult world as it so often seems on one's first innocent encounter with it.

The inhabitants of this microcosm are a cross section of humanity—a stationmaster dreaming futile dreams of promotion and spending far too much time with his backyard poultry farm; dispatcher Hubieka (beautifully played by Josef Somr), a shrewd womanizer whose successes belie his weird appearance and coarse manner; a girl telegrapher whose seduction by Hubieka is surely one of the great comic-erotic sequences in film history. Passing through, disturbing and rearranging the relationships of these human particles as electric charges re-pattern a field of iron filings, are the outsiders—a railway supervisor who combines Quislingism, pomposity and fatuity in a maddening manner; a girl from the resistance; a couple of girls with no resistance; a countess; an outraged mother; some German soldiery.

All of these characters are to some degree types, yet all are particularized by Menzel's uncanny eye for the telling detail, humanized by the spirit of compassionate satire that informs the entire film. A simple listing of those present indicates the wide, free range of the director's interest in the human animal under the stress of day-to-day existence, but it cannot begin to demonstrate his great gift for encompassing them all in his film without strain, without ever seeming to digress, without the slightest loss of dramatic tension. Again it is the brilliance of his selectivity that accomplishes this. He tells us all we need to know about all these people, but never one thing more than is necessary. His film is thus a miracle of compression, availing itself of the economies which modern film techniques offer the director, but never using them, as so many do, because their temptation is irresistible.

Menzel handles a variety of rapidly shifting moods with the

same ease that he handles his throng of characters. He juxta-
poses longing and laughter, despair and delight, rationality
with absurdity, and the result is a movie that comes closer to
capturing the texture of ordinary life as we ordinarily experience it than any contemporary movie I can readily think of.

That he does so without ever losing his sympathy—or ours—
for the most befuddled or obnoxious of his characters is a
measure of the warm, unsentimental humanism which is, despite his exciting technical mastery, Mr. Menzel's greatest
strength. Perhaps I can best sum up the magic he works by
noting that his film ends in sudden and shattering tragedy. Yet
as I left the theater, my mood was one of peaceful happiness—
as if I had been put in touch with man, with the world, in a
way that is in the last analysis inexplicable, but which is
extremely rare in this age of alienated and dehumanized art.

11/10/67

TITICUT FOLLIES

Titicut Follies is a documentary film that tells you more than you could possibly want to know—but no less than you should know—about life behind the walls of one of those institutions where we file and forget the criminally insane—in this instance the prison-hospital maintained for them by the state of Massachusetts at Bridgewater. It is a movie which avoids nothing as it relentlessly pursues the horrible truth of a horrible situation and in the process reveals once again the seemingly infinite capacity of man to visit inhumanity on his fellow man.

It has been regarded by critics, the public and the Massachusetts Attorney-General's office (which has been seeking in sundry ways to prevent its exhibition) as an exposé, and certainly it is that. We are assured by the film's producer-director, Frederick Wiseman, that the issues raised in it extend far beyond the boundaries of the Bay State, that, indeed, Bridgewater is, compared to similar snake pits elsewhere, a rather decent place. If so, we can be glad Mr. Wiseman took his cameras only to this one, for what he reveals of existence there is as harrowing as any normal viewer can stand.

The Bridgewater atmosphere is one of aimless hopelessness punctuated by outbursts of unthinking, almost ritualized violence. A psychiatrist turns an interview into a sadistic assault on such shreds of sanity as his inmate victim may still retain; or, with malicious cheerfulness, he force-feeds an old man—already near death—while we wonder whether the ash from the doctor's carelessly dangling cigarette is really going to fall into the glop being funneled into the convulsively shuddering throat; or the guards will vary their routine by tormenting— with words and a slap—a naked inhabitant of the violent ward who has soiled his cell in the night.

A society's treatment of the least of its citizens—and surely these are the least of ours—is perhaps the best measure of its humanity, its civilization; the repulsive reality revealed in *Titicut Follies* sickens, shames and forces one to contemplate our capacity for callousness. No one seeing this film can believe anything except that reform of the conditions it reports is urgent business, both as a matter of simple decency and as a symbolic act of concern for all who are desperately down-trodden.

Yet there is a dimension to the film that transcends the reformist. That, of course, is the aesthetic. Because it was shot with hand-held camera, edited with deliberate lack of slickness and eschews even a voice-over narration to neatly tie things together, cue our responses and lend it an air of conscious artistry, this dimension has been overlooked. But it is present— not so much in the merely adequate structure which involves cutting back and forth between a variety show put on by the inmates—the *Titicut Follies* of the title—and the daily life of the place, but in sequences quite casually thrown at us within the larger scheme.

Examples: An inmate delivering an interminable rational-sounding theory of history and politics which is, of course, totally mad; another inmate tonelessly singing to no one "The Ballad of the Green Berets," the lengthy lyrics of which he has for some reason perfectly memorized; a paranoid at first making perfect sense as he argues the case for his release until, driven desperate by the seeming incomprehension of his listeners, he presses too hard and begins to unconsciously reveal the depth of his illness.

The result in these instances is a shock of partial recognition, a sudden realization that insanity is a matter of degree and that these people are uncomfortably like us, their behavior only a comparatively slight exaggeration of that state we are pleased to call normal.

A similar identification is felt with the good folks of prison society—the rough-hewn but kindly head guard, the volunteer worker who somehow manages to organize a game of pin the tail on the donkey without self-consciousness or patronization, the simple-hearted nurse who finds her reward in a thank-you letter from a released inmate. The ordinary human decency of these people is extraordinarily touching in this context. It is what we like to think we would offer if we were the sorts who lit candles instead of occasionally cursing the darkness, and it is both poignant and maddening to realize that such goodness is not enough, that the dismal atmosphere created by the state must inevitably snuff out the little lights they—or we in their situation—manage to fan into flame.

A couple of years ago there was a great twittering over *Marat/Sade,* an artful theatrical representation of life in a nineteenth-century French madhouse. Much was made of playwright Peter Weiss's cleverness in turning the asylum into a microcosm in which we could observe all the world's insanity. It seemed to me that the work's self-consciousness diminished its force. It was too easy to take—safely removed from us in time and place, always careful at dangerous moments to remind us of its artificiality, of the fact that these were just a lot of actors miming craziness and not to worry.

There are no such easy outs for us in *Titicut Follies.* When we enter its microcosm, we cannot forget that its "actors" are there to stay, trapped forever in their own desperate inventions. The knowledge that they cannot wipe off their makeup, hang up their costumes and stroll over to Sardi's for a drink is what gives the film a power more forceful than any artifice can grant. When a work achieves that kind of power, it must be regarded as art, however artlessly or even crudely it generates it. Laying forth a social problem, *Titicut Follies* also tells us something about the human condition all of us share today, and that is

more than you can say about most of our more conscious
attempts at artistic statements these days.

12/1/67

Titicut Follies raised a nice extra-critical issue. *The State of
Massachusetts contended that Wiseman had, in return for permission to shoot in its Bedlam, granted the state the right to
approve (censor) his final print. It further contended that, in
effect, it had the obligation to act in loco parentis for the inmates, since none of them had the legal right to sign releases or
otherwise give permission to the producer-director to take their
photographs. It took Wiseman to court to enforce these rights
by preventing the distribution of the film. Wiseman denied
that he had, in effect, given the state rights to "final cut" (as
we say in the trade), and he made a persuasive (to me) argument that since he had publicly been hauling his equipment
around the hospital for months—obviously with the approval of
its administrators—the state was a little late in exercising its
prerogatives as guardians of the asylum's inmates. In fact, it
became clear to me as I followed the case that the state was
embarrassed for the public to see just what kind of a black hole
it had been maintaining at the expense of the taxpayers. Moreover, it seemed to me that there was another fundamental right
involved in the case—the right of the public to know about
conditions in the institutions it supports. Indeed, since the inmates had no legal standing, no way to speak for themselves, it
seemed to me there was no hope of improving their lot unless
journalists—and Wiseman was surely that—could gain access to
the place and make a report. It struck me as irrelevant that his
tool was a movie camera, not a pad and pencil.*

*In any event, I was asked to testify at Wiseman's trial as an
expert witness, asserting the artistic as well as journalistic merits
of the film. I thereby learned a valuable lesson, which is that the*

adversary system of jurisprudence is hopelessly inadequate for the discussion of issues that are, finally, aesthetic in nature. An imbecilically moralistic prosecutor kept trying to confine me to yes and no answers, despite the fact that there are no yes and no answers in criticism. An antique judge kept returning to the question of whether there was precedent in the movies of showing male genitalia (as indeed occurred in one pathetic scene), as if the sight of an aged and insane man naked could conceivably awaken prurient interest. The whole business was a farce—and a warning to me of what depths the state can sink to when its normally anonymous bureaucrats are exposed as derelict in their duty. For that was the true issue here. No one really gave a damn about the crazies, for if they did, they would not have been living for so many years in the squalid conditions Wiseman depicted. Indeed, if the state had exercised minimal humanity in its treatment of them, Wiseman would have had no film, but again there was no way within the confines of the trial to effectively raise this moral rather than legal point. The upshot is that the film at present may be shown only to professionals in psychiatry, law and corrections. Appeals have been taken to the Supreme Court, and, for a final irony, Elliot Richardson, the Attorney-General of Massachusetts who brought the action against the film, is now Secretary of Health, Education and Welfare in the Nixon Administration, for God's sake. My ability to maintain a reasonable tone in dealing with the movies was never more seriously tried than it was in this instance—Titicut Follies indeed.

THE GRADUATE

I am beginning to think that the most pernicious phrase of our age is that well-known battle cry "Never trust anyone over thirty." Personally, I couldn't care less if our junior citizens don't trust me, because I don't trust them either. But I notice a growing tendency among my fellow fuds—especially the artists and intellectuals—to try to ingratiate themselves with their adolescent critics by agreeing with them, and that disturbs me. There is something undignified—not to say masochistic—about one's deciding not to trust his own generation. In effect he is declaring that he does not trust himself, and I submit that the quality that best characterizes our time is not the revolt of our youth but the supine acquiescence of so many elders in that revolt. I regard this not only as disloyal to our own not totally dishonorable histories but unhelpful to the kids themselves, who need a strong-minded, but not rigid, older generation against which to test themselves.

The occasion for these geriatric musings is *The Graduate*, a film which starts out to satirize the alienated spirit of modern youth, does so with uncommon brilliance for its first half, but ends up selling out to the very spirit its creators intended to make fun of. Its protagonist, Benjamin Braddock (Dustin Hoffman), is introduced as the archetype of youthful angst, a sensitive lad whose collegiate triumphs in academics, athletics and campus activities fill his parents with delicious pride and fill him with an equally delicious disgust. By rights, his passage into the world of bourgeois striving should be smooth, but he loathes the whole idea of getting and spending. The more the adults around him urge him to take his first brisk strides toward success the deeper he sinks into a swoon of despair, the style of which is borrowed from certain nineteenth-century Russian novelists—a style that could not contrast more comically with the setting of upper-middle-class Los Angeles, preoccupied with sports cars, swimming pools and other sunlit status symbols, the awfulness of which director Mike Nichols catches with such wicked assurance.

Poor Ben. It is basic sex that undoes his enjoyable ennui. A determined young man can resist almost anything, but if his first seducer is an older woman (the wife of his father's partner, no less), he doesn't have a chance. His attempts to keep his cool when subjected to the consuming heat Anne Bancroft generates are hilariously pathetic, and the way he zigs when she zags will put you in mind of the best skits Mr. Nichols used to do with Elaine May. Mr. Hoffman is the master of an infinite variety of soulful stares, half-finished thoughts and phrases, and of a wonderfully wheezy expulsion of breath that occurs whenever he is up-tight, which is most of the time. His sureness of insight is delivered with such technical precision that I have no hesitation in calling it the year's most significant screen debut. Would that everyone connected with the film shared his sense of where he is and where he is going.

But once the May-September affair is established, things start to go wrong. Ben falls in love with his mistress's daughter (the lovely Katharine Ross), understandably upsetting her mom and causing a slightly sour stench to start pervading the comedy. We pass over the line separating farce from potential tragedy as Nichols and the scriptwriters, Calder Willingham and Buck Henry, try to compensate by subtly shifting their attitude toward Ben.

From anti- or at least non-hero, he suddenly starts to emerge as a romantic hero of the unhyphenated variety. Oh, he still fumbles and mumbles and trips all over himself, but the emotional distance from which we previously viewed him—a distance absolutely essential for satire—suddenly disappears. We find ourselves asked to stand shoulder to sympathetic shoulder with him as he attempts to rescue his (young) lady love from living death—marriage to a square.

The movie loses its shrewd. Sentiment replaces even-handed toughness, and there is an attempt to force our acknowledgment of Ben's final superiority over environment and elders. He is likable enough, and they are indeed ghastly. But he is also desperately self-absorbed and shamelessly spoiled. And while he is seen to strike the poses of exquisite sensitivity and sensibility, nothing in his talk or actions seems to substantiate his right to criticize, withdraw or revolt from the society in which he has yet to take a man's place. The failure of Nichols and company to insist on this proof strikes me as a fatal defect in artistic, not to mention social, responsibility.

We are distracted from this shortcoming by a succession of gags that ill suit the darkening mood of the film's last half and which, unlike the preceding humor, have no organic connection with character or situation. The true tensions generated by the generation gap are thus avoided and, along with them, the deepest comic possibilities as well. It's a shame—they were halfway to something wonderful when they skidded on a patch of greasy kid stuff.

1/19/68

THE STRANGER

I confess that I approached *The Stranger* with considerable trepidation. Albert Camus's novel, despite the vigor of its deceptively simple style, despite the marvelous clarity of its philosophy and psychology, seemed impossibly difficult to translate to the screen. Its setting—the Algiers of the writer's youth—is a country of the mind, easier for the realistic camera to distort than to capture. Nor did it seem likely that Meursault, the Stranger of the title, would make a very satisfactory central figure for a film. The modern archetype of the alienated man, he relates to the world only with distant contempt, internally expressed. He is a fascinating enigma on the printed page, but I surmised that the problem of externalizing his character and his malaise in dramatically valid terms would most likely be insurmountable.

How wrong I was. Director Luchino Visconti, a team of screenwriters and, most especially, Marcello Mastroianni as Meursault have made from *The Stranger* a film that can only be described as excellent—thoughtful, moving and faithful. Above all, faithful, for theirs is the kind of modest, self-effacing craftsmanship that serves rather than exploits its basic material. Eschewing the temptation to overcinematize the story, they have concentrated with commendable discipline on allowing the grave voice of Albert Camus to speak to us in a medium that was not his own. It comes through firm and clear, and true. Since this was a voice that both summed up and shaped the sensibility of at least two postwar generations, it is well worth the close attention this film forces us to pay.

Meursault is a clerk. He is supremely indifferent to his job, his surroundings, the people he knows (they can scarcely be called friends). The concerns, the strivings which ordinarily preoccupy most of us are absurdities to him. Only the sensations of the moment—the taste of food or a cigarette, the feel of the hot African sun on his flesh, the most purely physical aspects of sex—have any reality for him. The idea that there is any design by which these moments may be connected and given a larger meaning is anathema to him.

His mother dies and he feels inconvenience rather than sorrow. His firm offers him a promotion and he rejects it as meaningless. His girl friend suggests they get married and he announces that it is all the same to him if they do or if they don't. One day he goes to the beach with a small-time crook whom any ordinarily fastidious person would avoid but whom Meursault tolerates as he does everyone and everything—indifferently. The man has a fight with some Arabs, one of whose sisters he has previously beaten. Meursault does not get involved, but later, out for a solitary walk, he encounters the Arabs again, and when they appear to threaten him he kills one of them.

Tried for murder, he explains only that he did it "because of the sun." He offers no further extenuation and no remorse. It was an accident, like everything else in life, and he cannot be blamed if the heat temporarily forced him from his customary disengaged posture into the most terrible engagement one man can make with another—the taking of his life.

Meursault is doomed by his lack of repentance and by a string of witnesses who testify that his indifference to death is only an extension of his indifference to the customary standards by which we judge a man's fitness to live in civilization. To decent right-thinking people he is a moral monster who must be condemned—if not for his crime, then for his thoughts.

But of course he is not a monster. He is merely a man in

rebellion against the illusions which help the rest of us sustain our sanity, a man who has pressed rationalism to its outermost limits and is content to live on the brink of the darkest abyss, the place where even saints must fear to tread and which is, indeed, the take-off point for their sundry leaps of faith. Which makes him, perversely, ironically, a kind of tragic hero.

The artistic challenge such a figure presents is formidable. He is the embodiment not of observed human characteristics, as most fictional constructs are, but of a pure idea, the nature of which is such that our every instinct begs us to reject it. The problem is to humanize him so that we can open ourselves emotionally—not just intellectually—to his mind and his tragedy. I have never been certain that Camus himself solved this problem completely, especially for those who were not generally predisposed to his view of existence. The idea he represented clung unshakably to the mind, but Meursault the man had a way of slipping out of the reader's grasp.

The movie rectifies this defect. Meursault and his world are made palpable on film in a way they never were—for me, at least—on the page. This is not a matter of director or star adding a lot of helpful hints designed to cue our responses and make sure we get the point. It is, rather, an almost subliminal thing—the flicker of an expression in Mastroianni's face, the camera's eye falling briefly on a detail which helps concretize a story that is by its nature always in danger of becoming mythically abstract.

When, at the end, priest and Stranger meet in the condemned cell to discuss ultimate meanings, this attention to detail pays off. What seemed mainly an ideological duel in the novel here becomes a passionate struggle for the soul of an unpleasantly honest and courageous man we have come to care deeply about—not because we agree with him (we may or may not) but because we love him. He has already chosen death in preference to the conventional wisdom. Now he chooses damnation—if, indeed, there is a heaven. And this is a victory we can savor even if we believe he is wrong.

The Stranger is a muted, careful, even slow film that achieves *its* victory through an austere honesty that matches that of its hero. It is not a movie to engage casually and it may not please those for whom movies are primarily exercises in style or fashionable form. It does, however, place before us one of the key philosophical and artistic expressions of our time, and in illuminating it anew it inevitably illuminates the basic issues with which all of us must sooner or later grapple. It is, therefore, a film that any serious person must regard as inescapable.

2/2/68

In my time as a reviewer this is the only adaptation of a major novel of our period that turned out to be at least a near-great movie. It is also the only work of Visconti's that I thought supported the claims of his adherents that he was a director of world class. Again, this is one of those small, sober, intelligent and unsensational movies to which I am fatally attracted, almost against my will. I mean, for a boy brought up on an addictive diet of melodramatic genre pieces it is an odd taste and perhaps more reflective of my more intellectual tastes in literature than my normally more visceral tastes in movies.

On the other hand, it seems to me that although the earlier prejudice of serious film critics and audiences against "literary" movies was sound, it perhaps ought to be thought through again. Hollywood, of course, has tended to buy best-sellers and to make talky, static movies out of them that are execrable at any level. When it tackled "classics" the approach was gingerly, respectful and thus either laughable or dull. Hence the truism that it was bad or at least minor fiction—detective and western stories especially—that best survived the rigors of adaptation, since those who worked on them in the studios felt much freer to assert themselves and the demands of their medium for fairly simple-minded action. It now seems to me, however, that the sensibility gap has been closing for some time, especially in Europe. That is to say, that the best film makers share with the best novelists similar views of the human condition, and of the most effective fictive techniques for rendering it. Don't we appreciate much of the later Ingmar Bergman, for instance, in much the same way, and for much the same reasons, that we appreciate much of the most serious novels of our era? Can't the same thing be said of Antonioni, Rohmer, even Buñuel? And if, as I think, this is true, why should disapproval automatically attach itself to a careful adaptation of a work like The Stranger? It is no more static or talky than, let us say, The Touch (which is an original screenplay), no more psychologically oriented, no more, in the last analysis, a philosophical disquisition in dramatic form.

No doubt we will continue to have many bad adaptations of novels by movie makers, but we will also continue to have many bad movies regardless of their place of origin. What I'm saying is that the standard generalization about adaptation is, like all generalizations about the medium, not universally true and that we could safely lighten our baggage by throwing it out, judging each new case on its merits without reference to it.

CHARLIE BUBBLES

Here is Charlie Bubbles keeping an eye on things around the house: he has a television camera in every room and a nine-screen monitor in his study so he can see—and occasionally hector—friends and servants as they go about their work and play.

Here is Charlie Bubbles taking his secretary and would-be mistress on a visit to his old home town: he practically never gets out of his car or slows down to examine the landscape, preferring to keep the windshield and some distance between himself and the life that once he led.

And here is Charlie taking his son to a football match: they sit in a private booth and see the game through a glass dimly, cut off from the crowd, the play and from the possibility of participatory emotions.

Who is Charlie? What is responsible for his isolation? The rueful comedy that bears his ironically effervescent name as a title dramatizes his situation with great simplicity. He is a writer, up from the working class of Manchester, who in the course of becoming prematurely rich and famous has mislaid a writer's basic tool—the capacity to feel and to respond. Now he must pay a visit to his estranged wife and son, whom he has set up on a farm outside the city of his birth. His journey accidentally becomes an attempt—tight-lipped, monosyllabic and grimly weary—to re-establish his connections with life, people, his own history.

He fails—an act of will is no substitute for an act of faith—
and is last seen loosing the few remaining lines that moor him
to reality and drifting away from it all in a lovely surprising
symbolic sequence that is daringly different from the naturalistic tone of the rest of the movie, yet wonderfully right as a
climax.

Rightness, indeed, is the key to the film's success. In the last
analysis it is no more than a series of minor incidents pegged to
that most classically simple of story lines—a trip into the past.
Clumsily written or played, these vignettes and anecdotes might
have been like so many allegedly funny scenes in film these days,
only chancely comic and pointless. But Shelagh Delaney's
script has a way of lightly, precisely tapping the point of truth
in each of them. Albert Finney and the rest of the cast have
similarly good instincts, and they are handled by a new young
director—name of Albert Finney—who has had the wit to find
his own style and the confidence to stick to it. He has a fine,
subtle eye for the absurdity of soft and vulnerable human
beings trapped in the maze of hard cold surfaces of modern life
and moving with the speed of increasing desperation as they try
to find something in that wilderness of unyielding forms that is
quick and warm to the touch.

Movement implies displacement and that, finally, is the
film's true subject. No one is where he or she is supposed to be.
Charlie and his old north country friend (Colin Blakely) don't
belong in an expense-account restaurant in London, trying to
relate by throwing food at each other. They don't fit in
Charlie's house, either, for it is less a home than a repository
for the gadgets with which we vainly try to create environments
that work with instead of against the grain of our electronic
culture.

On the other hand, as Charlie's trip proves, you truly can't
go home again any more. The American girl (Liza Minnelli)
who accompanies him is looking for her family's ancestral roots
here, and all she finds is the rubble of reconstruction and a
frigidly moderne hotel, where she awkwardly offers herself to

the indifferently receptive Charlie. As for his wife (beautifully played by the slightly, deliciously, overripe Billie Whitelaw), she is an urban type who likes the idea of farm life but has trouble coping with its practical aspects. Her son, in the true spirit of the new times, lights up only when the television set does. Occasionally, to be sure, we glimpse someone who has stayed put, has resisted the lure of movement, but these characters are the saddest of all, since stasis is a kind of living death.

So there is no way out, nowhere to go and nowhere to rest. We retain from *Charlie Bubbles* a series of images of the sort with which I began this review: human figures blurred as they hasten past themselves shallowly reflected in the glass and metal of their surroundings, occasionally frozen for an instant in a numb and terrible self-awareness. Laughter dies, gives way to a pity which does not purge, only discomfits. *Charlie Bubbles* is a very modest thing, but like all good work in the minor keys it has a way of haunting the memory and catching us unaware in the small, lonely hours.

3/8/68

LA CHINOISE

If one is going to talk seriously about the movies of this decade, one must finally come to terms with that brilliant, maddening, prolific young veteran of the French New Wave, Jean-Luc Godard. In this country only his first film, *Breathless*, has been a popular success, and I sometimes think that for all his energy and daring, he will never have another. In the seven years since that sprightly, approachable little movie was released he has developed a highly difficult, individualistic manner that has polarized the film world, creating a small cult of worshipful disciples and a larger, if not more influential, group of opponents who regard him as a sort of Mau-Mau of the cinema, threatening not only its conventional aesthetic wisdom but, if I read them correctly, all of Western civilization as well. It is hard to build reasonably proportioned respect and understanding among ordinary moviegoers if the only reviews you get are either slavishly acceptant or furiously dismissive.

Godard is, I think, too interesting and important a figure for this kind of treatment; he must be saved from his friends and his enemies and, if possible, delivered to a larger audience, both for his own sake and its. His latest release, *La Chinoise* (*The Chinese Girl*), which is the first part of a projected trilogy, is a very good place to begin that process.

Early in his career Godard declared that what he liked best to do was show us individuals so obsessed with a single idea that they were compelled to follow it to its logical extreme and beyond—where, of course, madness lies. Until recently the metaphors he has used to examine the psychology of the True Believer have been mostly sexual and/or criminal. Now, however, circumstances have presented him with one that is, if not more apt, then more original and therefore more powerful.

That is the rise of Chinese Communism and, more to the point, the significance it is beginning to have for some young European leftists. To them Maoism is a force comparable to the religious reformation Luther launched in the sixteenth century, a force capable of violently purifying and reviving what seems to them a once idealistic institution that has grown excessively materialistic, even decadent. To them—amazing as it seems to us—Maoism looks like an attractive alternative to both Russian Communism and American capitalism.

I don't know if any of these youngsters have gone quite so far as the characters in *La Chinoise*—setting up a cell in a Paris apartment, where the short-wave set is always tuned to Radio Peking, the library consists entirely of Chairman Mao's infamous Little Red Book and the entertainment is mainly a stupefying series of lectures on and discussions of revolutionary theory—but Godard's vision of these curiously intense people is persuasively realistic. And chilling.

And comic. What always saves Godard's work for me is his superb sense of irony. His sympathetic fascination with the outsiders who always people his films rarely deteriorates into sentimentality. Quite the contrary—they are absurd creatures. In *La Chinoise*, for instance, adolescent inattention and ineptitude keep undercutting everyone's revolutionary fervor, as do the sexual crosscurrents which keep swirling about. And when these humorless idealists move from talk to action, things fall still further apart. They carefully plan an assassination and, of course, gun down the wrong man, then must go back and get the right one. Their bungling perhaps reads as a comment on the futility of revolution, the fact that they go unpunished for their crimes a comment on the impotence and fatuity of the adult world that has driven them to this desperate expedient.

Godard's attitude is summed up with admirable economy in the film's throwaway ending: the bourgeois friends from whom they borrowed the apartment in the first place return from vacation, and the would-be revolutionaries meekly surrender the pad and break up their cell.

In outline, I am afraid the picture sounds simpler, more straightforward than it really is. Indeed, what I have set down is only my interpretation of Godard's intentions. He hates to cue audience response to scenes and characters, hates to be in the position of begging them for approval. Working in the most seductive of the arts, he has therefore developed a carefully unseductive style—distant, elliptical, severely objective in its visualizations, arhythmic in its editing method. He alternates the pace and the mood of his pictures in an arbitrary, not to say capricious, way, always trying to keep you off balance, upset your expectations, force you to work at his art and thereby make you aware that it *is* art, not just a movie. Which accounts for the sequence that has by now become his trademark—a long excruciating scene where his normally restless camera sits on its haunches and peers like an unblinking cat at some endless discussion (in *La Chinoise* it is between a girl and a philosopher) that anyone else would cut out of the script without bothering to shoot it at all.

He is, in short, all the things his detractors say he is—pretentious, sophomoric, self-indulgent. But he is also all the things his supporters claim he is—a director who succeeds in capturing and bringing back alive some of the shyest, most skittish social and psychological demons of our time. Godard may never again make a completely satisfactory film, but at his best he remains one of our most sensitive and significant photo-journalists.

4/12/68

This piece seems unfinished to me now. I really intended to go on examining Godard's work as it appeared, but Weekend *followed very closely on the heels of* La Chinoise *in American re-*

lease, and it was so similar in tone and my response was so similar to it that I passed on it. Subsequently, as he lost his capacity to be ironic about the political metaphor, as he became more and more a committed revolutionary, I lost my taste for him entirely. I could no longer objectify my response to his films, so out of phase with his politics was I. But here I must confess that I could never develop the passionate partisanship of either his most avid defenders or his most vehement detractors. Emotionally I remained cool, neutral to him throughout. I'm now inclined, I guess, a little more toward John Simon's dismissiveness than I am to Pauline Kael's indulgence, but not very strongly so. The review's last sentence continues to stand as my infuriatingly uncommitted view of an artist whose work encourages most critics to passions I simply can't duplicate.

HOUR OF THE WOLF

Ingmar Bergman likes to speak of himself as a magician. The film maker, he notes, bases his art on the use of a machine that exploits a weakness in human vision in order to impart the illusion—not the reality—of motion and therefore of life. In other words, a highly complex art, and an industry hardly less complex, is based on a gadget that is fundamentally a toy to amuse and mystify children (or at least the child who resides in all of us). "Thus," says Bergman, "I am either an impostor or, when the audience is willing to be taken in, a conjurer."

There is both disarming modesty and admirable self-awareness in this statement, for I must confess that I have never been able to definitely decide whether Bergman is, indeed, a consummate magician or merely a mountebank. I change my mind from film to film and even from sequence to sequence in the same film. He is a journalist—not quite a philosopher—of the guilty soul, and the necessity to probe the unconscious states of his characters leads him to a heavily symbolic, sometimes expressionistic, style in which he has created (a) some of the most memorable screen images of our time and (b) some of the most annoyingly obscure and/or pretentious images of the same period. In short, he fascinates as he irritates, and all I know for certain is that the hold he has on me—and, I suspect, on almost everyone else—is based on his attempt, and ours, to resolve the basic tension between the artist and the trickster which exists in his personality and in his work.

It is no wonder that Bergman, so aware that his art—perhaps all art—is based at least partly on trumpery, should be obsessed with the tragedy of the artist figure who suddenly, mysteriously loses the power to cast his magic spells. *Persona*, released a year ago, and his latest film, *Hour of the Wolf*, both deal with this theme and are, in fact, twins more understandable and rewarding considered together instead of separately.

You will recall that in the former an actress loses her ability to speak and, as therapy, goes to live in an isolated seacoast cottage with a nurse companion of resounding normality. There the source of the artist's malaise is revealed. She is haunted by guilt over past failures to love and to respond to love, and she has come to believe she has lost the *right* to speak to the world. She also discovers a frightful cure for her condition. Her silence encourages her simple, healthy friend to blither on about herself, and the more she talks the more the nurse realizes that she is as guilt-ridden as the actress. By the end of the film, illness has been transferred from patient to nurse, and we have learned a terrible lesson: the artist must discharge his neuroses somehow; if he cannot do so in imaginative works, he will do so far more destructively by imposing them on other people.

Hour of the Wolf carries this logic one step further. The basic situation is the same. Again the artist blocked by guilts (this time he is a man and a painter), again the placidly normal companion (this time his pregnant wife), again the isolated cottage.

There is, however, one important difference. The companion will not allow herself to be drawn into the artist's insanity, perhaps because she is defending her unborn child, perhaps because she knows the wiles and dangers of her "case" more intimately than the nurse in *Persona* knew hers.

Anyway, the painter (played with his usual fine craftsmanship by Max von Sydow) cannot fight off his demons; they rise up to fill his mind—and the screen—blotting out every shred of reality until at last he attempts to kill his wife and succeeds in killing himself. In so doing he becomes the means of openly stating what was only implicit in the earlier film: that madness undischarged in art or in human relations must be discharged through self-destruction. Somehow or other it will out.

As a kind of journalist Bergman is always an objective observer of such phenomena, and he betrays little overt emotion over this denouement. He accepts self-destruction as coolly (one is tempted to say coldly) as he accepted in *Persona* the destruction of an innocent bystander. He is—as all his films testify—the sort of completely committed, perhaps self-absorbed, artist who has long lived with full awareness that the creative spirit can turn rogue, can destroy with the same passionate intensity that it builds. Indeed, such terror as one feels for the characters of these films is a direct product of Bergman's easy acceptance of this possibility. One imagines that the idea once frightened him; now it is merely another psychological phenomenon for him to examine and then objectify as art. (I will concede that this may be pure bravado on his part, even an act of self-romanticism, but I don't think it primarily is.)

Despite the dangers of subjectivism, I trust his motives in all this. They have, I think, a purity rare among film artists. His methods, on the other hand, are sometimes dubious. In *Persona*, for example, he took very great risks, striving for an elliptical austerity of statement that deliberately puzzled and frankly bored—particularly in the key scene where the exchange of personalities between the two women is consummated and symbolized by having the nurse repeat word for word the same interminable speech the actress has just given, the camera never wavering from a close-up on her, just as it never wavered from a similar shot on the previous speaker. I admired the daring of the sequence, the arrogance with which the artist forced us to accept it—and thought I might run screaming from the theater.

In *Hour of the Wolf* Bergman is back to his older, more

familiar tricks, mixing memories, visions and external reality in a deliberately confusing, though ultimately decipherable, way. There is also a very long dream sequence, perhaps the longest of the many he has filmed, and it is full of spectacular effects (including a long pan down the naked body of Ingrid Thulin). It is, on the whole, a more exciting film visually than its immediate predecessor, if not quite so memorable as *The Seventh Seal* or *Wild Strawberries*. Nevertheless, it seems to me something of a regression after *Persona*, a return to an easier, more superficial kind of magic making, a relaxation into the successes of the past instead of a development of the difficult, tightly compressed, highly charged manner, by no means perfected but infinitely promising, which he introduced last year. *Persona* perhaps explained itself too little, but it left us caught up in a mystery, powerless to keep our thoughts from returning to it. *Hour of the Wolf* explains too much (including, ironically, much of *Persona*) and thus allows us to escape from it relatively unscathed psychologically.

Still there are, as always in Bergman's films, those burning images of inner terror, etched forever in one's consciousness. At his best and at his worst the magician always leaves us with those. They are the best rationale for seeing everything and anything he makes, and they more than serve in the case of *Hour of the Wolf*. If it is a partial failure, it is so at the very highest level, and no matter how one evaluates it, the film further illuminates the dark and bloody ground of Ingmar Bergman's sensibility, which is, of course, one of the most important artistic sensibilities operating in the world today.

4/26/68

This piece marks an important intellectual turning point for me. I had been greatly troubled by Persona, so much so that I was unable to complete a satisfactory review of it and so stood silent about it until Hour of the Wolf, undoubtedly a lesser

piece, illuminated its predecessor for me. As I look back upon
it, I see now that I had simply been resisting the magic of
Persona, trying to close my mind against its persuasive power
because it upset all my convictions about Bergman. Excepting
Wild Strawberries and, perhaps, Through a Glass Darkly, I had
not at all liked his work. I respected his craftsmanship, of
course, but his metaphysical gropings seemed jejune to me, and
his descents into expressionism seemed to owe more to UFA,
circa 1920, than was generally recognized. In short, I thought
his films less original in concept and execution than many
believed. Moreover, in the late 1950s Bergman's obvious strain-
ing after seriousness was used, especially in middle-brow circles,
to condemn other traditions of movie making unfairly, as if he
were the first man to use the camera for purposes of philosophical exploration. In my opinion of those early films I was
undoubtedly reacting as much to the inflated claims of Bergman's admirers as I was to the quality of the works themselves.

Anyway, I should have been more alert to the gradual purifi-
cation of Bergman's style, his growth toward greater certainty
about his own beliefs, which freed his audience from the necessity of suffering with him through each and every change of
heart and mind. In short, self-absorption lessened, humanity
grew, and I did not attend his films with a mind sufficiently
open to observe this. Thus Hour of the Wolf was a breakthrough film for me, and my appreciation of Bergman's growing mastery has increased ever since. Among the contemporary
masters I doubt that he will ever have quite the place in my
heart that, for instance, Buñuel or Truffaut occupies, but who
can say? Bergman has changed and developed much more than
the latter, and it seems to me he is not done changing by any
means. That is very rare; movie directors don't as a rule exhibit
the kind of intellectual growth and experimental range Bergman has shown, the tendency being to develop a set of commercially viable tricks and habits and stop. Thus, the possibility
is that he will go on still further and the challenge will be to
keep up with him.

PLANET OF THE APES

Movie critics, of all people, should trust their instincts. When I saw *Planet of the Apes* a couple of months ago, I liked it. I just plain liked it—an ingenious, adventurous, humorous, deliciously spooky example of one of my favorite popular genres, science fiction, it was smartly made and contained a useful moral or two. I should have stood up and proclaimed my affectionate regard for the thing right off.

Any sensible child, as I will shortly demonstrate, would have done so automatically. But there are times when a critic, either out of self-consciousness or self-importance, cannot or will not respond as child, which is perhaps the worst of all possible errors when he is dealing with American films, since they have almost no art tradition and therefore impose a unique regressive obligation on those who would try to appreciate them at their proper level—an obligation that grows burdensome through excessive repetition, I might add. On the other hand, the number of altogether entertaining movie entertainments is, curiously, somewhat lower these days than the number of works that aspire, with somewhat more success, to the higher things (it is a strange and terrifying thing to live in the midst of the cultural revolution), and one really ought to stay alert and open to the genuinely good low-caste stuff—more alert, alas, than I was when I got up-tight and stodgy about *Planet*. Goodness of any kind is just too rare to pass lightly by.

Two factors contributed to my sense of guilt about this error.

One was the slowly dawning conviction that, damn it, *Planet* is the best American movie I have seen so far this year. Considering the competition, that is, perhaps, faint praise, but the movie is at least alive. By this I mean that it is alive to—and delighted with—its own possibilities. Care is taken to develop all the implications of its basic premise—the whole sociology of a world run by simians is exhaustively laid out for us—and there is none of that perfunctory air that often attends a movie that is depending on an oddly arresting gimmick and whose makers lack the wit or creative energy to do something with it. Even more pleasing, director Franklin Schaffner, screenwriters Rod Serling and Michael Wilson, and their cast are in no way tempted to let us know that they feel superior to the fairy story they're telling. So many of our commercial technicians, for reasons totally undiscernible to me, think they are better than their material and try to indicate it to us by invoking the distancing spirit of camp, creative people no less than critics being concerned to keep their cultural credentials in order, mostly by winking broadly at us, nudging us furiously in the ribs and saying, at least by implication, "Just kidding, folks, I'm really Shakespeare in drag."

The other and more important reason for this public recantation of my error of omission was my daughter's response to *Planet*. She's only four, but her buddies down the street liked the movie so much that they had to see it a second time—twenty-four hours after their first exposure—and she was invited along. Her inner life has not been the same since. The movie is on her mind and in her mind in a way that no other movie she's ever seen is.

Sure, they hooked her with the excitement of a crashing rocket, the exploration of desert and mountains, all those hairy, scary creatures tormenting Charlton Heston and chasing him all over the place, and so on. But they also taught her something—that animals and, by implication, all creatures different from her are capable of feeling. It taught her, she tells me in her own way, that they can be as scared of the unfamiliar and therefore as foolish and as prejudiced as more familiar beings (white Anglo-Saxon Protestants, for example) can be.

Now, we have preached this lesson to her, and she has been exposed to it as she watched bland kid stuff of the *Lassie-Gentle Ben* variety. But no one has had the wit before now to vivify it by a simple, radical reversal of the kind we see in *Planet of the Apes*, where creatures we are taught to believe are inferior are suddenly so superior that they have the power to lock up odd specimens like Heston in a zoo and run a few experiments on him to test the causes of his obvious inadequacy.

Yes, I suppose Erika was occasionally scared by the movie. But what is childhood without a few delicious cases of the creeps? (The violence depicted here is, by the way, not quite so intense as you'll find down at your neighborhood playground.) And what does a case of the creeps matter anyway if you learn something worthwhile from it and it is in part an authentic, totally engaging experience instead of just a way to kill a rainy Saturday, as most children's movies—and literature—are?

By the way, Erika just wandered by and asked me what I was doing. When I told her, she asked, "Are you writing about how we gotta see it again?" The answer, of course, was yes.

5/10/68

A FACE OF WAR

Even the title is unassuming—A *Face of War*, not *The*—
modestly implying that the experience of war has as many
interpretations as it has participants and observers. Its technique is in keeping with this spirit, low-keyed and straightforward. Producer-director Eugene S. Jones and a crew of three
simply moved in with the point squad of Mike Company,
Third Battalion, Seventh Marine Regiment, for ninety-seven
days in the summer of 1966 to record on film and sound tape
the quality of their lives in Vietnam. This is presented without
narration or musical score in a seventy-seven-minute film of
almost unbearable poignancy, a film which must rank with *The
Anderson Platoon*—and perhaps ahead of it—as one of the
great documents of our Asian agony.

The stuff of this film is the ordinary stuff of war—a patrol
through a rice paddy, a search for a sniper in a hamlet, the
destruction by land mines of a couple of troop carriers. The
conflict in Vietnam being more than most a hurry-up-and-wait
kind of thing, a great deal of footage is devoted to the activities
of the men when they are not actually in combat—an im-
promptu rodeo as they try to ride a peasant's panicky bullock, a
football game in ankle-deep mud, the treatment of villagers'
minor illnesses and accidents by medical corpsmen.

The peculiarity of the war is, of course, the shocking juxtaposition of the demands of war with the works of peace. Both
the little rodeo and the sick call are interrupted by the explo-

183

sion of mines and the necessity of attending to the ghastly consequences ("It hurts," a wounded marine says in shock, "it hurts"). The hunt for the sniper ends not only with his death but with the death of a little girl accidentally caught in the crossfire. Her last moments are spent in a circle of marines, and the anguish of their expressions, the sheer damned helplessness etched in the faces, is almost as terrible to behold as the child's senseless death.

One cannot help but reflect in this moment that an age that has produced the philosophy of the absurd has also produced, without really meaning to, a kind of warfare to match that philosophy, and that all of us—the child, her mother, the marines, even those of us who are merely distant witnesses— are equally helpless victims.

The point is driven home in another, longer sequence. A village that has harbored Vietcong is burned, its people weep, and up lumbers an armored vehicle of some kind. Its great metal jaws, cruelly pronged, open wide, and the people are herded in. The jaws grind shut, swallowing the entire population of a place, and off it clanks, uncomprehending. Technology has granted these people a kind of peace, but at the price of destroying the community they shared, the fabric of the only life they have known. It is as if this machine, only part of a much larger machine, runs mindlessly by itself, and again one has the sense that no one is really responsible, that the search for the machine's first cause is as futile as the search for the first cause of the universe itself. Yes, I think the machine could be stopped, but only locally and temporarily. In the twentieth century its soullessness must go marching on. That, of course, is the meaning of this war and one of the reasons it so fills us with dread and impotent rage.

There is, however, something more to be learned in Vietnam, and it is in showing us this less frequently observed side of the conflict that A *Face of War* earns its greatest distinction. We have heard a great deal about how this war is corrupting us, destroying our tradition and our morality. That may be so, especially in our political command posts, but the rot has not yet reached the men of M Company. Surrounded by, dependent on, ruled by, the engines of destruction, they remain triumphantly humane, roughly tender with one another and with the civilians they encounter.

One sequence is particularly telling in this respect. A peasant woman, attended by a midwife and one of their own medics, is giving birth, and a small group from the company stands around, unable to resist the ironic wonder of life beginning in the midst of death. Gently, awkwardly, with beautiful shyness, they welcome the child to a world that they, no more than anyone else, wanted to make. "Hey, tiger," they whisper as they reach out with tentative hands to touch the baby boy, exercising for the first time his right to protest. "Hey, little tiger."

Inarticulate they may be, but neither hope nor humanity has been trained out of them. Indeed, one feels that somehow both have been enhanced by the personal testing of an ambiguous war and by their youthful exposure to the blunt fact of mortality. One may be ashamed by the thing they have been asked to do, but one is not ashamed of them. Quite the opposite. That irreducible measure of goodness that is present in our national character, and which is too often ignored, is artlessly, uninsistently revealed by the brave men who appeared in—and made —this film. It seems to me that in this time when we search anew, as each generation must, for the meaning of who we are and what we are, the men of Mike Company remind us of something about ourselves and of our capacity for grace, even in torment, that we are in danger of forgetting.

5/24/68

It's just about impossible for documentaries to find an audience, and a documentary that speaks sympathetically about the men engaged in an unpopular war faces dismal prospects indeed. But

A Face of War, despite the fact it was seen by almost no one, is one of the great documentaries of a period when many were made but only a few—mostly those about rock music—found an audience. Indeed, the movie must rank with Fred Wiseman's examinations of the institutions of our society (the police, the schools, the hospitals, etc.) as an example of responsible use of cinéma vérité technique for serious journalistic purposes. Wiseman, of course, has found something of a home—and the chance to win Emmys—on educational television, but the commercial networks must bear heavy responsibility for not embracing cinéma vérité, which is ideally suited to the medium. If they had, it might have accustomed the mass audience to its style and created a market—to use a crass term—for the work of a talented group who are exploring the possibilities inherent in cinema's most interesting recent technological breakthrough— fast films, lightweight cameras and sound-recording equipment. Indeed, it's a scandal that the network news departments continue to avoid these techniques and, by so doing, avoid the examination of areas of our common experience that only these techniques can help us to investigate cinematically.

PETULIA

Let me put the matter very simply: *Petulia* is a terrific movie, at once a sad and savage comment on the ways we waste our time, our money and ourselves in upper-middle-class America. It is a subject much trifled with in movies these days, but rarely—if ever—has it been tackled with the ferocious and ultimately purifying energy displayed in this highly moral, yet unmoralistic, film.

Its strength stems from two sources, the passionate intensity with which director Richard Lester fastens his camera's eye on the inanimate artifacts of our consumer culture and the complex, highly charged (but subtly controlled) style—rather like a mosaic set in very rapid motion—with which he presents his vision of a world where the thing is king, an absolute sovereign holding all of us in thrall. The first master of the American movie, D. W. Griffith, thought film was uniquely qualified among the arts to examine what one critic called "the visible hieroglyphs of the unseen world," and they are, I think, the true subject of *Petulia*. A fully mechanized motel, a parody of a *Playboy* bachelor's pad, an inhumanly efficient hospital (a sort of medical factory)—what these hieroglyphs tell us about the true quality of our unseen world, the doomed hopes for ease and grace they contain! In a sense Lester is practicing in art what we all attempt in daily life—reading character by studying a man's possessions, which in the day of standardized people is a very useful gift. And from the place his characters choose to eat lunch, from the show flickering on an unwatched TV set in the corner, from the stuff they give their kids, we learn who his people are, what they really want, in a way that almost makes dialogue superfluous.

As for the style, it is the now conventionalized and commercialized one based on the quick cut and the deliberate jumbling of time sequence, which is no longer worth discussing, let alone deploring, since it is *the* style of the sixties. The point is that Lester uses it with superb natural ease. Too often in American films this technique is regarded as no more than an opportunity to show off, an extra added attraction tacked on for no discernible good reason. Here this style, which emphasizes the fact that movies are themselves a mechanically based art, works brilliantly; style and substance are organically, inextricably related, working like a reciprocating engine to drive home Lester's point.

By emphasizing its documentary merits I do not wish to suggest that there is no story in *Petulia*. It is a perfectly adequate little thing—a romance between the girl of the title (Julie Christie) and a doctor (George C. Scott) whom she sort of wins at a raffle. She is on the verge of a mental breakdown, driven there by a faggoty husband (Richard Chamberlain, who forgot his nice pills and is for the first time memorable) and his rich, devouring family, who give the kids every*thing* except understanding. Scott is on the verge of a social breakout, sick to death of material preoccupations, which seem to him a travesty of his profession's ideals and his own ideals about family life. For the length of the movie they twist and turn, attempting to elude the destinies their natures and the distorted values of their time, place and class impose upon them, but for all their venturings, both comic and grisly, they remain in the end pretty much as we found them, screwed-up prisoners of a screwed-up world.

This is, I think, a measure of the film's honesty, but there are others. Petulia and friend are nice enough to identify with, but they are not, finally, so charming or delightful that you feel like

indulging them to excess. Each has a hard core of selfishness
and foolishness that cannot be washed out; they contain within
themselves the very qualities against which they are in rebellion—how could they not, since they, too, are the creatures of
their era? Their tragedy is that, unlike the majority of their
fellow sufferers, they are aware of what's happening to them.
They are not the blind bourgeoisie of *The Graduate,* they do
not need an insufferably superior adolescent to show them
what's wrong with them. They know, they know—and still
they can't quite make it to decency and repose.

It is gut-grinding to watch them try, even when they make
you laugh. And laugh you do, in rueful self-recognition, for
Lester, his leading actors and screenwriter Lawrence B. Marcus
are confident and mordant throwaway ironists.

Still, the triumph rightly belongs to Lester. After the idle
pleasantries of the Beatle movies, the disappointing heaviness
of *A Funny Thing Happened on the Way to the Forum,* the
desperate preachments of *How I Won the War,* he has at
last controlled his enormous gift for movie making and placed
it in the service of a brilliantly conceived, carefully aimed,
splendidly detailed satire. He demands much of the audience, a
toughness, a stern ability to put down the desire—always
present at the movies—for the happy-ending cop-out. On the
other hand, he gives much—a rich, terrible examination of the
contemporary social and psychological malaise. It will be interesting to see if we are up to it, if this very fine film will attract
the large audience that other movies, working the easier, sun-
nier side of this same street, have gained.

5/31/68

*Petulia was on the whole more successful in examining middle-
class desperation than Divorce American Style, and though it
was unpopular with critics and the public, I continue to be fond*

of it. It has an essential tough-mindedness about it that seems to upset people. Part of the problem, I think, lies in the way such films are sold. For lack of a better term they are called comedies, and when they turn out to be at least as savage as they are funny, audiences don't know how to react to them— except to express disappointment and dismay. "Bad taste," they say, when in fact the subject of such films is national bad taste, and they confuse movie with subject. In this instance, Richard Lester's declining reputation—he was coming off two disasters, A Funny Thing Happened on the Way to the Forum, and How I Won the War—was no help. Preconceptions about him prevented many from observing that he was here attempting something he had not tried before, a sort of stylish realism, which suited him very well. It was a radical departure—almost as much so as A Hard Day's Night, his other good movie—and evidence of an attempt to transcend his previous limits and not, in my opinion, proof of a fatal lack of individuality or point of view. Maybe he's not a great director—surely he is not—but he is a man capable of putting on a good film every now and then, a capacity shared by many barred from the Auteur pantheon and thus a powerful criticism of the pantheon's validity as a critical tool.

WAR AND PEACE

One emerges from *War and Peace* exhausted and irritable. Since the length of the movie has been well publicized—is, indeed, the chief reason for curiosity about it—the tired condition of one's blood neither surprises nor dismays. Oxygen or a modest amount of alcohol will soon set it to rights. The irritation is less easily dismissed, for one has the feeling that it is not entirely the fault of director Sergei Bondarchuk and his cast of thousands that the policies of the film's American distributors in regard to this film are more than a little to blame for the restlessness it induces.

They have taken plenty of those classy ads (lots of white space surrounding small blocks of dignified prose in which their product is referred to as a "motion picture," an unnaturally toney phrase that always puts me on my guard), but in the really important matters they have treated *War and Peace* with a lack of respect usually accorded sleazy Italian sex and sandal epics designed for short runs at the bottoms of bills. In short, they have cut it and dubbed it and thereby ruined whatever merit it may have had. As you undoubtedly know, both of these practices are painfully common among movie businessmen, and since they betray a fundamental lack of respect for the artist and the uniqueness of his vision, they are reprehensible at any level; the worst B picture is entitled to fail on its own terms. When they are applied to something like *War and Peace*, a once-in-a-lifetime attempt to place on the screen a detailed, faithful rendering of a great work of literature that is also a national epic, a film that required five years of effort and unprecedented backing by the Russian government, these policies seem to me little short of demented.

Some fifty minutes are missing from the version playing in the United States, and though we are assured that nothing really important has been excised, this is patently not true. As usually happens when anti-artists start snipping around, it is the continuity, the connective tissue that gives a film its rhythm and its inner logic, that goes. The film you are being asked to pay as much as $7.50 to see has a bad case of the jumps; all too often you are unsure of how—or why—a character got from here to there, what the time sequence of events is. And it's all so stupid. If you commit yourself to a six-and-a-half-hour movie, what difference does another hour or so make? In for a penny, in for a pound, I say—the day is shot anyway.

As for the dubbing, it has the familiar effect of alienating audience from characters. You get fixed on those lips so obviously not speaking the lines you are hearing, you get to brooding about those radio-station voices reading instead of acting their parts, and it becomes impossible to sustain any identification with the figures on the screen. God knows, subtitling is not a perfect solution to the language barrier, but it is relatively unobtrusive, does not deny actors the use of their voices, which are, after all, the basic tools of their art, does not tamper with an intrinsic part of a film's design.

In the circumstances, it is difficult to offer an intelligent critique of Bondarchuk's work—and impossible to discuss his actors—but as a guess I would say it has its own deficiencies. Missing is the interesting theory of history as well as the Christian message Tolstoy was propagating in his novel (neither fits Marxist theory very well), and without this intellectual and moral underpinning the film lacks power and purpose. Its characters, all of whom had carefully calculated symbolic weights in the novel, now have little organic relationship to the great historical background against which they are placed and neither illuminate nor are illuminated by it. They are frankly flat and dull, and it is impossible to really engage oneself in their fates.

The isolation of the Soviet cinema from the stylistic revolution that has taken place over the last decade in Western Europe also hurts the film. It is heavy, square, old-fashioned and totally lacking in the visual stimulation one has by now come to expect almost as an inalienable right in movies that pretend to artistic seriousness.

That pretty much leaves the big battle at Borodino and the burning of Moscow to sustain interest. Both have a certain sweep and grandeur, but Bondarchuk concentrates excessively on the movement of masses, rarely favoring us with the telling, humanizing details—the faces in the crowd—out of which such masters of film spectacle as Sergei Eisenstein have patiently and painstakingly built their great action sequences. In particular, the story's emotional pivot, the lost wandering of the saintly Pierre (played by Bondarchuk himself) through the hell of Borodino, lacks the intensity, the sense of growing terror and pity, that can only be created by careful detailing. The burning of the capital and Napoleon's retreat are handled with greater sureness—proof, I suppose, that over the long years of shooting, the director learned a great deal by doing. Still, the feeling that the human element has been mislaid in order to concentrate on large-scale logistics persists. It is, ironically, a human enough failing, but coupled with the ideological blindness of the Russians and the commercial insensitivity of the American distributors, they lead me to think *War and Peace* is not worth the time or money it costs.

6/14/68

WILD IN THE STREETS

Wild in the Streets is one of those dumb-lucky movies that will draw an infinitely larger audience than it deserves because it deals with a subject—rioting youth—that is much on our minds and in our headlines these days. It does so in terms of our darkest, most delicious fantasy—that they might pass beyond the stage of mere disruptiveness and somehow take over our institutions and put us forcibly to pasture before we're ready to go. It has, therefore, stirred far more interest among critics and public than Grade Z quickies ordinarily do, and so it seems to me that a fair warning may be in order.

It is simply stated: cinematically *Wild in the Streets* is entirely devoid of intrinsic interest or merit, is, indeed, the veriest trash. Ineptly adapted from one of his own short stories by Robert Thom, it was less directed than slapped together by Barry Shear, and scarcely acted at all by a cast given no well-made scenes to play and no time to work on such material as they were provided. The impoverished atmosphere of the physical production extends to the moral and intellectual tone of the enterprise as well.

This lack of earnestness is disturbing precisely in proportion to the seriousness with which one takes the issues toyed with in this film, and I am afraid that I take them very seriously indeed. We are confronted in this nation today with something quite new in history—the mass alienation of youth, which means, finally, an alienation from our shared future. A phe-

nomenon that used to be a private and singular matter—a
necessary and, indeed, healthy part of growing up—is in the
process of politicalization. Youth is no longer a stage in growth;
it is now forming itself into a political and social class that has,
given the energy and intelligence of this generation, the potential of becoming a revolutionary elite.

Now, the people who made *Wild in the Streets* are only
dimly aware of this. Their premise—remarkably similar to that
of last year's *Privilege*—is that the kids might coalesce around a
pop singer and by exploiting an older politician's desire for
their votes (he favors lowering the voting age to fifteen) con-
trive to take over the nation, replacing democratic institutions
with a dictatorship of a new class.

All of this is graphically, if crudely, laid out for us, including
the concentration camps into which everyone over thirty-five is
herded and kept high on LSD. But in so doing, the point is
profoundly missed. I think it is symbolically right for the movie
revolutionaries to set up a system that would, the aging process
being so unfortunately inevitable, lead to their quick loss of
power. Our young radicals characteristically do not take a very
long view of the future. In no other way, however, do the
movie disruptionists resemble their real-life counterparts, few
of whom partake of the drug and show biz subcultures that
Wild in the Streets posits as revolutionary seedbeds.

But where the movie makers go completely wrong is ideo-
logically. They would have us believe that young people would
run wild in the streets in support of classic fascism—that is, in
aid of a clique hiding behind a single ignorant and psychotic
leader. But the fact is that the disruptionists of Columbia
University and of France are anarchists and nihilists; behind
their behavior lies a quite remarkably intense moral commitment that is infinitely more interesting and dangerous than the
simple power drive examined in this film. The latter could—
and would—be contained by conventional police and political
techniques. The former does not seek political power, but
rather a radical change in the entire sensibility of Western

culture and is thus impossible to deal with rationally, since such a change is not easily translatable into specific negotiable demands. Indeed, since the taking up of political power is abhorrent to anarchist ideology, you cannot satisfy them even by abdicating to them.

The special terror posed by the anarchist—and what a movie it would make—is more subtle than you would ever guess from *Wild in the Streets,* for he presents the possibility of an infinite chain of absurd, unpredictable, disruptive incidents that cannot be cooled by reason, compromise or mild repression. A free society is thus left only with a hope—that the fever will subside before drastic measures are taken by the quacks who are inevitably called in on hopeless social cases.

In the context of this larger reality something like *Wild in the Streets* is not even a good, useful fantasy. It trifles with, trivializes, a serious issue by irrelevant sensationalism (at the same time comforting the thoughtless by implying that the troublesome element among our young are just a bunch of weirdo hopheads not really worth more than a pseudo shudder). In fact, it seems to me an almost perfect example of the kind of imbecile commercial culture against which our kids are quite right to protest. A film by and for old sold-out men, it represents—even granting them some seriousness of original purpose—an attempt to cram into an inappropriate, inadequate and antique frame of reference a phenomenon that had, before they began, transcended that frame. It can only appeal to members of the Then Generation trying to join the Now Generation without undertaking the effort of thought.

7/26/68

Some three years have passed and in certain details it is now clear that this review lacked prescience. It appears now that the alienation of our youth was less massive than I thought. Some

very persuasive studies have indicated that the media were concentrating on the picturesque froth on top of the generational
brew and missed the stolid, flat-as-ever majority below. Then,
too, there is obviously a closer correlation between the drug-
rock scene and such political activity as persists. Finally, there
is a certain amount of sucking up to the kids in this notice that
puzzles and angers me as I look back on it. What could I have
been thinking about that week?

On the other hand, some of the review remains, for me, valid.
The movie was terrible, technically and aesthetically, and the
"lunatic charm . . . nightmare gaiety" Pauline Kael found in
the film was, I think, largely to be found in the good thesis
about "Trash, Art and the Movies" she used this movie to
expound rather than in the film itself. But the lasting point is
that the kids are not well enough organized, individually or
collectively, to get any very dangerous fascism going here. For
almost by definition fascism requires getting your shit together
and keeping it in that state for longish periods of time. Most of
them can't keep a modest-sized commune going for more than
a few months. They are, as I said, nihilists if they're anything.
But even that's probably too dignified a term for a generation
of hitch-hikers, drop-outs and pot-heads.

So the review is half-right, half-wrong. But the failure of the
film, after the initial hoo-ha, to exercise any permanent hold on
the imagination of anyone of any age indicates to me that in
gross terms I called the shot correctly. I'm letting it stand here,
however, mostly as an example of the kind of heat 'n serve
passions that reviewing on a weekly basis sometimes engenders.
How quickly they cool! How distant they can seem after the
passage of only a very short period of time! If I had this one to
do all over again, I wouldn't.

RACHEL, RACHEL

Rachel, Rachel turned out to be a discomfiting movie for me, one that calls into question a widely held assumption that I, among many others, have always maintained about the movies. It is clearly a film undertaken in a spirit entirely too rare in the American film industry. That is to say that in this case a star (Joanne Woodward) and a screenwriter (Stewart Stern) discovered a novel (Margaret Laurence's *A Jest of God*) that was to them something more than a mere "property." Instead, it was a difficult and delicate thing that challenged and excited them as artists, something they felt they simply had to make. They apparently encountered enormous difficulties in obtaining the relatively modest backing they required, and it was not until Miss Woodward's husband, Paul Newman, put his plentiful clout behind the project by agreeing to direct it that they could go ahead.

Everyone involved thereupon did his work with taste, conviction and solid, sometimes brilliant, craftsmanship. Stern's script, despite a tendency to tell rather than show, rings with gentle irony and rueful truth. Miss Woodward proves again that she is perhaps the only major female star of our day capable of genuine naturalism, submerging self and image in a subtle, disciplined performance that avoids showiness, excessive sentiment, self-consciousness. As a director, Newman is anything but the bouncing boy-o we are accustomed to seeing on our screens. He has a sensitive, slightly melancholic eye for something most American movies miss—the texture of ordinary life—a feel for emotional nuance and a technical sureness —he is neither too radical nor too conservative—that are quite remarkable in a first film.

In short, all the elements of an excellent movie are here, and yet, somehow, I emerged from *Rachel, Rachel* appreciating it, respecting it, but strangely unmoved by it. Why, I wonder, does a rightly motivated movie go wrong? The trouble is that the story itself is simply too slight, too familiar to fully engage us at this late date. It is merely a slice of the thirty-fifth summer of a spinster schoolteacher, acutely aware that life is about to get so far beyond her that she will never be able to catch it again. She is nagged by problems common to her type—persistent virginity, a sickly aging mother to whom she is nurse-companion, memories and missed opportunities that are really too inconsequential to support the psychological weight they must carry for her (and for us).

The movie records her ambiguous triumphs over these afflictions—loss of virtue substituting new problems for old, the partial, probably temporary, neutralization of Mom, a breakout from her small-town existence that is no more than vaguely hopeful—and properly so in the circumstances. It is all very right, very believable, very honest. One sympathizes. But in the last analysis, sympathy is a mild emotion, really no more than an act of murmured civility that implies in its very expression a basic irreducible alienation from its object.

Could the movie makers have forced us across this gap? I don't know. Perhaps their basic material is just too true to be good dramatically, too much like unexciting, unclimactic, unresolved life to be an exhilarating or emotionally purging experience. Perhaps everyone was just a trifle too careful, to craftsmanlike, and so failed to take the kind of risks that by their very daring stimulate us even when they fail or only partially succeed. Perhaps you have to tempt the danger of falsification in order to succeed in this damnable art.

But, as I said in the beginning, I believe in the spirit in

which this project was undertaken, and the results cannot be said to shatter that belief, only to raise a few questions about its universal efficacy. I would hate to think anything I might say here would harm this film at the box office, because, like all such attempts at artistic integrity, it is a test case, the performance of which will be carefully watched by the money men. In any case, it is always possible that my failure to fully respond to *Rachel, Rachel* may lie in some defect in my own sensibility, some flaw not shared by others.

I think, therefore, that you should test it for yourself. As I have indicated, it contains many rewards, not least of which is an almost perfect supporting cast. In it, one must mention Estelle Parsons, touching, funny, achieving a marvelous individuality in her characterization of another old maid, trying to dissolve her loneliness in revivalistic religion while suppressing a leaning to lesbianism. Equally good are James Olson as the tricky stud who liberates Rachel sexually—decency and maleness warring quietly beneath his fast talk—and Kate Harrington as Mom, somehow achieving depth in what could have been nothing but a stock role.

Rachel, Rachel is, I think, less than the sum of its parts, but in intent and in much of its execution it is a good deal more than one is used to getting at the movies. That is an ambiguous kind of recommendation, but then, *Rachel, Rachel* is an ambiguous kind of movie.

10/4/68

Too careful, too careful. What I really thought was that it was a bloody bore. They had pasted signs all over the place saying: "Caution, Serious Artists at Work. Proceed at Your Own Risk." I should not have allowed myself to be taken in so easily. One of the troubles with reviewing movies, however, is that you can't help being aware of the non-artistic problems creative people have to surmount, and the question of motives—in this case, I'm convinced they were of the highest—does come up and can influence the reviewer. In this case, no great harm was done, since the movie was certainly respectable. Better for audiences to be bored in a good cause than in a bad one, I suppose.

WARRENDALE

Warrendale is a touching movie. I mean that quite literally, because it is a documentary in the *cinéma vérité* style about a Canadian institution which pioneered a therapy for severely disturbed children based upon making constant physical contact with them, most especially in the course of "holding sessions" where, cradled in the arms of a staff member, free of the danger of harming themselves or others, the kids are encouraged to vent their fears and angers as openly, as violently, as they feel they must.

Despite the placid connotation of the phrase, these holding sessions are anything but peaceful. It may require three adults to secure the child, and his cries and the psychologist's shouts mingle in an uproar that has the physical aspect of a wrestling match, the tonal quality of a family brawl. The method openly admits what is only implied in other forms of psychological work—that what is going on between patient and therapist is nothing short of a struggle for life. Since there can be no more dramatic confrontation than that, one leaves *Warrendale* exhausted by the terrible effort at communication yet exhilarated both by the possibilities inherent in the process and by the people who make it work.

There is, of course, a theoretical rationale for the therapy at Warrendale (a residential institution where the children live in mixed-age, mixed-sex groups of twelve in small houses, with staffers functioning as parents). As explained by Dr. John

Brown, Warrendale's founder, who has since opened a series of similar institutions, it goes something like this: As infants we all experience the world largely through touch and taste at first. The other senses take in more information than we can process. We gain our "basic humanizing experiences," the sense of being loved and wanted, through touch. It has been proved that infants will die if they are totally denied this reassuring knowledge, and even some deprivation of it can cause severe disturbance. Undoubtedly some of the kids at Warrendale (many of them from orphanages) need to be held precisely because no one ever did so. Still others, whatever happened to them in infancy, have come to so distrust all forms of communication that they can only be put in touch, as it were, with themselves and reality by tactile experience, which "cannot be distorted in the same way that verbal communication can be distorted."

Not that it is easy even to establish this most primitive rapport. The kids fight it through sullen withdrawal or hysterical physical resistance. Over months, however, they come to see that physical contact is not being used for crudely manipulative purposes, is in no way hurting them, and so, grudgingly, they begin to trust, expose their true feelings, and emerge, shy and scared and still hurting, from their self-made prisons.

To see this happen is to be witness to a miracle. Moreover, to see how encouraging the rest of the kids are when one of their number opens up—no matter how violently—is especially enlightening for an up-tight middle-class adult long taught to disapprove of such naked emotionality in others and to repress it in himself.

In short, there are social implications in *Warrendale* (an indictment, if you like—in the very presence of these children—of the way we ordinarily conduct the business of life) that transcend its value as the record of a revolutionary technique.

But it is as raw, simple human drama that Allan King's superbly made film is most memorable. The final section shows

what happens in one cottage when the children must be told
that their cook, a much-beloved figure, has suddenly died.
"How the hell can I explain it to a kid if I can't explain it to
myself?" one young woman asks. But the decision is to try—to
hide nothing. The staff knows full well that some of its charges
will freak out, and two teen-age girls do just that, quickly
passing the point where, at another institution, drugs or re-
straints would be called into play. Bringing them back from
that point, getting them to accept death as both fact and
mystery and, most important, as a loss for which they must not
personally feel guilty, is a sweating, screaming agony—a drama
as terrible as any I have ever seen on film. There is a victory of
sorts. That is to say, peace is restored and life goes on. We
know we have seen only one incident on a long journey, a
small, precious, hopeful sign and nothing more. Yet the point
is made. One can only admire the intelligence that can imagine
so radical a cure for so radical a disease and, even more, the
human beings who have the courage and the patience to see it
through.

10/18/68

HOT MILLIONS

Hot Millions is the kind of movie that worries me a lot. By contemporary commercial standards it doesn't have much going for it. The stars, Peter Ustinov, Maggie Smith, Karl Malden, Bob Newhart, are well known to be pleasant players, but they have little demonstrated clout at the box office. The story is not based on a big presold hit play or novel but is merely a humble original screenplay by Mr. Ustinov and Ira Wallach. The director is a newcomer named Eric Till, and no one's heart can be expected to leap up when his credit flashes on the screen.

No, *Hot Millions* doesn't list among its assets any of the items usually supposed to guarantee success. It is trying to get by on talent and a good idea sensibly and funnily executed, and I really don't know, in this day of supercharged, superheated, relentlessly modish comedy (*Duffy* springs vulgarly to mind), whether this is enough. I do hope so, for *Hot Millions* is one of the sweetest, nicest, most pleasurable movies you could hope to see—you relax into it as you do into comfy old carpet slippers.

On its surface the plot will seem, I'm afraid, depressingly familiar—a fairly elaborate attempt to embezzle a million pounds from the London office of an American conglomerate called Ta-Can-Co. (*Sounds* right, that name, which is a minor detail, yet a measure of the thoughtful care expended on the film.) But don't be alarmed. Where most crime pictures concentrate on the technical details of the job at hand and on fashionability of dress, décor and attitude, *Hot Millions* focuses on character and on a situation that faces all of us, criminal and ordinary citizen alike—technological unemployment.

Ustinov is a professional embezzler about to become redundant, as they say in England, because the computers have made it seemingly impossible to juggle the books in the traditional manner of his calling. He must modernize his operations if he is to bend the machines to his sly will. The machines, of course, are resistant to mathematically sophisticated tampering, but Ustinov finally beats them—and incidentally delivers the movie's essential message—by resorting to humble and very human means: he gives the key unit a smart crack in the shins with a pail borrowed from a scrubwoman.

His principal problem, appropriately enough, is also a human one, namely the girl who lives down the hall from him and coincidentally becomes his secretary. She is the very model of humane inefficiency, managing to lose one job as a meter maid because she lacks the heart to pass out tickets and another as a bus conductor because she's more interested in helping people on and off the vehicle than she is in collecting fares. She's not long for Ta-Can-Co. either, being unable to change a typewriter ribbon and frequently tardy as well.

In this role Maggie Smith, best known for her Shakespearean roles, is marvelously vital, never merely coy or adorable, as an old-fashioned girl, too feminine, sensible and independent to be folded, stapled or mutilated by a machine-made, machine-dominated system. She is a perfect match for Ustinov's embezzler, who is at once dreamy and practical, a shy, lonely man with a paradoxical gift for smoothly confident talk. A supremely intelligent comic actor who through the years has gained increasing control and subtlety in his work, Ustinov has never been better than he is here.

In short, the two of them give us real people, characters with unexpected depths and genuine feelings. Their high moment—and the film's—comes when they discover to their mutual amazement that they love each other. Trying to evade the quietly wolfish Newhart, she has invited Ustinov over for dinner. She's in the kitchen burning bangers when he sits down idly to play the piano. She hears, picks up the flute he never knew she played, and starts accompanying him. The looks of sudden wonder they exchange, the vision of a lifetime of wonderful duets opening before them is tender, touching, true and entirely typical of a movie that always runs at a human pace and never outgrows human scale.

Like so many movies these days, *Hot Millions* does not regard the theft of money from a large faceless institution as a serious crime. It is, instead, regarded as the individual's revenge on the big-money bureaucracies which are insured by still other bureaucracies and won't miss the loot anyway.

The thing that sets this well-directed movie apart from the others is that its people do not succumb to the styles and values of their institutional enemies, insist instead upon going quietly against their grain and the grain of their times. They aren't cynical, sophisticated, hard or brittle. They are, however, more honestly, more humorously, more humanely intent on doing their own thing than a dozen self-conscious rebels of the James Coburn type. Their adventure—which comes out neatly and nicely for all concerned—is only a small thing, perhaps so small that its clear, sweet voice will be drowned out by the brassy uproar emanating from our screens. I do hope not—for its sake, our sake and the sake of comedies as yet unborn.

10/25/68

Such a sweet, gentle film. Such a flop. They threw it into the Music Hall in New York, where it simply could not fill that giant screen or compete with the Rockettes. Then it got the kind of reviews that might have meant good business if it had been playing in theaters accessible to the kind of audience that pays attention to reviews, an audience which does not go to the

Music Hall ever. As a result of this wanton mishandling it made a poor track record, and that caused exhibitors to shy away from it. Which meant that the audience that continually cries out for this kind of comedy never got a chance to see it. This is the sort of thing which happens endlessly in the movie business and which saddens and infuriates me. Of course, Hot Millions is not great art, but it is the kind of film that provides decent entertainment and can arrest the drift of the mass audience away from the medium—if that audience knows about it and can find it playing somewhere.

BULLITT

Bullitt is not a sensational movie—at least in the common usage of that term. But it is a movie of sensation, by which I mean that the director, Peter Yates, has aimed at making as palpable as possible those aspects of the physical world encountered by a San Francisco police detective working on a very lively and dangerous case that, logically enough, creates in him a state of consciousness in which he is preternaturally aware of both the menace and the promise (of clues and cues) in familiar surroundings.

You know how it is when you are concentrating very hard on a problem. All your senses are peculiarly alert, you seem to see more—in more detail—and to hear things more acutely, more analytically. That's the way it is with the title Shamus in this picture, played with unwonted clenched-fist tightness by Steve McQueen, who has not given such a well-disciplined performance in years.

As we gumshoe around the city with him looking for the persons unknown who bumped off an alleged mobster he was supposed to be guarding until he could testify before a Senate crime-investigating committee, director Yates forces us to share the cop's furious concentration, achieving this remarkable feeling of identification—no, oneness—with the protagonist by daring means. He deliberately avoids that pell-mell pacing that propels us mindlessly through films of this type. Instead, he lingers musingly on environments, probing at them with his camera until, for example, you can almost smell the cheap hotel room where the attempt on the witness's life was made, so you can feel the tension in the operating room where the surgical team tries to save his life, feel on your flesh the chilly sterility of the autopsy room where at last he rests in absurd death. It is the same with less morbid matters—the examination of some suitcases for clues, even the watchful concentration of the policemen as an electronic gizmo whirls and whirrs, receiving and printing out an electronically transmitted photograph of a suspect.

By contrast, action and death come quickly, without warning. A door is opened, the hired killers appear, the shotguns blast and two men are bloodily, grievously wounded before they—or the audience—can quite comprehend the fact. McQueen is riding along in his car, observes that he is being tailed, reverses positions and is suddenly the pursuer in a wild car chase through the roller-coaster streets. Thanks to nothing more complicated than sound basic movie making (intelligent camera placement and editing), this becomes an action sequence that must be compared with the best in film history. The final run-down, gun-down is almost equally well made and far more original—McQueen and criminal lunging around an airport in the dark, dodging not only each other's shots but the big jets as they take off and land.

Were you to stop and think about it, the logic and motives of *Bullitt*'s plot are, to put it politely, strained. And some may object to the total lack of depth in its characterizations, although I think their one-dimensionality, their almost abstract quality, represents a perfectly intelligent comment on the brutal amorality implicit in people whose only meaningful orientation is to whatever job is at hand—an orientation, as we have lately seen, that is as common to presidential candidates as it is to policemen. Indeed, Yates and screenwriters Alan R. Trustman and Harry Kleiner make a considerable point about the perfunctory quality of McQueen's private life. There is a marvelous throwaway shot of him buying a week's supply of frozen dinners without even looking at their labels, for example. But the real sign of what his work has done to him is his relationship with his girl friend (Jacqueline Bisset). He hardly notices her—and she is both very nice and very beautiful—is stunned when she calls his attention to the moral stench of the world he perforce inhabits. It is only when she is around that he and the film lose that alertness to nuance I mentioned before. Enough said, and said with understated irony.

It is almost impossible, on the other hand, to say enough for the style, based on careful attention to detail, which redeems this film, lifting it out of the category of the routine crime film where, by rights, it belongs, making it something worth the attention of the serious audience. The trade press reports that it went some $200,000 over budget and resulted in the cancellation of a long-term contract between McQueen and its producers. If this is true, an injustice has been committed. Careful shooting on location costs money, but it should be obvious, even to a movie executive, that in this case a rare bargain has been obtained. To punish people when they strive for quality—and particularly when they attain it—is false, even dangerous, economy. It is the kind of thinking that in the past silenced some of Hollywood's best talent and it ill suits an industry that is pretending maturity at the top of its press agents' lungs.

11/22/68

Kenneth Hyman, in charge of production at Warner Brothers when this movie was made, later told me (I thought he was a very civilized fellow, incidentally, and not at all the legendary mogul type) that there was another side to the story related in the last paragraph. Seems the star, as is the wont of that peculiar breed, insisted on an awful lot of expensive perquisites, not at all necessary to achieve quality, as he ego-tripped through this production and that my natural bias in favor of artists over businessmen was, in this case, misapplied. It's plausible, though nothing is ever provable in these squabbles. The fact is that there is an enmity between producers and artists that stretches back almost to the beginnings of the movies, and they now approach each other with such mutual suspicion and hostility that it is a miracle they get anything done at all. Back in the days when the whole industry was fat and rich, the costs of their enmity could easily be absorbed. Now, however, the question of survival is at hand, and it seems to me that actors like McQueen can no longer afford to regard producers like Hyman as automatically being the class enemy. Conversely, the producers have got to stop treating all "talent" as just naturally willful children, patronizing and cheating them reflexively. If they don't hang together they are going to hang separately. In short, some sort of community spirit is going to have to come over the movie makers—and that's going to mean an end to half-million-dollar fees to actors (maybe even an end to $100,000 fees) and a greater willingness by producers to relinquish the "standard of the industry" which insists on huge crews, heavy equipment and all the rest of the paraphernalia that runs up production costs. Everyone is simply going to have to scale down, and there now exists a technology that can enable them to do so— if they're willing. And if they can begin to work with some degree of mutual trust. The first step, I think, is to remove the cost pressure from all of them, and that will mean getting technicians to experiment with the new techniques and agents to cease their insistence on monumental "above the line" costs for properties, players, directors, etc. "Fat chance," I hear someone murmuring. Probably so. But what choice do they have, really?

THE LION IN WINTER

There is one good thing about *The Lion in Winter*. It sent me off into a pleasantly nostalgic reverie about an old radio series called *The Bickersons*, in which Don Ameche and Frances Langford played a funny married couple who were always on each other's backs about something or other. Hadn't thought of them in years, and just recalling the sound of Ameche's exasperated drawl as he cried, "Aww, Blaaanche," set me chuckling to myself.

Unfortunately, most of the dialogue in the script, which James Goldman has adapted from his own play, would have rung truer spilling out of your old Crosley than it does from the mouths of Henry II of England (Peter O'Toole), Eleanor of Aquitaine (Katharine Hepburn) and their three wretched sons. At the very least it is anachronistic. At worst, which is often, it is ludicrous: all these people rowing around in barges, gobbling roast boar, heartily draining their silver goblets and exchanging one-line zingers in the modern idiom.

That is by no means the end of the movie's defects. The plot is based on a historical incident—the squabble between Henry's sons over succession to his throne. The old man himself favors, for reasons that persuade no one, his youngest, the almost literally drooling idiot, John. The queen leans toward Richard, known to history as "The Lion-Hearted," but here revealed as a fag beneath his ferocity—Mom loved him not wisely but too well. Skulking around as an also-ran is Geoffrey.

Nobody likes him, since he is an inveterate sneak, liar and plotter, though if anyone had stopped long enough to think, they might have realized that these qualities grant him a natural aptitude for statecraft quite lacking in his rival siblings. This nest of vipers—which includes the androgynous King of France and his sister, betrothed to Richard, mistress to Henry, but sort of pleasant anyway (one longs to inquire, "What's a nice girl like you doing in a place like this?")—scheme, scream and snivel through a plot so labyrinthine as to defy description. It is perhaps a measure of its pointlessness to note that after two hours it comes out exactly where it began, as do the principal characters, who develop not a cubit beyond their caricature introductions.

All that effort and no resolution, no point. Well, perhaps Mr. Goldman is one of those writers who find historical characters, incidents and settings useful in lending distance, perspective to archetypal moral confrontations and thus illuminating some contemporary issue. So it was for Jean Anouilh in *Becket*, which also featured Henry II, who was, coincidentally, played by O'Toole in the film version.

No such luck. All we have here is a nasty little struggle for power among a group of people who are all equally repugnant and among whom it is impossible for the viewer to choose even the least offensive for purposes of temporary identification.

Anthony Harvey, the director, has, of course, mounted the thing in the manner of other Very Important Pictures—another *Becket* or *A Man for All Seasons*. There is much picture-book photography, static but stunning, a heavy emphasis on the contrasting textures of stonework, velvets, brocades and all the other historical whatnots that must have cost Joseph E. Levine a pretty penny. Harvey has also encouraged—or allowed—his actors to carry on in the grand manner. As in bad Shakespearean productions, there is a lot of posturing and much aimless grappling among the actors but no fully developed, carefully choreographed action scenes, and, naturally, lines are not so much spoken as richly vocalized. Of the two stars, it should be noted that Mr. O'Toole comes on too strong for a man motivated by intimations of mortality, while Miss Hepburn is just too nice to play Eleanor as the grasping, conniving creature Mr. Goldman apparently conceived her to be.

In short, *The Lion in Winter* is a mess. And a fraud—an elaborate attempt by all concerned to make us believe we are in the presence of a literary-cultural event when, in fact, buried beneath all its trappings there is not even a basic beginning for a simple meaningful dramatic conflict. This is Hollywood and Broadway—show biz—aping the manner of high culture without having the faintest idea of what constitutes a substantial play of ideas or of character. They should stick to *The Bickersons*.

Unpublished

This review went unpublished because the film had been praised in the course of a production story in an earlier issue and the magazine's policy—since changed to something less monolithic —was not to encourage contradictory statements in different departments. I print it for the first time because my feelings about this film led me into the worst public quarrel of my life as a critic. It was named best picture of the year by the New York Film Critics the first time I participated in that group's balloting, a choice that so offended some of us that we briefly resigned—an action that led to reform of the group's voting procedures. I still think this was a wretched movie—a pseudo-intellectual pseudo-epic that, I must say, still angers me.

Faces (see below) was the film that the dissidents in the NYFC squabble were mostly supporting. The contrast between the two films powerfully illuminates the essential absurdity of these awards and the tradition that demands that critics compile "ten best" lists at the end of the year. The only thing the two movies have in common is that they are physically long strips of celluloid exposed by one machine and projected by another. I don't make ten-best lists, and I probably should not join in these balloting revels either. They may have made some sense when the American studio product was dominant and the vast majority of films were made under similar terms and represented roughly comparable points of view. Now, however, we are truly comparing apples and oranges (and even artichokes), and these listings and ballotings are increasingly occasions on which we demonstrate adherence to aesthetic ideologies, and the winners, as was the case of Z in 1969, are often not the best pictures but the best compromise at which we can arrive, after demonstrating, in the early going, where our hearts truly lie. It's all fairly fatuous, but it would be harmless if the NYFC vote didn't have some commercial value for the winners and some influence on the Academy Award balloting, which comes later and which really adds millions to the box-office take of the winners.

FACES

At this point it almost seems superfluous to heap more praise on John Cassavetes's *Faces*, and yet I can't resist the impulse. This is, I think, a great and courageous film in which Cassavetes has dared more than any American director in recent memory, and it is important to understand the nature of what he has done.

There is no point in dwelling long on the more obvious aspects of his experiment. Yes, his actors—all small-part movie players, except for his wife, Gena Rowlands—worked without salary, their reward to be percentages of the profits, which were by no means certain. Yes, the theme is unpromising—a middle-aging couple experimenting with infidelity to relieve the emptiness of their marriage. Yes, the film is grainy and superrealistic in a way that is inevitable when acting is in the improvisational style and recorded by a hand-held camera operating in very close quarters.

These qualities have led to a few dissenting dismissals of *Faces* as "a home movie." But this charge confuses style with substance and misses entirely the compassionate intelligence which Cassavetes—who also wrote the script—brings to his subject. He has a shrewd and highly moral vision of the special quality of affluent middle-class life in America, *circa* now, baby. And for all the superficial looseness of the film, he never once loses track of his point. On the contrary, he keeps boring in on it from every possible angle.

Infidelity is really only a device to heighten Cassavetes's true subject, the banality of the way too many of us live. His couple, John Marley and Lynn Carlin, are battered by this banality, sick, sad and tired, searching unconsciously for warmer and more human lives. Unable to define or to express what they want, each of them stumbles into potentially melodramatic situations that end up near to tragedy but nearer still to comedy.

Herein lies part of the film's originality, for customarily in our movies and plays and books infidelity is played firmly within one mode or the other. In *Faces* our expectations are endlessly jostled, as are those of the main characters. Marley, for example, thinks he might feel feeling again if only he can bed an ordinary little tart he meets in a bar (Miss Rowlands). But when he goes to her, he finds a party in progress and he is forced into a numbing round of back-slapping, falsely hearty male camaraderie. He must cover his really quite desperate need with strident jokes and the miming of a good sport's role.

Meantime, his wife and her girl friends are out on the town, assuaging their loneliness and boredom at a discotheque, where they acquire a gigolo, beautifully played by Seymour Cassel not as the traditional snake in the grass but as a cheerfully bouncing puppy. They take him home, lewd visions dancing through their heads, pleasantries more appropriate to a PTA meeting on their lips as they attempt to deny—mostly to themselves— their true desire.

Husband finally makes it with prostitute and it's nice and all that, but not quite the all-purpose answer he sought. Wife makes it, too—and nearly kills herself in remorse and shame when she learns a similar truth. When they confront each other in the gray morning-after light, one can almost taste the ashes in their mouths.

As a writer, Cassavetes has an uncanny ear for the sounds, at once funny and terrifying, that we make to fill the silent spaces in existence. As a director, he has the courage to make a long film in just eight scenes, stretching our attention spans (attenuated by TV and the voguish quick-cut style) almost to the breaking point, holding us with lovingly wrought physical details and closely observed psychological nuances. In the course of these endless scenes he gives his actors a chance to develop their characters in a way that is unique in movies; this is one of the few films I know in which one can sensibly speak of the excellence of its ensemble playing. Indeed, the actors obviously worked together so long and so intensively that their work finally transcends the normal criteria for acting. They are behaving, not playing.

Do not infer that this film is dreary or depressing, no matter how it may seem in outline. Cassavetes is one of those remarkable artists who have learned to dissect us without at the same time learning to despise us. Somehow, without resort to sentiment, special pleading or falsification, he makes us share the healthily curious, oddly loving spirit in which he approaches his subjects. That is the light that illumines a dark work and which, perversely, cheers us as we emerge from a film that is truly and deeply an experience.

1/17/69

IF . . .

If . . . reminds me of a hornet. According to aerodynamic theory, any creature so woefully misdesigned is not supposed to be able to fly at all, and according to such theories of movie construction as I hold, a mixture of film moods and methods like *If* . . . shouldn't be able to get off the ground either. But it does—angry, tough and full of sting.

It begins as if it is going to be just another in that long line of nastinesses about English public school life—perhaps more sharply observed than most, a little more intense in its feeling about these institutions and the boys trapped in them. Along toward the middle, however, it becomes clear that grimly humorous realism is only a small part of director Lindsay Anderson's intention. Without warning or explanation he modulates into the fantasies of escape, rebellion and destruction shared by the school's three least tractable scholars.

By the end of the film they—and we—have shared in fancy the charms of a ferociously eager cafe hostess, disrupted the school's annual military maneuvers by using real bullets, and staged a full-scale bloody guerrilla attack on the Founder's Day exercises. And we have been smoothly but forcibly transported from our traditional position of coolly objective observers of human behavior into experiencing what it is like to live again inside the skin of an adolescent. One is reminded how very sweaty and feverish it is in there, difficult to breathe because the space is crowded with dusty cartons of conventional wis-

dom left there by careless adults and the fantasy a kid manu-
factures for himself out of misapprehension and undischarged
imaginative energy.

Anderson has called his film "a vision," and like all good
visions there is nothing escapist or comforting about it. It will,
I am sure, puzzle and anger a good many people. Many will
observe that Anderson has borrowed much of his style from
Jean-Luc Godard. Like the Frenchman, he divides his film into
sections—each introduced with a title—and, of course, his
casual unexplained leaps from reality to unreality are right out
of Godard's film can. But he, too, does it well, and he forces
our close attention and strong emotional response with the
technique.

Nevertheless, and it's greatly to his credit, he is an English-
man. Which means that he shares with his country's best
novelists and film makers a taste and skill for characterizations—both of people and institutions—which has never been
one of Godard's strong points. Godard's people are nearly
always abstractions, intellectual constructs, designed to help
him illustrate philosophical theories. Anderson, by contrast, is a
former documentarian who can reveal the public school's character simply by letting his camera prowl its corridors and
rooms, precisely and economically presenting the evidence of
its seedy and irrelevant traditionalism. He is equally good at
personifying a lonely new boy, a fatuous faculty member, a
sadistic upperclassman with a glance or a shard of dialogue.

A public school boy himself, Mr. Anderson has obviously
thought hard about what happens when unformed adolescents
come into conflict with rigidly formed institutions. The result
is that his film is *felt*. I stress the point because youth is a
terribly attractive subject for movie makers today, and one sees
so many films (Hall Bartlett's *Changes* and Jacques Demy's
The Model Shop are two recent examples) that do nothing
with it beyond taking an attitude of rather squishy, patronizing
tolerance for youthful angst. Anderson alone transforms psychological and sociological data into a passionate personal

statement. He really remembers what it was like growing up absurd.

Some may object more strenuously than I have to Anderson's use of borrowed avant-garde techniques to revitalize material that is excessively familiar. As I said at the outset, the overall design of If . . . , considered with scientific detachment, is quite disconcerting. Sometimes, indeed, one feels as if he is about to turn black and blue from the pounding and jarring administered by Anderson and a very gifted group of young actors as they endlessly shift their emotional gears. But one does not so much attend this movie as submit to it.

2/28/69

STOLEN KISSES

When director François Truffaut is in a good mood, as he obviously was when he made *Stolen Kisses*, it is always ten o'clock in the morning of a sunny summer's day and he is an alert, relaxed adolescent allowing his frolicsome imagination an hour of free play. Satirical insights, romantic longings, dreams of adventure play a skittering game of tag through his incorrigibly comic sensibility. The world, when we see it through his eyes, is transformed into a garden of delights, and the inhabitants thereof become sportive children with brief attention spans, much energy and a capacity for only momentary dismay. Tragedy here is a pratfall, fate is a funny coincidence and death only the topper to a running gag called life.

A Truffaut movie can be a heavenly haven for today's overburdened movie audience, but it can be a special kind of hell for a reviewer trying to capture and imprison between straight lines of type a joyousness that is communicated by the director in the bounce of a character's walk, the quality of the light on a scene, the seemingly improvised juxtapositions of slightly off-center characters, the surprising—but never wrenching—twists in the development of the story. The essential stuff of Truffaut's art is, in short, evanescent detail that has a way of evaporating in your hand when you try to grab hold of it for sober, sensible critical discussion.

I suppose *Stolen Kisses* is best described as a comedy of misplaced enthusiasm. We meet young Antoine Doinel (played, incidentally, by Jean-Pierre Léaud, who was the little boy in Truffaut's first film, *The 400 Blows*, and who has now grown to deliciously awkward adolescence) as he is about to be fired by the army. Yes, fired, not discharged. He is not a draftee. He enlisted and then proved himself too inept even to be entrusted with the modest responsibilities of a peacetime yardbird. The officer handing him his papers suggests he not overmatch himself in civilian life—a nice job as a tie salesman perhaps?

Sound advice. For Antoine is soon screwing up as hotel night clerk, private detective, TV repairman. He has energy, good will—and entirely too much unfocused imagination. His head swathed in clouds of romantic imagining, he can never quite see where he's putting his two left feet. His love affairs—with a pretty young student and an even prettier older woman—are particularly hopeless. Each in her turn must try to ensnare him, not because he's too shy but because, in his ardor, he keeps rushing right past them.

Perhaps one gets a better idea of Truffaut's game by concentrating on some small aspect of it. For example, the business with Mme. Tabard, the older inamorata. He meets her when his detective agency assigns him as an undercover agent to the stockroom of a shoe store owned by her husband. And why does a shoe store need a secret agent? Easy—because the owner wants to find out why no one likes him. And why don't they? Equally elementary—because he's so crazy he goes around hiring detectives to find out why he's not popular.

Nicely meshed, I think. Especially when you remember that Antoine is such a bad detective that his employer's only choice is to fire him (hard, since he's such an amiable lunkhead) or to find cases so ridiculous that he can't harm anyone by stirring around in them (much easier, considering the condition of the world as Truffaut sees it).

This leads me to a more general point about Truffaut's work. The superficial looseness of his style, the way he makes difficult comedic leaps look easy, has been much admired and much imitated—with disastrous results. What the imitators miss is the half-hidden, half-mad logic at work in his films. It serves his films as a well-designed set of eccentric cams serves a sophisticated machine, keeping its disparate parts whirling without colliding and thus jamming the works.

Which does not mean that everything in a Truffaut movie is finally and firmly explicable. He has a tantalizing gift for leaving a few loose ends dangling. We are never, for instance, given the slightest explanation why a chic, cool, serene lady like Mme. Tabard ever got mixed up with a loony like her husband or what in the name of sanity makes her respond, however briefly, to a goof like Antoine.

Well, that's Truffaut for you, simultaneously observing that life has its funny little patterns and its funny little mysteries as well. And somehow making the not inconsiderable point that the awareness of their simultaneity is the beginning of wisdom, without ever losing that prankish, and above all youthful, spirit that has animated his work from the beginning. Though it is not so richly textured, I think *Stolen Kisses* is easily his best thing since *Jules and Jim*, further evidence that he may be the finest comic artist now working in the movies. Anyway, his company is one of the great pleasures presently available to us.

3/7/69

THE RED AND
THE WHITE

The Red and the White is to my knowledge the first feature by
Miklós Jancsó, a Hungarian director highly acclaimed in Europe, to be released here. Given the remoteness of his subject—
a series of small incidents in the civil war between Bolshevik
and counterrevolutionary forces in Russia in 1918—and the
film's general lack of glamour, sex and name personalities, it is
not going to be easy for audiences to find. And even if the local
art house does play it, pictures like this one have a way of
disappearing almost as soon as they appear. Perseverance and
alertness are therefore required if this remarkable film is going
to get the sort of reception it deserves.

It is not an avant-garde enterprise. Rather, it refers us back
to the great epic tradition of the early Soviet cinema (the
Russians co-produced it with the Hungarians). Eisenstein, of
course, springs to mind and, even more to the point, Alexander
Dovzhenko, who so powerfully juxtaposed the innocent beauty
of the land with the terrible beauty of men at war (especially
old-fashioned unmechanized war) to underline the bitter irony
of human destructiveness.

As with Eisenstein, there are few characters, in the traditional sense of the word, in Jancsó's film. Or rather there is
only one character, a collective one, in *The Red and the White*
—a people at war among themselves. Some faces stand out in
the crowd: a White Army nurse who falls in love with a Red
soldier; a Cossack tormenting and humiliating a peasant girl he

suspects of harboring a fugitive; one White officer proudly refusing to collaborate with his captors, another volunteering to do so, and both somehow engaging our sympathies.

People are not really Jancsó's subject. It is the sweep of war that preoccupies him, and it is in the images of its ferocious energies and absurd cruelty that the movie comes close to greatness. Though this war was won in history, it is not "won" in the film. Here all is flux, and with each change in the fortunes of war we see only a reversal of roles, not a change in the basic behavior of men caught up in battle. Each side implacably hunts down its fleeing enemies in the spirit of avenging angels; each treats captives with casual brutality, convinced of the historical necessity of its inhumanity; each leavens its cruelty with a capricious compassion that offers the spectator not relief but a peculiar intensification of horror, emphasizing as it does our sense of being adrift on a sea of random senselessness. The random quality of war's exactions have rarely been laid before us as openly as they are in *The Red and the White*.

What one carries away from the film is not a story as such but rather a collection of sequences that are burned, perhaps forever, in one's consciousness: hundreds of Red prisoners crowded into a narrow street in a fortresslike monastery and given a sporting fifteen-minute head start before their captors begin rounding them up like wild animals; a group of retreating soldiers panicked by the appearance of that novel engine of destruction, a strafing airplane; the nurses from a hospital conducted into a wood, given ball gowns and asked to dance with a group of officers while a military band provides the waltzes of an era now passed beyond recall. This last is rich in poignancy and suffused with a strange tension.

Then, at the very end of the film, there is the most memorable of all the film's memorable sequences, one of those moments of revolutionary heroism that have long been the specialty of the Communist cinema and which, whatever one's political convictions, have about them an aura that can only be termed noble. A small party of Red soldiers—Russians and some Hungarian volunteers—top a rise and see spread out before them the great valley of the Volga River. They must cross it to find safety, but between them and the river's bank stands an impenetrable mass of White soldiers. To advance is, of course, to die. But retreat (and further wandering) is unthinkable. And so they enter the valley—singing the Marseillaise.

It is possible to see this scene as pure politicalized sentimentality, the sort of thing one would ordinarily sneer from the screen. I am sure, however one reads it, it served Mr. Jancsó's purposes, reassuring the two state-controlled film industries that underwrote his venture about his political correctness. To me, however, far removed from the historical moment he is investigating, and frankly caring less about his politics than his art, the scene is too moving, too deeply felt, to be understood merely as an empty propagandistic gesture. One cannot remain content with such a simple reading of it.

These are men who have broken out of the confusion Mr. Jancsó has so graphically recorded in his earlier scenes. They at last have purpose, direction and a comforting goal—rejoining the main body of their army and a more rational war than the absurd guerrilla affair in which they were caught up. Now, at the last moment, they are thwarted, and death—unambiguous, peaceful and, in the circumstances, honorable—seems infinitely preferable than a return to the insanity they hoped they were leaving behind for good. They are to be understood, finally, not as military or political heroes but as existential ones. Camus, I think, would have understood them better than Stalin.

5/2/69

LONESOME COWBOYS

Show me a cowboy who rides sidesaddle,
and I'll show you a gay ranchero.
                             —ERNIE KOVACS

That one-liner, which I heard the late great comedian throw
away one time, is as accurate a summary of Andy Warhol's new
movie, *Lonesome Cowboys*, as one can make. But the point of
one of his films is never to be found in its content, but simply
in its existence, whether it happens to be twenty-four hours
long, as one of them is, or twenty-four minutes, as one of them
might perfectly well be. None of the matters usually brought
up when we talk about films—story, style, technique—has any
relevance to his work. Indeed, I have no hesitancy in admitting
that I left *Cowboys* ten minutes before it was over, on the
grounds that since it had no beginning and no middle it probably didn't have an ending either. It seemed to me at least as
important to get to my lunch appointment on time as it did to
hang around and see whether Viva, his current superstar, got
debagged one more time.

    Do not misunderstand; the film did not suddenly reach some
new low in "tastelessness" or stupidity. I will not pretend
that walking out was any kind of critical gesture. As an act it
was neither more nor less significant than any of the gestures
one observed on screen. Like them—like the entire movie—it
was just something one felt like doing that day. Indeed, the

only important act we make regarding a Warhol film is walking in; after that it clearly makes no difference to him what we do, how we respond.

In the profoundest sense, therefore, Warhol is impervious to criticism. Implicit in the act of reviewing any work of art is the assumption, shared by critic, creator and audience, that the work is always potentially a "question for further discussion," as a study guide might have it. One assumes that the artist may want to engage, if only in the privacy of his own mind, in some sort of dialogue with his auditors, while they in turn may wish to observe the "development" in his technique and sensibility from work to work. But clearly Warhol engages with no one outside his coterie (he lives—and eventually will die—on the quality of his publicity, but that is another matter), and there is no development worth speaking of in his thing.

To be sure, *Cowboys* was shot in thirty-five millimeter (a first for him) and had an unprecedented four-day shooting schedule, but he remains firmly rooted, technically and aesthetically, to a point in film history around 1904–05, when the first American story films were being shot. Like the primitives, all he does is borrow a real setting, place amateur actors in front of it and instruct them to improvise dialogue and action based on a rough outline. A genius can stretch this technique to masterwork lengths (i.e., Griffith's *Birth of a Nation*), but Warhol cannot or will not.

It is fair to say that he knows only one thing, for as Robert Mazzocco has shrewdly pointed out, his works in all media are repetitions of a single simple juxtaposition, that of "the mindlessly banal and the haphazardly corrupt, or of the totally outrageous and the totally bloodless." It is, he notes, a peculiarly American juxtaposition, and I would venture to say that is the basic mix in about nine-tenths of our popular culture. Warhol's virtue, if he may be said to have one, is that in his essential stupidity he makes the contrast between the two very stark, stripping away the platitudes and hypocrisies with which we customarily attempt to unify these contradictory elements.

There is something basically funny in *Cowboys*, for instance, about skinny, androgynous Viva, so obviously the creation of the Now Culture, impersonating a frontier hooker, something weirdly engaging about the cowboys being fruitcakes—borrowing mascara from one another or using the hitching rail as a *barre*. What Warhol has done is to place faggery in the context from which we have drawn our traditional sustaining masculine mythology—a corruption and a banality together again, you will observe—and we are surprised and annoyed to find genuine laughter being jerked from us. Surprised because it occurs in the midst of the acute fatigue Warhol's lack of intelligence and technique (and his aggressive desire to administer shocks to the bourgeois sexual sensibility) customarily engenders; annoyed because one wishes to return his very real contempt for us with contempt for him. Our laughter spoils the perfection of our disdain and has, for some critics, created a problem: how to explain away that laughter?

Some have leapt to the conclusion that he is beginning to emerge as a self-conscious rather than unconscious satirist, and *Cowboys* has been here and there written up as a genuine spoof—sort of *Support Your Local Sheriff* in drag. That is, I think, rather too long a leap to make on the basis of the evidence before us. Indeed, I would say that he is still considerably less an artist than Kovacs, who found a form for the same basic juxtaposition (or absurdity or insight) more appropriate to its importance than a two-hour movie. The most you can say for Warhol is that he is, as Mr. Mazzocco says, "sophisticated by default."

Specifically, he has lingered long, and one suspects for want of a better idea, at this business of corruption and banality endlessly combined and recombined, as a child out on a nature walk will linger over some small thing—an odd-shaped stone, a dandelion gone to seed—while the adults have hurried on in pursuit of larger quarries. Returning to hurry the laggard, we are interested to observe that, yes, the thing is pretty or interesting in its humble way and, yes, one is pleased to see the child using his eyes. But it is a nuisance when he keeps pausing, slowing one down with observations of similar trivia dozens of times.

To this, one might add another point. Obviously, his sensibility was formed entirely by the media culture, so by practicing journalism on himself he can also, in a way, journalize the entire culture that made him. But, in the nature of things, a journalist cannot transcend his subject, while the artist can—and must. Which is another way of saying that journalism is not art, although increasingly the distinction eludes us, since both now confuse the mere assertion of self with the creation in the one case of a genuine report on an event observed, in the other of an art object.

There is, of course, something delicious about a mass culture that gave Warhol his subject and the ready-to-wear sensibility he applies to understanding it celebrating him as if he were an exemplary rebel against it instead of the model prisoner of it. But there is something frightening about it, too. People are always asking critics about the so-called underground film, and it always turns out they're asking about Warhol. He has pre-empted the field, leaving no audience for the more serious independent artists who work below our normal sight lines. Indeed, it is risky to attempt to criticize him, for criticism is instantly converted into still more publicity, the piece that attempts to understand him becoming, all disclaimers to the contrary, an endorsement.

So let me be very clear. I don't think Warhol or *Lonesome Cowboys* is any good. I don't even think he is an artist, avant-garde or conventional. He is just very, very important—too important to go on mindlessly denigrating or trying to ignore, as if he were just a fad like hula hoops. He may, like them, quietly disappear. But like his soup cans he is endlessly replicable in this culture of ours.

6/13/69

TRUE GRIT

There is a moment of true glory in *True Grit*. It occurs late in the film when at long last John Wayne must face up to—and face down—Lucky Ned Pepper and his bandit gang. It is one against four as Wayne informs Lucky Ned that he has only two dismal choices—either to be shot within a minute or to surrender and be taken back to town for hanging. Ned retorts that this is "bold talk for a one-eyed fat man."

A look of rage, contempt and truly delicious anticipation of immediate bloody action illuminates Wayne's countenance, and crying, "Fill your hand, you son of a bitch," he takes his horse's reins between his teeth, spurs him to a mad gallop, and with his six-shooter blazing from one hand, his rifle (which he handles like a toothpick) barking from the other, he proceeds to ride his opponents down.

Watching, one shouts, laughs and, unaccountably, feels tears beginning to tingle. For one feels one is witnessing not just the beginning of a good movie's climax but, perhaps, a full-throated valedictory for a tradition. Here is Wayne, the last of a great generation of western heroes, committing himself again to an action that at once affectionately parodies and joyously summarizes the hundreds—thousands—of similar moments that have preceded it in our film history. And there is a tremendous sense of relief and release in the way he goes about it.

One has wondered how long he and the western could maintain their vitality, for in recent years there has been a

steady decline in standards, in creative interest, in the form—
too many attempts to pump false life into it. One had feared it
might be coming to the end of its long trail, and so the
strength of one's response to *True Grit* and this, its highest
moment, is conditioned by the context in which it appears.

It probably represents the final flaring of a dying flame, not
its rekindling, but that matters less, perhaps, than the interesting, delicate balance it achieves between two forces. It is quite
conscious of the humor implicit in the strange hold the conventions of western fictions have exercised on our collective
imagination; at the same time it maintains a decent respect for
the honest values and emotions that have time and time again
compelled us to return to this material.

The success of Charles Portis's best-selling novel was based
on this and on two other factors as well. It offered, first of all,
an essentially anti-heroic view of the west, which certainly suits
our present mood. Only its teen-age narrator-heroine, Mattie
Ross—shrewd, brave, moralistic (a typical adolescent, in short)
—is truly good. The purity of her character illuminates through
contrast the soiled, spoiled—if satirically defined—natures of
the people she encounters on her quest to avenge the murder
of her father, among whom one must definitely number the
rogues who ride with her on her great adventure—Rooster
Cogburn (Wayne's character), conducting his affairs as a U.S.
marshal in very dubious style, and La Boeuf (Glen Campbell),
a vain and venal Texas Ranger. This vision—scarcely unique—
was freshened, intensified, made delightfully palatable by
Portis's resort to and rescue of the old vernacular style, with its
arresting antique locutions and metaphors—a way of talking
and thinking so old as to seem brand-new.

The success of the film, in turn, is based on its faithfulness to
the author's intent and style. Screenwriter Marguerite Roberts
has sensibly retained most of his best dialogue intact, and
director Henry Hathaway has, in effect, used Wordsworth as
his production designer: "Every prospect pleases and only man
is vile"—if comically so—in his visualization of the Indian

Territory setting. Hathaway is seventy years old and has been
making action films since 1933, so he knows instinctively, it
seems, when he may invoke our laughter at the conventions of
the western, when he must retain his seriousness about them.
His visual style is as simple as Mattie's moral style (young Kim
Darby is marvelous in the role) and as direct as Portis's prose
style.

But perhaps the most important element in the film's triumph is John Wayne. He has discovered what's funny about
the character he has always played (one has observed him
working toward this knowledge in several recent movies), and
now he gives us a rich double vision of it. He is himself, and he
is himself playing himself—an exuberant put-on that seems to
delight him as much as it does us. At his age and station in life
it is a true and gritty and hilarious thing to do. Whatever else
he does—and I hope it will be much—*True Grit* represents, I
think, the true climax of a great and well-loved career—if not as
an actor then as an American institution.

6/20/69

*This review is the product of a lifelong infatuation with John
Wayne, an infatuation that transcended politics (my line has
always been that if we allow the Paul Newmans of the movie
world to express their congenial political views, we owe people
like Wayne the right to be reactionaries) and may even transcend common sense. Anyway, I had written favorably about
Wayne long before True Grit, and I mention that in order to
dissociate myself from those reviewers who rather patronizingly
granted him high marks for this piece of work after ignoring
for years the fact that every bit as much as Bogart, Cooper,
et al., he had created a subtle heroic American archetype and
had done so with a skill deserving of as much interest as has
been lavished on them posthumously. Indeed, I think Wayne*

has done work that for years has represented a kind of modest excellence in a very special line of endeavor—movie-star acting (for want of a better term). Anyway, he deserved his Oscar and he deserves from critics the kind of affection audiences have long since bestowed on him. You don't survive as long as he has without intelligence and a certain subtlety of self-understanding.

MIDNIGHT COWBOY

Hurrying through Forty-second Street or one of its equivalents (which exist in every sizable American city), we have all at one time or another brushed against Joe Buck, the Midnight Cowboy, or Ratso Rizzo, his friend. And if we have been so careless as to meet their importunate gaze, at once sly and bold, we have wondered about them—where they came from, how they live and even, cruelly, why they live. If we are honest, we must admit that we see them in less than human terms, as members of some alien subspecies essentially unknown and unknowable to us.

It is the great virtue of director John Schlesinger's film that he insists upon the humanity of Joe and Ratso; it is its great defect that he never really proves it. What he does prove is that there is a direct relationship between their queer, sad, violent habitat and our own. Grabbing us by the arm, he forces us to slow down and look—really look—at the neon wilderness through which his cowboy rides. The grind-house movies, all-night pizza parlors and shooting galleries are, he insists, the places where our commonly held visions of glamour, escape and heroism are reduced to parodistic least common denominators. Here we can clearly see the lunatic nature of the dreams we all share; here we can see all too well the price of living too deeply in the media-manufactured fantasies.

Beneath gaudiness we perceive that Joe and Ratso are not exactly strangers. The former is an up-to-date version of the

eternal rube. His steed may now be a Greyhound bus, his
cowboy clothes and manners may reflect not experience (despite a Texas upbringing) but the influence of popular culture,
his hope of a high-priced career as a stud for hire to Eastern
womankind driven desperate by their effete, hung-up mates
may be comical; yet he remains heir to the long line of country
cousins who have bought the Brooklyn Bridge from Ratso's
forefathers. And the latter, with his wheedling voice, his scut-
tling quickness, his muddled cynicism (which grants him
understanding of how the system works, but not quite enough
shrewdness to make it work *for* him), is the city's timeless
spokesman.

We are to understand, I think, that these archetypes have
been flawed, rendered more than traditionally vulnerable by
their times. Like the tawdry environment they inhabit, they are
the products of ceaselessly, carelessly exploitative society. Controlled and consoled by viciously moronic ideas, they are on a
lifelong bad trip and utterly unable to end it.

It is a bit much. There is no end of easy targets in modern
America, and Schlesinger is neither so clever nor so daring as he
thinks he is in banging away at them. Still, it must be admitted
that he has this social background firmly in focus here, however
we value his effort. What's disastrously wrong with the film is
its foreground fuzziness. Despite the superb ease of Jon Voight
in the title role and the hard work of Dustin Hoffman as Ratso
(he is apparently determined to remain what he naturally is, a
great character actor, instead of becoming merely another
movie star), Schlesinger never comes to grips with their characters as individuals. To be sure, each has been given an explana-
tory wretched childhood, while Joe has a sexual trauma and
Ratso a game leg to further illumine their drop-out status. But
that's not quite enough to engage us sympathetically.

They must be seen as literally lovable, and so, in the desperate penniless adversity they share, a beautiful masculine relationship begins to take shape. Slowly (much too slowly) we are
asked to observe that their essential dumbness may be a form

of exemplary innocence, their inability to cope with reality a form of purity, the unacknowledged love that grows between them a kind of salvation, a sweet triumph over a mad, decadent world.

But it just doesn't work. One could accept mutually exploitative, explicitly stated faggery. Trained the hard way in human misuse, one could imagine them using one another ill in their agony. To what, however, can we attribute the pretty impulse that overtakes them, converting them from dull louts (whom we have been encouraged much of the time to laugh at) into tender comrades? How are we to accept the delicate suggestion that if we will only look closely at the top of the dung heap we have been so relentlessly exploring we will find a dear romantic pansy flowering there?

Only as a fake, I fear. Or as the act of desperate men copping a plea. Anyway, it is not the moments of hard truth that are difficult to take in this film. It is the sweet nothings it disingenuously whispers in our ear that finally repel us.

6/27/69

EASY RIDER

Easy Rider is in the smallest—sociological—sense a historic movie. For in it the motorcycle is for the first time on screen converted from a malignant to a benign symbol, and the kids who ride are seen not as vandals or threats to the established order but as innocent individualists in desperate unavailing flight from the System.

Sheer romanticism? Of course. But then the endless cycle of cycle-gang pictures to which we have been subjected in recent years is also an exaggeration, a commercialized compound of the worst figments of our most dismal imaginings about what's going on across the generation gap. At the very least *Easy Rider* is a useful corrective. At its inconsistent best it is an attempt to restate in vivid contemporary terms certain ageless American preoccupations.

In form it is a loose, lovely-to-look-at, often laughing, often lyric epic about two young men (Peter Fonda and Dennis Hopper, who respectively produced and directed the film and collaborated with Terry Southern on the screenplay) who somehow believe the American Road is still free, open and fit for decent adventurings. They—and we—should know right at the beginning that they are probably doomed to discover otherwise. They are seeking a pure and purifying experience—a refreshed intimacy with their senses as well as the land and its people. But the means by which they finance their trip (the

proceeds of junk smuggling) and their goal (New Orleans at
Mardi Gras) are, in that order, impure and trivial.

Still, at first it seems the road retains its legendary qualities
as a place that promises escape, a way of changing one's luck.
These promises are, of course, important to all of us—always
have been—and as they proceed eastward (an interesting reversal of our traditional westering impulse), our hopes about
the quality of the experience we are sharing with them rise.
They investigate two aspects of the simple life—stopping
briefly at a family ranch and for a longer time at a hippie
commune where idealism and impracticality co-exist in nicely
loony fashion. Sitting around the campfire with the shaggy type
who is their guide to the commune, Fonda inquires whether he
has ever wanted to assume another identity. Well, maybe
Porky Pig, comes the reply.

It's funny in context, anyhow, and an indication that the
film is not going to ride easy on youth's present sure sense of
superiority to the adult middle-class culture. Its makers are
more sympathetic to the kids than to their parents, but the
deck is not entirely stacked. Later on in a small-town jail they
encounter an alcoholic civil liberties lawyer (wonderfully
played by Jack Nicholson). He springs them, and they attempt
to spring him from his bag (largely parental) by taking him
along to New Orleans. Among their first suggestions is a
liberating joint or two of pot. But, in the movie's best scene,
they discover that even with the aid of pot they can't match
the half-mad visionary intensity their straight friend achieves
just by thinking about UFOs. The joke is on their attitudes
and expectations—and on us. For the implication is that the
paranoid style increasingly evident in middle-class life may be a
form of mind bending at least as funny—and ultimately scary
—as the drug scene.

Indeed, it is that paranoia—based on a fear of freedom—that
ultimately turns this movie into tragedy. Even speed cannot
turn Mardi Gras into the liberating carnival of the spirit and

the senses they hoped it would be. It is too up-tight. And the road to it and away from it does lead through modern America, and inevitably they must collide with the casual unthinking brutality of a nation that talks much of freedom but will not tolerate radical personal expressions of it, will on occasion mindlessly kill dreams it does not understand and approve.

Easy Rider often fails to develop fully and exploit its best dramatic and comic potentials. It often lacks the technical skill to realize all its ambitions. Most damaging of all, perhaps, is its failure to let us really know its principals. Fonda comes on as an inarticulate novice saint, while Hopper gives off a vague air of anarchical menace, but neither really lets us inside his skin. They are too much in love with the idea of themselves as victims to show us the defects and imbalances that led them off on their quest—and to the sad waste of its ending. But despite all this, and a rather self-congratulatory air that hangs over this determinedly independent production, the film is, at least, alive, and glad about it, in a way in which few commercial films are these days.

7/11/69

I wonder how many others had an experience like mine with Easy Rider. I came to it at the end of what I recall as the most dismal season of all releases that I can remember. One American film after another offered evidence of an exhaustion of creativity and of the remaining strength of the genres. None offered any evidence that movie makers were looking for forms, techniques, personalities, ideas that would bring our films into some congruity with life as we were experiencing it. The night before, I had seen The April Fools, and though it was no worse than anything else I had recently seen it was distressingly no better. And then came this now famous film. I'm glad to see that I didn't entirely blow my cool over it, for it was, in the last analysis, a thin little movie that never realized all of its potentialities, never gave evidence that it understood all its own implications. On the other hand, it was fresh and improvisatory and, I think, less a product of commercial calculation than some of the other successful "youth" pictures. Fonda and Hopper in a simple intuitive (and as we have since seen, inimitable) way captured the mood of a historical moment in a way that moved me largely because they were such primitives. One had the feeling, as E. B. White once said of Thurber, that if they ever got good, they'd be terrible. In any case, I think I'll always be grateful to Easy Rider for reawakening in me at a moment when it had almost flickered out a feeling for the possibilities of the movies. I suppose some other movie would have done so, but the fact remains that this was the one that did.

THE WILD BUNCH

The Wild Bunch is the first masterpiece in the new tradition of what should probably be called "the dirty western," and I doubt that it can be widely tolerated, let alone appreciated, without some understanding of the new set of feelings about the frontier that it, unlike the films that established this tradition, *consciously*, and therefore artfully, summarizes.

The traditional—or "clean"—western is, as a rule, no more firmly located in time than a dream is. Indeed, the western has generally been understood as the dream work of the American collective unconscious, referring us endlessly to a lost Eden that we probably never truly inhabited. Peopled by characters who were conveniently, unambiguously good or evil, we observed in this dream that on those comparatively rare occasions when they killed one another they usually did so for an understandable reason, with minimum pleasure and with a minimum flow of blood and agony. Death in Eden was a convention rather than a stinking reality.

Not so in *The Wild Bunch*. Its simple story of an aging, morally moronic bandit gang in fruitless search of one last major robbery is mostly a convention to get us from the terrible massacre that immediately follows its first-reel failure at this task to the even more terrible (and quite suicidal) one that concludes the film. It is only in these moments of mass death that the film is, ironically, completely alive, only in them that director Sam Peckinpah's enormous talent seems completely

committed and fully extended—so much so that I am prepared
to state that they rank among the very greatest action sequences ever made. Moreover, they make a vicious and very
contemporary point, which is that when death comes in whole-
sale lots, when there is no way even of counting the bodies,
there is no way of feeling anything about it except a strange,
sick, frightening exultation. We are here arrived at a point far
beyond good guys versus bad guys; we are, as the saying goes,
beyond good and evil.

Well, this sort of thing—without Peckinpah's intensity of
realization—has become increasingly familiar in the dirty westerns of this decade, and a lot of people, myself included, have
regarded them as at best an attempt to bring some demyth-
ologizing realism to bear on our history, at worst a part of the
general escalation of sensationalism in popular culture. There
is, however, a good deal more than that going on in *The Wild
Bunch*.

The Bunch do not live in never-never land. They ride
through the teens of this century, at a point when Frederick
Jackson Turner and other historians had officially closed our
frontier, and the Bunch are feeling it—so much so that they
attempt to ride right out of our history and into Mexico's,
where they are not yet anachronisms. This careful location of
the movie's time and place strikes me as the key to its success.
For although the physical closing of the frontier is some
seventy years past, the date of its psychological closing is much
more recent—say about five years ago—and we are still feeling
that. Anyway, in the mid-sixties it became generally obvious
that we were finally and irrevocably an urban nation, that such
a nation required a radical redefinition of its concepts of
community and individualism so as to eliminate, among other
defects, the underclass (mostly black) that had supported its
previous definitions. Vietnam was (also among other things) a
failed attempt by a western President, quite conscious of his
region's historic safety-valve role, to externalize the frontier and
keep it alive for another generation. Indeed, it is almost too

easy to observe that the underclass of the sixties has been charged with "taming" (or to use the updated word, "pacifying") this fake frontier, just as the nineteenth-century underclass performed the same function on the real one. An acquaintance of mine, lately returned from Vietnam, tells me that so far as he can see there is nothing in civilian life that can support the "imaginative intensity" ordinary soldiers bring to fighting the war there, and certainly a similar statement could have been made about pioneering, else why has it dominated our imaginations for so long?

These are, perhaps, very large statements to pin on a movie. Still, it seems to me that the dirty western has throughout the sixties been groping about in our violent past, unconsciously searching for some historically true objective correlative that would help illuminate our present sense of desperate psychological dislocation. In *The Wild Bunch*, helped by co-writer Walon Green, cameraman Lucien Ballard and a cast of old worthies (William Holden, Robert Ryan, *et al.*) and new ones (Jamie Sanchez, Warren Oates), Peckinpah has brilliantly concluded this search. The promise of *Ride the High Country*, in which as early as 1961 he modestly and rather wistfully explored similar terrain, has finally been fulfilled in what may someday come to seem one of the most important records of the mood of our times and one of the most important American films of the era.

7/25/69

MEDIUM COOL

Medium Cool—the title has two obvious meanings. It refers us, by the simple reversal of McLuhan's fashionable term, to television, for which the film's protagonist (Robert Forster) works as a cameraman. And it alludes to Forster's own emotional climate, which he is seen struggling to escape for the length of the movie.

More important, however, is what the title suggests about the entire nation's predominant attitude toward violence, an attitude that has grown ever more common—without our being completely aware of its growth—since we became enmeshed in the media web. Haskell Wexler, the great cameraman who also wrote and directed *Medium Cool* as his first feature, is suggesting in it that we have become voyeurs of violence, at once disturbed and titillated by it as we vicariously participate in it via television. He is saying, I think, that whether we pretend to deplore or ignore this material we get a cool kick out of it at the deepest levels of our being. And that as a result we are hooked on the stuff, requiring ever stronger doses to feed our habit, just like the other junkies.

Item: Forster and a girl friend getting so turned on sexually by the semi-fraudulent violence of a roller derby that they leave early to rush home.

Item: A *cinéma vérité* sequence in which we are invited to observe a group of middle-class ladies taking shooting lessons. Their interest and excitement are comically but frighteningly out of proportion to their need for this form of adult education.

Largest item of all: The fact that Forster is seen at the outset as rather like a surgeon, unable to pursue his profession if he lets himself become involved in his subjects' lives or thinks about the social effects of his work. He is fired when he follows a black militant's story further than his station's management thinks necessary. He's caught the thrill of their activities—who needs understanding?

It turns out that he does. And once he is free to lift his eye from his viewfinder, he begins really to see. At which point, of course, he begins really to feel, not only about his subjects—he involves himself with a young mother and her son who have exchanged the poverty of Appalachia for the poverty of a Chicago slum—but about himself and what he has been doing. And he is appalled by the contribution to anarchy that "professionalism" (i.e., emotional neutrality) can make.

In this state of heightened awareness he signs on as a cameraman covering the recent Chicago Democratic convention. Into its violent orbit his Appalachian "family" is accidentally drawn, and out of it a final tragedy, appropriately accidental, evolves.

The power of the media to magnify events and to involve the unprepared and the innocent in history is powerfully demonstrated in these sequences, though I am not sure Mr. Wexler has entirely solved the aesthetic and technical problems that arise when fictional characters are juxtaposed with great events. He gives us a more intimate view of the Chicago riots than TV ever did ("Look out, Haskell, it's real," a voice on the sound track cries as a canister of tear gas explodes near the film maker), but he never quite succeeds in melding his people believably with his superb documentary footage. Nor does he make his interpretation of their motives or the larger meanings of their acts entirely clear or dramatically sharp. One must read a good deal into *Medium Cool*.

But that, of course, is no bad thing. It is refreshing to have an American film released by a major studio that is not "well made" in the conventional sense, that does not insist on reducing everything to a single simple point and that bears the mark of a single creative hand. Any reservations about *Medium Cool* fade to insignificance beside the importance of Mr. Wexler's achievement. His is, I believe, the first entirely serious commercially sponsored basically fictional film born of the time of troubles through which this nation has been passing. Alone of American movie makers Mr. Wexler has asked one of the difficult, pressing, *right* questions that hover constantly in the back of all our minds. He does not pretend to solve the problem posed by television's mindless ability to convert real violence into a peculiarly grubby form of surreality simply by its presence on the scene. But by posing it in fictional rather than purely documentary terms he has intensified our awareness of the problem's human dimensions. In short, he has been about the proper business of the concerned artist, which is not drafting manifestoes but trying to understand what's happening to us all.

8/15/69

PUTNEY SWOPE

I have tried my best to cop out on Robert Downey's *Putney Swope*. It is the first of his films to get a full-scale aboveground release and therefore the first to expose to general view the talents of a very rare mole—an undergrounder with a real sense of humor, an ability to make us laugh at his work intentionally.

I suppose I should have leapt forth with a combined news bulletin and warning for the faint of heart. But frankly, on first viewing I wasn't at all certain the great world was ready for Mr. Downey, because his stuff is often rough, crude, vulgar—in a word (the meaning of which is no longer clear to me) tasteless. Nor did I think that he has as yet put it all together—matching his gift for surrealistic social comment with complete technical mastery and a sure sense of when a joke is over.

I still don't think he has arrived at that point, but a couple of things have happened since *Putney Swope* was released. To begin with, in an almost unprecedented gesture of contempt, the New York *Daily News*, which rates movies by awarding them up to four stars, granted none at all to *Putney*. It seems to me that any picture getting zilch on a scoreboard that automatically gives a couple of twinklers to the average Vincent Price chiller can't be all bad. Then, through a series of circumstances, I was obliged to see the picture a second time, in an audience composed of young theater people. Their uncomplicated delight in it opened my ideas to a simple fact, which is that its virtues far outweigh its defects.

These last can be summed up as mostly structural. The premise—that the black title character accidentally becomes head of a powerful ad agency, which he promptly renames Truth and Soul (or TS for short) and from which he fires all but a few token white staffers in order to replace them with a complete range of dark militants—is no more than a thin clothesline on which he closely pegs a dizzying succession of one-liners, blackouts, quick satirical sketches and simple shockers. Downey works in too much, works out too little, with ideas, situations, characters popping in and out of focus too often, too quickly, too carelessly. The film never develops the richness, the rhythms, the cumulative momentum one senses could have been there had a little more time and discipline gone into its making (though his budgetary limitations surely account for the former defect).

Still, as Putney says upon accepting the TS presidency, "I don't believe in rocking the boat, I believe in sinking it." So does Downey, who has Putney and colleagues doing their damnedest to punch holes in most of the basic premises that keep us afloat. Chief among them is consumerism. In the commercials they make for such clients as Ethereal Cereal, Lucky Air Lines and Face Off (a pimple cream for adolescents) they replace the usual euphemisms, evasions and hypocrisies of ad land with blunt promises of visceral satisfactions (on Lucky Air Lines, for instance, the hostesses cease to be sex symbols and become full-scale sexual objects housed in a harem on every flight). In short, innuendos become full-scale promises to fulfill the desperate needs we vainly hope the purchase of goods and services will fulfill. It may not be soulful, but it is truthful—not just about the cynicism with which we are often manipulated but about the feebleness of our most common definition of happiness as well.

Downey claims his sociopolitical beliefs may be summed up as "paranoid anarchy," and he flails about at institutions other than consumerism with a fine impartial fervor. The intellectuals get it in his first sequence, when a McLuhan-like media guru descends on Manhattan, his helicopter flying the skull and crossbones and the stars and bars, while he is dressed in his true colors (Hell's Angels garb, with his club name—Mensa— scrawled across his jacket). The politicians? Well, he imagines the President of the United States as a midget, one of whose advisers endlessly mutters bad jokes in his ear, another of whom is a tycoon-pothead-anti-Semite. The blacks themselves? They end up by selling out, as corrupted as anyone else by proximity to the cash and power nexus.

It's all, as *Mad Comics* would have it, "humor in the jugular vein," a vein which, I think, suits our time somewhat better than the Wildean or Shavian modes. It has the raucous truth of a cry from the balcony or the bleachers—the kind of Bronx jeer that has long been the specialty of the nation's yeoman democrat, a man who sometimes misses certain subtleties but has always managed to hang on pretty well to the basic truths. There's vigor in this vulgarity, health in these hee-haws, the strength of wind to blow away those disinfectant perfumes with which we have attempted to hide some of the bad odors our society has been giving off lately. In all, *Putney Swope* is a kind of *Laugh-In* for adults—without Darling Dan and Adorable Dick to help us swallow our medicine.

8/22/69

BUTCH CASSIDY AND
THE SUNDANCE KID

It is *The Wild Bunch* for people who couldn't stand *The Wild Bunch*. That is to say *Butch Cassidy and the Sundance Kid* is funny instead of grim, elegiac instead of horrifying as it treats the same theme as the earlier film—the closing of our western frontier and the consequent technological disemployment of its bandit population.

The new film is distinguished by William Goldman's genuinely humorous gag writing (the well-known novelist is so drawn to these characters that on one occasion he used Sundance's real name, Harry Longbough, as a pen name) and by wonderfully lively performances in the title roles by Paul Newman and Robert Redford. The former imparts to Butch the easy good nature of the most popular guy in the frat house; the latter gives Sundance the cool competence, the canny reserve of a star athlete. Both are more interesting than your standard good-bad guys and there is between them something quite rare in our films, a real masculine relationship, the terms of which remain unspoken, the depth of which is greater than they know.

It is deeper, perhaps, than either Goldman or the director, George Roy Hill, knew. For although this is a highly entertaining, extraordinarily pleasant movie, I found I could not completely give my heart to it. For one thing Goldman shares with his brother James (who wrote *The Lion in Winter*) is what seems to me a near-fatal attraction to anachronistic dialogue; it makes you laugh all right, but it also often destroys one's sense of mood and time and place. There are also some strange emphases in Hill's direction—for example, a comic bike-riding sequence with Newman and Katharine Ross that is apparently included as an excuse to get a really terrible song—the worst thing in Burt Bacharach's entirely inappropriate score—into the film. A long chase, the heart of the film, in which Butch and the Kid for the first time confront the frightening new efficiency of the Pinkerton detective agency (and see the hand-writing on their wall), never develops the tension it should, because Mr. Hill prefers the pursuers to be understood as artful abstractions—the forces of modernism, I guess—rather than as menacing individuals. Perhaps worse than that is the manner in which the impact of the final tragedy is dissipated. Butch and the Kid have fled to Bolivia in search of a frontier that is still open. But it is a mess, and instead of getting a sense of growing desperation and of impending doom, we get . . . more jokes. There, at last, Butch must do what he has never done before, kill in order to avoid being killed. It should be a moment of high drama, but—typical of this section—it is glossed over by the use of that new (and already used-up) convention of screen violence, death in beautiful slow motion. The result is that when Butch and the Kid are finally, fatally trapped by the local soldiery, we do not feel as much as we should, care as much as we want to care about their fate.

It seems to me that all along the way in this movie the people responsible for it have taken the easy crowd-pleasing choices when really there was no need to do so. The analogy between the situation of these men—their way of life radically chang-ing, their frustration over what is happening to them growing—and our own situation is neither difficult to understand nor hard to take. I confess I don't entirely understand why Gold-man and Hill did what they did. They are not hacks, and they are not without talent. The thought nags at me that perhaps the western is an essentially primitive form best undertaken by people with direct and simplifying sensibilities (the master of the form, John Ford, springs to mind). Goldman's sensibility is basically modern and urban (as witness his fine script for *Harper*), and perhaps, despite his obvious love for this material, he does not entirely trust it. The same may be true of Hill, whose best is a fable about city kids, *The World of Henry Orient*.

Well, I do not want to overthink this. *Butch Cassidy and the Sundance Kid* is a perfectly harmless and quite entertaining film and one's basic complaint is only that it comes close to being a good deal more and didn't quite make it.

10/24/69

HIGH SCHOOL

There is good nostalgia and—less familiarly—bad nostalgia. It is the latter form of this somewhat suspect emotion that is induced by Frederick Wiseman's *High School*, a wicked, brilliant documentary about life in a lower-middle-class secondary school in Philadelphia. Watching it, the upper centers of the brain register the correct feeling of dismay bordering on despair as the dreariness of this educational environment is revealed to us. A little deeper down, however, I think almost any graduate of a public school may very well experience the film as I did, with a certain odd, and by no means creditable, sense of relief.

There has been such an earnest effort to reform the system in recent years, so many studies, so many experiments with new teaching methods and technologies, that I expected the film might reveal a fundamental change in high schooling as a basic human experience. The social critic in me certainly hoped that was the case. On the other hand, one is, after all, an Old Boy of public education, bound by a certain sentiment to those forms of hazing nearly everyone has suffered in the process of growing up absurd in this country in this century.

And that is where the relief comes in. For *High School* proves that newer generations have not escaped these traditional torments. If Mr. Wiseman's example is as typical as I think it is, they not only survive, they actually flourish in the 1960s. You will be glad to know, for example, that it is still possible to find on your average faculty a petty sadist to manage the hall monitors and that he continues to pad the corridors, harassing the guilty and the innocent alike by his fervent desire to check their passes. At a slightly higher level you will still find that assistant principal whose rage for simply conceived discipline and order can shout down the fundamental adolescent hunger for more subtle forms of justice. Indeed, to me the film's most potent scene involves such a character's inability even to listen to a student's very plausible excuse for an act of minor rebellion, so intent is he on reading his standard lecture on the need for deportment moronically defined. Out of such acorns of experience grow, no doubt, the mighty oaks of college anarchy.

One resorts to irony about such matters mainly to keep from blithering in anger. And then one finds oneself reduced to helpless laughter by the nonsensical pedagogy these amateur cops are serving—a serious young English teacher playing Simon and Garfunkel records in an attempt to stir some interest among the kids in poetry; a more traditional-minded colleague earnestly reciting "Casey at the Bat" while her charges register a wide, exquisite range of boredom; a home-ec teacher, humorous and practical, putting on a fashion show and trying to teach her student models the rudiments of good posture and good taste and then a little later attempting to come to grips with a prejudice against her black students which, though admittedly mild, is so deeply ingrained that she can momentarily escape from it only by pretending that it does not really, really exist.

It's all funny in a sad sort of way, and then toward the end of the film it ceases to be funny at all. First we overhear a halting conversation between an athletic coach and one of his former players just back from Vietnam. They are discussing other kids from the school who have served there, exchanging information on who was killed, who was wounded, who is still intact. A little later at an assembly a teacher reads a letter written by another graduate just before he went into action over there. Ostensibly it is an attempt to express gratitude for the way in which the school has prepared him for life. Actually, however, like the talk between coach and athlete, it is an unconscious effort to reconcile the disparities between the reality of life and the middle-class fantasy about life that is propagated by the school. The gap between the two is, finally, too deep for irony, too appalling to go on laughing about.

The school houses an obviously expensive space flight simulator, and to the obvious excitement of the student body, boy "astronauts" fly in it for days, eliciting congratulatory wires from the real astronauts at the end of their adventure. I'm sure the PTA and the Board of Education can point to this piece of hardware and prove, as materialistic parents do, that they have "done everything" for their kids. It is the singular merit of Mr. Wiseman's film that it definitively proves this argument just won't wash.

Closely following his *Titicut Follies* and his Emmy Award-winning *Law and Order*, the film also definitively proves his claim to being our most distinguished practitioner of *cinéma vérité*, using the technique not merely to document the lives of pop singers and show folk, but to seriously examine the quality of our institutions. As this is written, *High School* has had exactly one theatrical showing, a lack of exposure entirely too typical of serious documentaries. If we care as much about good film as we claim to nowadays, it should have thousands more. We need it as much as it needs an audience.

9/12/69

BOB & CAROL &
TED & ALICE

Bob and Carol are the swingers. He's a documentary film maker, and one weekend they journey out to the Esalen-like institute which is to be his next subject, there to participate in an encounter group. Result: they see the future and discover that it works—for them at least.

Ted and Alice are the squares. They are the kind of old, old friends whose companionship is so taken for granted that neither couple has noticed they really have nothing in common any more except the history they have shared.

Anyway, Bob and Carol (Robert Culp and Natalie Wood) want to introduce Ted and Alice (Elliott Gould and Dyan Cannon) to their new state of grace. The latter are appalled and titillated by that prospect—appalled when Carol follows a restaurant waiter all the way into the kitchen in an attempt to relate to him as one human being to another; titillated when they discover that Bob has casually slept with a girl in San Francisco, confessed and found his wife ever so modern and understanding about it. To be sure, he has to work a little harder when he discovers Carol exercising the same freedom in his very bed with the local tennis pro. But he manages—mixing a round of drinks and serving them, amid strained small talk, right in the bedroom they all now share.

In the retelling it sounds, perhaps, a little sour. But on the screen it is not. Neither is it black, farcical, desperately chic. To put the matter simply, *Bob & Carol & Ted & Alice* is as sweet

and charming and funny and, above all, *human* as any comedy
that has been made in the United States in this decade. Indeed, one has to delve much deeper in movie history to find apt
comparisons to it. In the thirties Myrna Loy and William
Powell gave us our first believable vision of a sophisticated
modern marriage. A little later Hepburn and Tracy revised and
expanded that vision in the lovely series of marital comedies
they gave us.

But in the fifties and sixties the movies have proved to be
neither very funny nor very helpful when they tried to report to
us from the front lines of the battle between the sexes. We
have been too preoccupied with kinky kicks, not enough concerned about what Benjamin DeMott calls "the texture of
domestic dailiness." And that, really, is the basis of this film's
success. Its people look, act, talk like real human beings, and
they move through an achingly familiar suburban world. If,
perhaps, the majority of us are not yet putting the new morality into everyday use, these four people make us realize how
genuinely tempting it is, how easy it can be for the people
DeMott calls "competent, caring, functioning" to experiment
with it. And it is perhaps a measure of how far we have come
from the great days of Kate and Spence to note that it now
requires a team of two couples to fully recount our follies and
troubles.

There are scenes in BCTA that will come to seem, in memory, the perfect measures of our contemporary domestic des-
perations in this "transitional" era. The best of them is an in-
bed quarrel between Ted and Alice that may be the longest—
and is surely the funniest—such scene in Hollywood's history.
It summarizes so many issues that cause us anguish and anxiety
—the statistics of Kinsey and Masters, the psychological by-
products of the pill and the pursuit of prosperity, the half-
explained (and half-digested) news and advice we have received about the new ways men and women are supposed to
relate to one another. It is a great scene—at once hilarious,

discomfiting and, finally, a little sad and more than a little thought-provoking. Other sequences are almost as good. For example, there is Alice head-to-head with her analyst—a maddeningly non-directive type who offers little more than monosyllabic encouragement (but no real assistance) in her struggle to understand herself. At long last she surfaces with a precious insight—only to have her doctor turn very directive indeed. It seems her hour is up and he firmly directs her right out the door. It seems to me a perfect paradigm of the way our calendars and schedules defeat almost every attempt to understand ourselves and the world.

But I mustn't give the impression that all the humor in the picture stems from the struggles of the squares to get with our brave new world. The smugness of the swingers—so sure they have hitched a ride on the express train of history, so endlessly understanding of everything and everybody, so earnestly helpful to each other and to their friends as they try to make it to the promised land—that is a joy, too.

In fact, one of the great pleasures of the film lies in the way all four principals keep surprising us with their excellence. One has no sooner decided that Miss Wood is doing the best job than one changes his mind; clearly Mr. Gould is best. But no—here is Miss Cannon being brilliant. And now look here—Mr. Culp has topped her. One finally gives up. They are all marvelous—wonderfully contrasting types, always in control of themselves and their material. When, finally, the movie reaches its climax in an abortive spouse swap during a Las Vegas weekend ("First the orgy, then we'll go hear Tony Bennett"), one leaves them with real regret. And with real admiration for the beautifully observed, very original script by Paul Mazursky and Larry Tucker and for the former's superb direction. If there is a criticism to be made, it is of the very last sequence, an expressionistic business out of tone with the rest of the film and quite unnecessary. It is, however, a very small regret and one quite overshadowed by the memory of the first film that has dared to be intelligently witty yet decent and compassionate about people caught up in a sexual revolution no one fully understands.

A false reputation precedes *Bob & Carol & Ted & Alice.* The night I saw it the audience was determined for a reel or two to treat it raucously, as if it were another heartless, mindless satire of an increasingly familiar type. In time, however, the boyish shouts and girlish giggles died down, replaced by another kind of laughter—the thoughtful kind which accompanies at least a degree of rueful self-recognition.

10/3/69

OH! WHAT A
LOVELY WAR

I cannot remember a movie I looked forward to more keenly than *Oh! What a Lovely War,* and I cannot remember one that has more deeply disappointed me. This is, however, a more than usually subjective reaction, and perhaps in fairness to the film I had better indulge in a little autobiography in order to explain myself.

In 1964 my wife and I happened to be in London, and one night we happened to drive past the theater where Joan Little-wood's original stage production was running. We had vaguely heard about it and so, having nothing better to do, we stopped the cab and went in. What we saw was a revelation: seventeen young actors and actresses re-creating with the aid of a few sketchy props and settings the mood of an entire nation (Britain) at war (World War One). Their material consisted, most significantly, of the popular songs of the period (mostly cheerful and romantic) placed in stark contrast with the songs (mostly cynical, and generally set to the tunes of hymns and folk songs) that the Tommies were making up in the trenches of France. A similar contrast was made out of literary mate-rial—official dispatches and speeches being played off against the more truthful words researchers were able to dig out of the diaries and reminiscences of the ordinary soldiers and nurses (and those few officers who had the eyes to really see what was going on at the Western Front).

It was all so simple. And so powerful. On that little stage, to the accompaniment of a rickey-tickey orchestra, Miss Little-wood and her tiny troupe made us see—and feel—not only the horrible futility of this war but the death of the old confident age King Edward inherited from Victoria and the birth of a new age—our own, with its loss of faith not only in God but in the institutions that control power within it. The work, a collaborative effort for which no single author took credit, was, of course, the most potent anti-war statement I have ever seen. But it was something much more than that—a great human document, perhaps, or a statement of belief in the good sense, the beauty of ordinary man. It is hard to name its quality, even though I have thought a good deal about it. Possibly it is enough to say that it affected me more than any theatrical work I can remember.

And now one must confront the movie Richard Attenbor-ough, that gifted actor, has made of *Oh! What a Lovely War*. Its heart is surely in the right place, and it makes a conscientious attempt to find the cinematic equivalents of Miss Little-wood's theater piece. But it doesn't work. It doesn't work at all.

To begin with, the youthful improvisatory quality of the original is gone. All kinds of great names from the English theater (Olivier, Gielgud, Richardson) have been recruited to do bits, and though individually most of them are quite good, collectively they are not. By their presence, and quite without meaning to, they have the effect of co-opting the work, if not for the establishment, then for the official culture. In place of the small, simple unadorned stage we now have gaudy Brighton Pier for a setting. It is, of course, a famous amusement park and one understands the temptation it must have been to Attenborough. But it is not really an apt metaphor for the Western Front and the notion of having John Mills, who plays Sir Douglas Haig, the British commander, as the ticket-selling impresario of the place quickly wears thin. Moreover, by so specifically locating his film on the pier, Attenborough creates an insoluble stylistic problem for himself. He must have scenes in the trenches and that means cutting away from Brighton to a representation of the front. It is not quite real, not quite expressionistic. It looks, alas, like your standard backlot movie battlefield, and each time we are transported to it we are jarred aesthetically instead of shocked emotionally. Then, too, the movie's cast of thousands—or at least hundreds—is a mistake. A handful of people, each of whom is obviously playing several characters, are effective as symbols of that abstract entity, man. The very act of changing masks, as it were, reinforces our sense of each player's universality. But a lot of people is simply a lot of people. We cannot get hold of them, identify with them, feel for them and with them.

Finally, and perhaps most inexplicable, is the film's wretched treatment of the songs that were the very heart of the theatrical experience. The verses the Tommies made up in the trenches made no overt political statement. Nor did they speak in terms of rage, anguish, self-pity. They were, in fact, perversely cheeky, full of the common soldiers' cheerful contempt for the ineptitude of their officers and for the ruling class that they represented. They were an attempt to maintain sanity and autonomy in the midst of what must surely have been the most dehumanizing war we have yet conducted. The contrast between these little pieces of folk art and the context in which they were created was almost unbearably poignant—and stirring. In the film they can scarcely be heard at all—they are for the most part heard as background music or as transitional fragments. Their wit—their wonderfully saving wit—is simply gone. And I could weep, for *Oh! What a Lovely War* was one of those experiences I have always wanted to share with as many people as possible. And now it's been ruined. Looking at this monstrosity, will anyone believe in its original greatness, a greatness in no need of inflation?

10/10/69

COMING APART

I suppose most of the discussion of *Coming Apart* is going to revolve around whether or not it violates "contemporary community standards" in its treatment of sex. That is, let me hasten to say, a fair question, for the movie is extraordinarily blunt about, and singularly preoccupied with, naked bodies and with certain widely practiced but rarely photographed uses to which those bodies can be put by libidinous human beings. Indeed, in its unwillingness to avert its eyes from them the film can only be compared, alas, to *I Am Curious* (*Yellow*). Still, contemporary community standards are in such a shambles that no honest man can say with any certainty whether an object of art (or commerce) really exceeds them. Moreover, *Coming Apart* does at least deal with our community, not Sweden's, and it does so, I believe, in a way that is altogether more interesting, psychologically and cinematically, than that rather heavy-handed exercise. Which seems to me a very important point in its favor.

It is, in fact, one of the very few illuminating—not to say harrowing—portrayals of a schizophrenic crack-up that I have ever seen on the screen. The fellow coming apart is a married psychiatrist (Rip Torn) who has taken a bachelor pad where for reasons of illusion and delusion he pretends to be a photographer. The place is equipped with a hidden movie camera which he uses to record the results of his unscientific but totally dedicated study of an amazingly accurate cross section

of New York feminine life that he lures into its range. The film
we watch is supposed to be the film that camera has exposed
and that is where the technical interest of the film lies. For
director Milton Moses Ginsberg must hold our attention over a
long span, using only the one fixed angle available to this
camera and without any of the editing devices available to the
directors of less radically simplified films (the convention is
that scenes start when the protagonist flips on a switch, end
when he switches it off or the camera runs out of film). I'm not
going to dither on about the inventiveness Ginsberg displays in
discovering ways to vary his work—staging action at different
distances from the camera, making use of the edges of the
frame and off-camera voices. All of that will someday make an
interesting piece in one of the film journals, but it seems to me
technique is only of consequence if it in some way reinforces
our comprehension of a director's larger meaning, and this one
does so.

That hidden camera is the logical extension—no, the *re-
ductio ad absurdum*—of our age's insistence that experience
must be passed through some recording-communicating
medium before it can become completely real to us. Of course,
the end result of our media lunacy may very well be the opposite of what is intended; it is likely that it is a dissociative force,
preventing us from getting in touch with emotional reality.

Certainly Mr. Ginsberg wants us to observe that there is a
correlation between our coolly voyeuristic state as we watch the
hidden camera's film unroll and that of the psychiatrist who
has, with similar coolness (coldness might be a better word),
decided to act out his fantasy life in front of it, regardless of its
effect on his loved ones off stage or his partners on stage.

It's all right for him in the beginning, when the emotional
stakes are low. A casual encounter with an aimless chick who
used to be one of his patients, a comic engagement with a
masochist ("Hurt me," she cries. "How?" he inquires, eager to
please but puzzled about method), a sad encounter with a
teeny-brained teeny-bopper who develops inhibitions when she

remembers her baby is asleep in the carriage she has parked over there in the corner. The trouble develops when the chick (played by Sally Kirkland with a perfect air of dumb desperation) would have him take responsibility for her. That, of course, is precisely what he is trying to avoid, and things start to come unstuck quite quickly thereafter. The older woman whose rejection apparently triggered this strange interlude rejects him anew, suggesting that he really ought to pull himself together. Shortly thereafter his wife traces him to his lair and she too observes that he is rather farther along in the process of disintegration than he knows. The point is that man cannot live by fantasy alone; reality, dismal as it is, sustains us, is essential to us, much as we hate the idea. And when Miss Kirkland returns one last time in order to wreck his little world (and its camera), we see just how fragile fantasy is. For when the apartment is destroyed, its owner is too. It is not, I think, a tragedy, which may be the film's chief defect. It is merely an ending. And if you asked me if the same basic point could not have been made without so much frankly displayed sexual activity, I would have to reply that it could have been. Easily. Surely the motives of the film's makers must be questioned. Surely the motives of anyone who decided to avoid it could not be questioned. But the effect of the film is powerful, not least because of Rip Torn's really brilliant performance as he transforms himself from a man making a half-serious experiment in living to a creature ensnared in a trap of his own devising. I despise the currently fashionable paradox that works of art that offend traditional morality are often more deeply moral than those that do not dare such transgressions. And yet in honesty it must be recorded that Coming Apart does have a morally instructive dimension. It may or may not have been made in the spirit of art, but for some people—among whom I number myself—it has the effect of art, and very troubling art at that.

This one I feel I have to defend. In 1969 there was no dearth of defenders for I Am Curious (Yellow)—me among them. I felt that, of course, it should be seen. On the other hand, I can't say that I found it very interesting or particularly revealing about the sexual relation, and the correlation it attempted to establish between sex and politics seemed to me tenuous indeed. By contrast this film, shot on little more than a sexploitation picture budget and dealing at least metaphorically with our growing sense that nothing is real until we have passed it through some sort of lens, seemed to say something quite vivid about our way of life. I couldn't deny that it was a cheap little thing, but cheap little things have a way of revealing ourselves to ourselves in a way that more pretentious, more carefully thought out works do not—since the more time and effort that is put into a movie, the more time and effort goes into rationalization, a kind of softening of focus in order to protect the investment. (That's where the fascination of B pictures has traditionally been found—in their artless and direct catering to common fantasies.)

In many respects this was a nasty little film—a lot nastier than Petulia or Bob & Carol & Ted & Alice, but I think, for all my talk about the necessity for a humane point of view in movies, that there is a need for nastiness in them as well. Our novels report to us the bad news that we use one another badly in life, and I think movies must sometimes do the same thing—no matter what the lady critics have to say about the matter. Anyway, the film died the death. And a year later Life ran a picture of a motel that caters to honeymooners exclusively. Among the amenities it automatically provides is a camera for each couple so that they may conveniently record, and thus make real, their first connubial grapplings. All I'm saying is that Coming Apart illuminated with discomfiting candor a reality that is increasingly familiar. And though reality is not the highest end to which a movie may aspire, it is a necessary beginning.

DOWNHILL RACER

One of Hollywood's most cherished folk beliefs is that movies about athletes are doomed to box-office failure. Even after television made sports fans out of everyone, regardless of age, sex, creed and color, that article of faith was never seriously tested, simply because until now no one has made a really good movie about sport.

But now at last we can determine if quality can overcome alleged audience indifference, for *Downhill Racer* is precisely what we have waited so long to see—a small, tense, expertly made (and, on occasion, surprisingly funny) film about a newly chic form of athletic competition—Alpine skiing. The story is as clean and simple and invigorating as I imagine it must be to *schuss* down a good slope on a cold clear day when the snow is just right. Boy wants to become champion, boy becomes champion after a period of trial and peril—that's all there is to it, and, really, that's all there is to any sporting endeavor, which is why we are all so mightily drawn to it in these complex times.

That simplicity, that insistence on the heart of the matter, winning or losing, is not the least of *Downhill*'s virtues, and there are others of equal importance. Quite obviously, they include capturing on color film the sheer beauty of the white world in which the racers live. Here the director, Michael Ritchie, a young man making his first feature, splendidly exploits a couple of fine paradoxes. From a distance the skiers seem to have the effortless grace of birds in flight. Close up, though, he makes us see that they are engaged in a pounding, brutal, breath-stealing ordeal, and the contrast between the way downhill racing looks and the way it is gripped me as strongly as anything I have recently seen on the screen. Then there's the other paradox—that this agonizing effort takes place, unlike that of any other sport, with the competitor alone in a sea of silence. Only the wind of his own passage and the whoosh of his skis on the snow accompany him—an oddly peaceful accompaniment to so violent a competitive effort. It seems to me that anyone, whether he cares about this sport or any sport, must respond to these paradoxes. I know for certain that I could have watched them ski on forever, despite the fact that I've never done it and, sedentary coward that I am, hope never to be dared into trying it.

Still, there is a good deal more to *Downhill Racer* than its aesthetically pleasing exploitation of previously untouched cinematic territory, and that is its careful exploration of the character of its central figure. A press sheet from the producers carelessly speaks of the skiers as professionals, when they are, of course, by common winking consent, amateurs. In fact, the press agents speak more truly than the various international committees who rule sports like skiing. They are pros in everything except name, meaning that they accept the most rigorous forms of discipline (including self-discipline) because they love the sport with an intensity no amateur can, love it so much they are willing to devote their *entire* lives to the pursuit of excellence in it. That they should, as the hero of this film does, expect and receive rewards commensurate with their dedication seems to me only honest and realistic. The cynicism belongs to the gray old men who insist on the pious pretense that sport conducted at this level is otherwise mostly because they wish it were.

Anyway, David Chappellet, as Robert Redford plays him, is such a driven, driving competitor. He races by their rules, but he plays life by his own. The good of the team, the honor of the nation, the pleasures of tradition are nothing to him. He's there because he's good—and potentially great—and that's the end of sporting platitudes. Redford gives us a kid who is tough, innocent, vain—a taker who gives of himself only when he's on the hill racing, but then gives all of himself. In short, he is what all great athletes are—an individualist pushing out against the limits of his sport, which are the conventions of style, otherwise known as "the way we've always done it," and history, otherwise known as the record book.

He's not an entirely pleasant fellow, but no one hell-bent on radical self-improvement is. The reward for success in this endeavor in sport is, of course, social improvement as well, and Redford knows the gentleman athlete is obsolete because rude kids who saw what winning could do for them socially and economically elbowed him aside in their effort to earn what was his by birthright. It is this complex figure, rebelling against his coach (Gene Hackman), vulnerable to a sophisticated girl (Camilla Sparv), that Redford gives us in all his surprising complexity—the definitive jock, one of the central symbolic figures in the inner life of modern men. The intensity of the challenge he flings out, the coolness with which he tries to cover the intensity of his need to win are sometimes comic. But what he learns in the end, in the moment of his biggest win, about the transitory nature of victory and the role that luck plays in achieving it, is not funny at all. It is good, strong, purging stuff—as is all of *Downhill Racer.*

I guess the conventional wisdom still stands: Downhill did not do well financially. But unlike most movie reviewers I do care a great deal about sports, remain fascinated by the psychology of the athlete and think that the winning-losing metaphor, in which cramped space he must define himself, is a key one that many of us have borrowed, with rather unpleasant effect on our own lives and the quality of our society. I remain convinced that this laconic, tough-minded little picture is the best exploration of all this that we've had on screen and wish that more movie makers would push out into this relatively unexplored territory. And that audiences would go along with them. If it is acceptable to study, in fictional form, the creative processes of art, why is it not equally acceptable to examine the creative processes of the athlete, who works under analogous pressures and who is, as a rule, engaged in much more photogenic activities?

ADALEN '31

Commercially, the question is this: Will the huge American audience that made *Elvira Madigan* one of the mightiest hits ever to play the art houses come out in similar numbers to see a really good, but much more complex, much less romantic, movie by its gifted director, Bo Widerberg?

His new effort, *Adalen '31*, shares two of the qualities that distinguished its predecessor: its photography is extraordinarily beautiful, and the fact that it will end in tragedy is known right from the beginning, when a title announces that it is based on an incident that occurred in the Swedish town named in the title. There, in 1931, five people were killed when soldiers fired on workers peacefully marching to protest the importation of scab labor to break a strike they had mounted against a wood pulp plant. (The film is dedicated to the memory of these five accidental martyrs.)

But where *Elvira* was a dully developed, dramatically unaccented trip down a path too straight and too obvious to be interesting, *Adalen '31* leaps with life and with a marvelous variety of incident. With quick deft strokes Widerberg captures microcosmically one of those rare historical moments when the forces of change are harshly outlined against a background of tradition everyone concerned had regarded as immutable.

He states the conflict in his opening shots—the silent gloomy factory towering over a sun-splashed landscape that is

still, despite the industrial intrusion, essentially rural. He develops it by introducing us to a family that has nothing but its
fundamentally decent instincts to guide its response to the
strike, which is, of course, merely the local manifestation of a
worldwide socioeconomic upheaval. Those instincts, as Widerberg wrenchingly proves, are not good enough to protect them.

Only the youngest child, pattering innocently behind her increasingly desperate elders, touchingly fascinated by the unend-
ing (but to her still wondrous) trivia of existence—her father's
morning shave, her mother doing the laundry, a fishing trip—is
somehow safe from chaos. One brother, slightly older, is en-
tranced by the miracles of modernism, joins his gang in manu-
facturing wings, hoping that they may try to flap into flight by
leaping from a barn roof, and is the first to pay a modest price
for progress—a bad landing and a broken leg. The eldest boy, a
teen-ager, swings on the new music—Dixieland—and can actually get Stockholm on his crystal set. With class lines breaking
down, however, he is also able to enter into a love affair with a
girl from the right side of the tracks, the factory manager's
daughter, no less. Which turns out to be confusing to him and
disastrous to her—pregnancy ending in abortion.

The boy's parents, in a way, close the circle. The wife insists
on maintaining domestic routine—her husband has a clean
white shirt each morning to armor him against his idle day. As
they drag on, as his fellow strikers grow more restive and violence flares between them and the strike breakers, he insists on
the efficacy of negotiation, even rescues one of the scabs from a
mob at considerable risk to himself. This, of course, represents
innocence, too. But it is of a kind quite different from his
smallest child's. It is willed innocence, despairingly applied
against the tide of history, a tide which soon sweeps him up
and quite casually destroys him at the bloody climax of the
film.

Obviously, there are analogies between Widerberg's distant
Adalen and our own situation, which is equally prerevolutionary. Obviously, too, there will be radicalized viewers of the

film who will find its sheer beauty, its nostalgic air excessively sentimental. But it seems to me that distance lends understanding to the subject. There is no question about which side engages Widerberg's sympathy. He merely suggests in a low and reasonable voice that though something was gained in that struggle—and in all the labor struggles of the 1930s—something was lost as well, had perhaps been lost before it began, when the whole world acquiesced in industrialization. What was lost was not merely the innocence we witness being destroyed here. There was, as Widerberg shows us, a pace and a texture and a scale in the life of that little town that was proportioned to the size and capacities of ordinary people. The picture ends with the eldest son in mourning for his father but resisting an appeal for full-scale revolution, insisting instead on the need to fully understand what happened in Adalen, '31. It is no cop-out. It is, indeed, subtle and intelligent of Widerberg to insist on this point, for it is what transforms his movie from mere ideology into humane and affecting art.

11/7/69

Saving, perhaps, The Organizer, this is the most sensitive exploration of men on strike that I have ever seen, and one has to wonder where the New Left (and, for that matter, the Old Left) was when it played briefly here. No doubt the quiet, nonexhortative tone hurt it with the politicalized, though there can be no doubt where Widerberg's sympathies lay. No doubt, too, the subject matter put off the huge audience he had found for the really awful Elvira Madigan. But the response to this movie disappointed me almost as much as the response to The Thief. Bad release and promotion hurt the film, of course, but again one must wonder about the devotion of what's left of the movie audience. They could find their way to movies like this if they tried, if they cared about the art as much as they claim.

TELL THEM
WILLIE BOY IS HERE

Twenty years ago a screenwriter named Abraham Polonsky was given his first opportunity to direct one of his own scripts and the result—*Force of Evil*—has enjoyed a reputation as an unacclaimed masterpiece in certain quarters (and quarterlies) ever since. However slight the film's actual merits may have been, there is some rough justice in its underground repute. For Polonsky was blacklisted for his political beliefs shortly after its release, and two decades had to pass before he was allowed to make a movie again.

So the first thing to say about that effort, *Tell Them Willie Boy Is Here,* is a word of thanks to Universal for belatedly attempting to redress the wrong done Polonsky so long ago (though, of course, there can never be adequate recompense for the stupid and cowardly theft of twenty years of a man's professional life). One goes to *Willie Boy* hoping it will be a triumph for its writer-director and prepared to make quite a few concessions to a man forcibly prevented from practicing his art for too long a time. One comes away reluctantly admitting that *Willie Boy* is no more than a pretentious B picture, enlivened by a couple of good action sequences and deadened by the belief, common to Polonsky's generation of film makers, that concern for serious and real social issues is an adequate substitute for art.

In *Willie Boy* we are treated to the news that racial prejudice is bad. The title character (Robert Blake) is an Indian who claims his bride (Katharine Ross) by the ancient tribal method of capture, in the course of which he kills her father. "That's murder," cries the surrounding white community, a good excuse for hunting down Willie Boy as a way of venting its hatred of Indians in general, of this one in particular (he's uppity), and of recapturing, circa 1910, the good old frontier days when the only good redskin was a dead one, etc., etc. Sundry unexceptionable points are developed as the chase proceeds: that mass hysteria and a lynch-mob psychology are easily generated, that do-gooding liberal meddling with a minority culture is almost as devastating as ignorant intolerance, that a good man (Robert Redford, who plays the sheriff reluctantly leading the chase) can be forced by social pressure to do evil.

But while Polonsky gets all his messages straight, his sense of character remains primitive. Blake's Willie is just James Dean in Man-Tan, Miss Ross's Indian girl is of the wooden, or cigarstore, type. Redford's character is supposed to represent a sort of least common denominator, growing from naïve job orientation to awareness of the social immorality in which he is caught up. Unfortunately, Polonsky neglected to write (or at least shoot—there are large discrepancies between the synopsis handed out at screenings and the film as shown) any scenes of him struggling with self and society, and so the character who is potentially most interesting never really comes into clear focus.

William Pechter, a dismal critic, whose only known service to film was keeping Polonsky's name alive through the years, has called him "the richest literary talent to have appeared in American film," and I'm sorry to say Mr. Polonsky appears to have taken such notices seriously. So we have lines like "You'll never catch Willie, Sheriff, he's like a cloud." And this exchange: "It don't make no sense." "Maybe that's the sense it makes." Polonsky even hauls out the famously fatalistic last thought of his best-known script, *Body and Soul*, and has Willie repeat it almost verbatim: "One way or the other, you die in the end." So the rich literary talent turns out to be imitation Odets, tough and laconic and full of pregnant overtones. It was a false—if entertaining—style years ago. Now it seems merely quaint, especially in a period western, far removed from the urban milieu where it was born.

To put it briefly and bluntly, *Willie Boy* is a confused and fragmentary piece of work, not unbearable to watch, but not very interesting either. How it might have been with Mr. Polonsky's talent had it been allowed to develop normally we will never know, but the only deep feeling we develop as we watch *Willie Boy* is for that which might have been, not for that which is.

11/28/69

This film demonstrates very clearly what happens when you try to cram everything—even the western—into the political metaphor. There has been in many of our recent westerns a strong desire to draw an analogy between our treatment of the Indians and our war in Vietnam. But it doesn't really work, because history does not repeat itself in sufficient detail to make such analogies persuasive. Times do change. The suggestion of parallels between then and now in The Wild Bunch seems artful and interesting to me, but heavy-handed Agitprop of Polonsky's sort finally infuriates me with its simple-mindedness and its lack of attention to the basic demands of movie making.

THEY SHOOT HORSES,
DON'T THEY?

They Shoot Horses, Don't They? is an attempt to make a good major movie out of Horace McCoy's good minor novel (now thirty-five years old) in which that weird fad of the thirties, marathon dancing, is used as an existential metaphor. The book cannot quite stand the strain of its transition to an expensive screen property. But that basic metaphor—people exerting themselves to the point of madness, even death, in an absurd activity and in pursuit of an illusory prize—holds up splendidly.

The early reviews have been at some pains to point out the defects in Sydney Pollack's movie and, for the most part, I cannot quarrel with them. He too often substitutes eclectic borrowings from currently chic movie styles for a strongly individual point of view. The color camera does unintentionally prettify the carefully dismal dance hall that is the movie's only setting. Jane Fonda—intelligent and capable—is all wrong as Gloria, the girl so defeated by the marathon and by life that she asks her partner (Michael Sarrazin) to put her out of her misery—which he obligingly does—at the end of the film. She works hard, but she just can't make us believe that she is not a born survivor.

All right, all right. But I still think TSHDT is, flaws and all, one of the outstanding movies of the season. It has an intensity, an energy, that is sustained without letup from start to finish, and those are qualities that, even in such significant films as *Easy Rider* and *Alice's Restaurant*, we get only in isolated sequences. It is good to find a film with the craft—and the passion—to maintain them throughout. Equally important, the movie is very tough-minded, almost to the point of coldness. It makes no attempt to romanticize the children of the Depression forced to live out this squalid nightmare because they had no better economic alternatives (even losing, they get free food and a roof over their heads). There are no politics in the film, no incitement to useless riot. It knows there is no redress this side of heaven for the human condition.

What it gives us in sickening profusion are images of suffering—of dumb animal pain—that will probably stay etched in memory forever. A pregnant Okie girl and her husband dragging themselves around the floor, a movie extra (Susannah York) dressed up like Harlow, hoping to be discovered by a talent scout (even the fantasies of these characters are pathetic), then devastated when it is her partner who gets work—ten days in a Monogram western. Most affecting of all are the sprints—crowd pleasers in which the exhausted dancers must don track suits and race around the floor for ten minutes —the three couples last over the finish line to be summarily eliminated. These are masterfully handled by Pollack—the first of them as a frenzy, the second in slow motion, which is for once used effectively to vary pace and to freeze the anguish of the struggle in virtual caricature.

Finally, one must say a word about Gig Young, who plays the promoter-emcee of the marathon. He has been a durably likable light comedian for almost thirty years. Now he lets his image go. "Yowsah, yowsah, yowsah," he cries in endless false cheer, burbling on to the freaky audience at his freak show about how the competition and "these wonderful young people" represent the true spirit of America, and the fact that he just may be right is, perhaps, the most chilling aspect of the movie. Backstage he is a whiskey-soaked cigarette-voiced cynic who got into this line of work when religious revivalism soured on him. A character developed from a few lines in the novel, he embodies the true mordant vision of Horace McCoy—one of the best and least-recognized of our "tough" writers—and if Gig Young doesn't get an Academy Award for his devastating portrayal of human devastation, there is no justice.

Which is an odd thing to say at the end of a review of *They Shoot Horses, Don't They?*—since that is precisely what the movie has been telling us with an urgency that quite overrides its defects.

1/23/70

M* A* S* H

Ordinarily the letters MASH, besides spelling a familiar word, form one of those outrageously ironic military acronyms standing, as it happens, for a unit known as a Mobile Army Surgical Hospital. However, if you drop three little asterisks into it thusly, M*A*S*H, those letters are magically transformed into something wonderful—the title of one of the best and funniest movies I've seen in years.

In its infinite, mysterious wisdom, the army has established a MASH unit in what must be the largest mud puddle created by the Korean War. Moreover, it has assigned to it a group of irredeemably civilian medicine men, caught up in the doctor's draft and determined (a) to practice all the best and latest techniques of their profession and (b) to retain as much as possible of the free-wheeling atmosphere of the medical school dormitories from which they have but lately graduated.

From this situation it would have been possible to make one of those mild little army farces that became so familiar to us during and after World War Two. But director Robert Altman and screenwriter Ring Lardner, Jr., are intent on playing a much more savage game. When their doctors are not knee deep in mud, they are knee deep in the blood of the casualties that stream endlessly through their installation. They quickly recognize that they will not be able to preserve their sanity—much less their humanity—with mild little japes like stealing the distributor head off the colonel's jeep or by staging a night of funny amateur theatricals. Their struggle is much more desperate than that, the agony in which they are involved too real, too horrible.

Altman insists we understand that point; the stream of jokes flows right along with the flow of blood in the surgery, until finally they intermingle in such a way that one is in the curious position of laughing hysterically at the same time one is averting his eyes from the spilling guts and gore. Moreover, you should go to M*A*S*H forewarned that its humor is not, as they say, in good taste. That is because war is not in good taste either.

For example: the particular nemesis of the young doctors (Elliott Gould, Donald Sutherland, Tom Skerritt) is a veteran incompetent, whose commission and degree amount to a double license to kill. Of course, whenever he loses a patient he drops to his knees, prays up a storm and insists that God's will has been done. They drive him literally mad—and begin the process of reforming the hypocritical R.A. nurse who has been his chief supporter—by bugging the bed they share and broadcasting over the public address system the sounds of their lovemaking. Not nice. Not nice at all. But in context, funny as hell. And a great big helping of just deserts.

There are several other servings almost equally delicious. They have, for example, a lovely treat for the commander of a hospital in Japan who is more interested in proper military courtesy and proper uniforms than he is in providing proper medical care—and who compounds that felony by refusing to treat needy civilians in his facility. They also have a grand climactic surprise for a general whose inane pleasure it is to organize "morale-building" football games while a war is going on—and who makes a nice thing out of betting on them.

But the good guys of M*A*S*H are not just a bunch of merry pranksters on a spree. They are best understood, I think, as Robin Hoods of rationalism, robbing from the rich stockpiles of madness controlled by the people who make (and manage) wars and doling it out in inoculating life-saving doses to the little guys caught up in the mess. They may be vicious in their persecution of the pompous, the petty and the paranoid, but they have a wonderful tenderness with outcasts and underlings and innocents. They manage a miraculous and elaborate cure for a dentist who is suicidal over an imagined loss of virility, they do their best to medicate their messboy out of the draft, they are marvelously kind to a chaplain who is hopelessly befuddled by the sheer speed and amount of living and dying that goes on in their cramped compound.

I have nothing but awed admiration for the way Altman has managed what is obviously a precarious project, one which could have gone all black on him. Or, more likely, have been betrayed by a lack of courage on his part. The thing has a loose, improvisational quality about it—as if his actors were encouraged to be as inventive as possible. But it is never slack, careless or indulgent of their whims or the director's. Every scene is both tight in execution and rich in detail. All concerned are sure about what they are doing, what they mean to say.

What they mean to say is not going to be easy for some people to take, for M*A*S*H challenges us as few comedies—few movies of any kind—challenge us. It asks us to see with some of the alertness, some of the courage its makers did. Some will turn aside from it, but a film like this is what the new freedom of the screen is all about. It redeems a great many of the abuses of that freedom that we have endured in the past few years.

2/20/70

PATTON

Patton bears (in the ads, not on screen) the subtitle A *Salute to a Rebel*. This is an obvious attempt to lure young pacifistic audiences in to see what must from the outside appear to them to be a standard color wide-screen hard-ticket biography of a legendary hawk. I guess they want the kids to think of George S. Patton as the ultimate four-star hippie.

It is a ludicrous thought, but the picture they are so earnestly trying to sell is anything but ludicrous. It is, in fact, one of the most interesting now playing, for the simple reason that Patton was one of the most fascinating near-psychotics ever to achieve prominence in America in any form of endeavor.

"Rebel" does not begin to describe him. He was a polo-playing poetry-writing cavalryman quite seriously convinced that he had lived through several previous incarnations as a warrior hero, and a man mad to practice the old military virtues—honor, courage, super-patriotism—in a world that, though it still goes to war, prefers not to glory in or glorify that activity. Slapping battle-fatigued soldiers, killing mules that got in the way of his lightning advances, blithely suggesting that as long as his Third Army was in position to do so at the end of World War Two it might just as well keep going and polish off the Russians, Patton had nothing but contempt for such hypocrisy. Wearing his ivory-handled six-shooters and the dashing uniforms he designed himself, with his obscene simple-minded exhortations to his troops (a slightly laundered one, delivered in front of a huge American flag opens this movie and sets its surreal tone), he was a liberal's nightmare, all our worst fantasies about the military mind incarnate and rampant.

Moreover, he was the antithesis of the great American military tradition—all those good gray *kindly* men (from Grant and Lee to Eisenhower and Bradley) who have abhorred war and regarded leadership in it as a terrible burden to be taken up reluctantly and dropped gratefully. Patton purely loved it, believed it his destiny to lead a great army in mighty battle. It was in his openness about this love that, even his critics concede, he made his strongest claim on us. Command—life-and-death power over thousands—is a joy, and the American pretense that this is not so is a pain and a bore. It was good of Patton to bring the matter into the open where we could all deal with it, distasteful as the subject is.

Any movie inescapably glorifies its subject. There he is, larger than life, the center of our attention for a couple of hours. Such exposure cannot help but engage our affection, however reluctant we are to surrender it. This is especially true of someone like Patton, who, with his wildly exaggerated personality, his inability to hide any thought or emotion, comes to seem literally superhuman, even (God help us) rather endearingly funny—especially when he is played by that grand actor George C. Scott, who communicates such infectious joy when he has a really juicy part like this one.

Yet the film is carefully honest. Much of Patton's dialogue is taken from the historical record, and Franklin Schaffner has directed it in a deliberately flat, straight style, which increases our sense of objectivity about the man. He may have been crazy as a coot, but he was also a genius of mechanized war, very likely the only one we had when we discovered we needed one. Thus *Patton* makes us think hard about this paradox: that though we civilians despise the military mind (of which his was virtually a caricature), we have yet to devise a way of getting along without it. These emotional DPs, pursuing their anti-diluvian dreams of glory, do serve us. Pacifists had better go see *Patton* and study the face of their enemy, their savior, their brother.

2/27/70

FELLINI SATYRICON,
THE DAMNED,
ZABRISKIE POINT

In the numberless interviews Federico Fellini has given out in the course of publicizing his new film (pretentiously known as *Fellini Satyricon*, despite the fact that it relies quite heavily on the *Satyricon* of Petronius for the incidents that serve to trigger his imagery), he has seemed to want to have it two ways. On the one hand he has insisted that his film has no "meaning" in the conventional sense of the word; on the other he has with equal firmness insisted that there is an analogy between the decaying society he has placed on screen and our own. He has also flung out a challenge: we must not bring to his movie any preconceptions about what a film should or should not be. If we do, and if we insist on them, we run the risk of being judged out of it, not with it. The kids, he says, dig what he's doing, apparently because of their almost divine cultural innocence.

Maybe so. But in evaluating Fellini's film, his unresolved contradiction about intent is more significant than the challenge to join the youth culture (such challenges becoming, like patriotism, the last refuge of scoundrels). In any case, the best films of the past few years have forced us to abandon the conventional expectations we used to take to the movies. We know, without Fellini telling us, that they are likely to be free-form voyages of self-discovery, attempts to reveal in public the private preoccupations of their makers. Which means that his *Satyricon* is hardly the radical departure Fellini thinks it is. Nor is his sensibility as he reveals it to us here so profound or so disturbing as he thinks it is either. Quite the opposite; his is a mind of truly stupefying banality.

In form, the film is merely a series of incidents in which a young decadent, Encolpius, journeys with a friend from one unspecified place to another across a scenic, hellish imaginary landscape of Fellini's own devising. Each turn in his path brings him face to face with some spectacular new depravity. Very often these are revealed to us in quite striking imagery—the wedding on a slave ship of a homosexual pair, the abduction of an albino hermaphrodite and dwarfish oracle from its grotto, an encounter with a mock minotaur in a labyrinth. Equally often, however, the imagery is simply an attempt to wow us with spectacle, as in a visualization of Petronius' most famous scene, Trimalchio's banquet. But striking or not, none of the incidents may be said to advance our understanding of plot or character, conventions Fellini has totally abandoned. Nor can they be said to help us penetrate deeper and deeper into the director's mind, which, given a mind worth penetrating, would have been both interesting and a valid rationale. In tone and development the incidents turn out to be curiously repetitive (Fellini's preoccupation with the homoerotic is, shall we say, a drag). And before long whatever sense of adventure we had felt over the opportunity of exploring his inner life with him is dissipated. We begin to feel that we are trapped in an ill-catalogued but highly specialized junkyard.

The work can only be understood, I think, as ritual, and in fairness I should note that on the night I saw it many in the audience assumed attitudes of near-religious veneration. They must have been either transfixed or experiencing the early stages of catatonia, a condition I would have welcomed if only to stop the St. Vitus's dance of my cramped, protesting limbs.

Ritual, of course, implies celebration, and so we must ask what Fellini is asking us to celebrate—his own virtuosity or his vision of decay? The first is impossible, for however powerful his images, they are not enough to sustain us all by themselves for the length of his picture. That leaves us with his vision—

and with the contradiction I mentioned at the beginning. If the film has no conventional meaning, if it is no more than a dredging operation in his unconscious, then we are forced to the conclusion that he is a man without sufficient wit, intelligence or maturity to hold our attention for very long. If, on the other hand, we are to accept his insistence that there is an analogy between his imaginary world and our own, we are forced to the conclusion that his vision is severely limited.

Regrettably, one finds the *Satyricon* confirming what one has suspected ever since Fellini abandoned the neorealism of his early, best films, which is that his mind is very nearly empty. Rattling around in it is this one big feeling—that ours is a time of almost total degeneration, out of which there may arise some new, as yet undreamed, civilization. This may well be true (or untrue), but one is obliged, if one is an artist, to do something more with the proposition than persist in illustrating it with ever more baroque, ever more hysterical demonstrations of it. It is obvious that one cannot be "faithful" to Petronius, if only because the work survives as mere fragments. Even so, his tone—cool, ironic, mocking—might well have guided Fellini, as it guided F. Scott Fitzgerald in the creation of the finest modern work suggested by the *Satyricon*, which is, of course, *The Great Gatsby*, that model of economy, clarity and resonating power.

One begins to imagine, however, that Fellini is not as impervious to outside influences as he would like us to think. For his *Satyricon* climaxes a period of a few months in which the other two leading Italian directors, Luchino Visconti and Michelangelo Antonioni, have loosed similar visions upon the world. One begins to think that along the Via Veneto some kind of communal sensibility is operating, for their films are also studies of decay. Indeed, Visconti's *The Damned* may well be the most curious of them all. In some ways it is the most conventional movie—an intricately plotted attempt to examine through the microcosm of a great Krupp-like family the conditions that gave rise to Nazism in Germany some forty years ago.

But the microcosm turns out to be a distorting lens. One emerges from *The Damned* with the strong impression that the yeast causing the rise of the Third Reich was exotic depravity—transvestism, child molestation, incest. No one denies that the prewar German power elite was, to put it mildly, an unhealthy organism. But to imply a cause-effect relationship between sexual perversion and political perversion is both historically inaccurate and socially irresponsible. For it has an odd, insulating effect on us, making us feel that totalitarianism is a rare bloom, one that can flower only in very special soil. There are, to be sure, plenty of arguments against the "banality of evil" explanation of fascism, but it does have one great virtue: it makes us aware, banality being an omnipresent fact of human existence, that evil can happen here (or there or anywhere) at any time. To render Nazism exotic, a once-in-a-lifetime phenomenon, is to miss the point. Granted Visconti does so in grand operatic style (imagine Verdi trying to write a Wagnerian opera), granted that such an enterprise by its very strangeness will catch unforgettably in the mind. Even so, it is a dismal movie.

Antonioni's *Zabriskie Point* shares some of the defects of its competitors. Like Visconti, he is a stranger attempting to make sense of a strange land (in this case, modern America). Like Fellini, he is here (for the first time in his distinguished career) primarily an imagist, untrammeled by any strong storytelling compulsion. Nevertheless, he is artist enough—and more than enough—to have overcome these defects. But in telling such a story as he has to tell—about a radical youth wrongly suspected of killing a cop in a campus riot and of a hippie girl who is sort of like, you know, drifting and of how they meet in the desert and make love in the wasteland and then part, he to be killed, she to be radicalized by his needless death—he gets distracted. Like so many European visitors, he falls under the spell of the American vastness, the enormous emptiness of our spaces. There is great beauty in some of his visions, but there is also, for a man of his caliber, a dismaying familiarity about many of them. We are, I think, to understand that the empty land is the objective correlative of an emptiness of spirit he found here. But that, too, is a cliché and no better than a half-truth. There are moments, particularly in the early portions of the film, where I imagined Antonioni had satire on his mind, and not merely satire aimed at the established establishment targets but at our hare-brained revolutionaries as well. Alas, he does not stick with it. Or with anything very long. The tensions he has created in his best work (*L'Avventura, Blow-Up*) through the use of mystery stories with existential overtones is missing. So is the psychological richness he is able to create with wordless glances and gestures. Even the most striking images in *Zabriskie Point* lack the rich texture, the overtones of meaning that he has achieved in the past. One never feels compelled to engage with him, to wrest from him those meanings that he has yielded up so stubbornly in the past. The uniqueness of *Zabriskie Point* in his canon is not that one rejects it, finds it a failure. That is a disappointment for which we are prepared when we confront the work of any artist. What is odd is the superficiality of the experience we undergo, the ease with which we escape it. I expect that with Fellini; I never expected it, am amazed to find it in Antonioni.

3/20/70

THE BALLAD OF
CABLE HOGUE

One great subject obsesses director Sam Peckinpah. It is the closing of the American frontier around the turn of the century. He has made other films about the west, but his best work is that in which he gives free rein to his complex feelings about this historical event. Mostly he seems to believe that we took more of our sense of identity, as individuals and as a nation, from the frontier than we realize (or perhaps are willing to admit), and that we have been lost and drifting ever since it ceased to offer us the potential of personal freedom radically and often violently defined.

In *Ride the High Country*, almost a decade ago, he gave his most balanced, most carefully controlled statement on this subject in a film of surpassing beauty and subtlety, a film which, incidentally, gave Randolph Scott and Joel McCrea the roles of their lives to close out their careers as western heroes. Last year, in *The Wild Bunch*, which I think was probably the best American film of the year, he presented a more violent version of his vision, here and there flawed, but at the very least a masterpiece of the action director's craft. Now, in *The Ballad of Cable Hogue*, he takes up his great theme in a new mood— comic, elegiac, leisurely and peaceable. I think it is less than his best work—but a great deal better than about 90 per cent of the stuff to which we are ordinarily subjected at the movies.

Rambling and episodic in development, the film really does have the improvisatory, folkish, legendary quality of a ballad (though the temptation to present such a piece as musical accompaniment to the picture is, thank God, resisted). It recounts in deliberately simplified—almost childlike—terms the title character's abandonment in the desert (without food, water or weapons) by his prospecting companions; his discovery, when he is nearly dead of thirst, of a spring that both saves and changes his life. For it is located on a stage line and is the only water for a very long way. There he opens a modest hostelry and there, after years of profitless wandering in the wilderness, he prospers.

Much besides material prosperity comes to him as he waits by the side of the road—a fraudulent preacher (David Warner) whose relationship to the film's main line is ambiguous, but who is at least an interesting character; a good-hearted prostitute (Stella Stevens) with whom he shares a lovely idyll that seems to make the desert bloom; a chance at last to revenge himself on the men who left him to die out there in the first place. His final visitor, however, is the modern world, automobiles jouncing along the stage track, and with it comes death, as it always does in a Peckinpah movie. But the manner of its arrival—casual, humorous, surprising—and the manner of its greeting—graceful and even charming—is done with a sense of beauty and irony that was, for me, overwhelming.

I don't want to discuss in detail the last sequence of the film, since so much of its effectiveness depends on your being unprepared for it. This much, however, should be said—that it is so good and right that it entirely disarms the vagrant critical thoughts that had been gathering before its arrival. For one must admit that the humor implicit in some of the earlier scenes is not fully realized on screen and that some of that which is realized is disappointingly familiar, with archetypes too often dwindling into clichés. More than once Peckinpah and his film are saved simply by the fact that Jason Robards is present in the title role. His Cable Hogue, a man who talks frankly and openly to God, a man of sentiment, rough-hewn common sense and primitive capitalist shrewdness, is a wonderful character—a walking summary of the pioneer virtues as Peckinpah sees them. It is, in short, a dream role—the best Robards has ever had in the movies, and he is more than up to its demands; indeed, one suspects he was born to fulfill them. A lesser actor might have stomped and shouted his way through it, but he manages to shade the role with marvelous delicacy, in the process providing Peckinpah with the rock-solid foundation for a movie that is dangerously careless in some aspects of its carpentry, creaking and swaying as it shifts under the pressures he applics to it. Even so, it is a curiously compelling film. Like a child's playhouse, we come to love it not for its perfect symmetry but for the open way it expresses the feelings of its creator.

3/27/70

WOODSTOCK

Fairly early in *Woodstock* (*The Movie,* as the ads helpfully subtitle it) Joan Baez comes on and in that incredibly pure and beautiful voice of hers sings, "I dreamed I saw Joe Hill last night," an old radical song I haven't heard since my days as a parlor pink almost twenty years ago, when we used to gather round the low-fi and listen to Paul Robeson's recording of it, singing along with him occasionally. At that point I began to feel pretty good about *Woodstock,* and I stayed with that feeling throughout this three-hour filmed record of last summer's famous "three days of peace and music."

Miss Baez's song was quite simply a very useful reference point, a thing I was surprised to discover could be shared across generational lines. I don't really think these kids have any more right to strong emotions about a martyred IWW organizer than we did back in the fifties; the song generates for them, as it did for us, a kind of false nostalgia. None of us experienced the simpler emotions, simpler social ideals, of what seem to have been simpler times, but we profoundly wish we had. So that much at least we share.

Indeed, it seems to me that the entire Woodstock experience may have been in the last analysis an exercise in nostalgia. Here was this terrible mess—too many people, too much mud and garbage, not enough food, shelter, medicine—and yet it was governed peacefully by no authority figures more menacing than the guys manning the public address system. Compensat-

ing for the inconveniences the crowd endured, certain amenities, in particular good music and plenty of pot, were available, and there was very little crime and less anti-social behavior than the average New Yorker endures every day of his
life.

In consequence there was much talk, over that P.A. system
and in the crowd, about Woodstock being temporarily the
second largest city in New York (untrue, incidentally) and
thus by implication a model of the humane and pacifistic
manner in which the youth culture would govern if given the
chance. The analogy, of course, is false. All Woodstock really
proved is that this generation can rise to uncomfortable occasions as well as any. But they all knew their agony was finite—
you can't starve to death over a weekend—which is precisely
the opposite of what the urban dweller knows.

So the lesson of the Woodstock experience is more modest
than you may have been led to think. Still, Michael Wadleigh's
film shows the kids were clearly good-natured, cool, funny.
There are wonderful vignettes—a girl who lost her sister "during Richie Havens" and wants to find her "because she has to
be in court on Monday"; a boy who shrewdly notes that
"people who are nowhere are coming because they think
people who are somewhere are here"; best of all, a stoned cat
who is under the misapprehension the film makers are doing a
movie about the Portosan equipment, accepts it as a way-out
example of doing your own thing, and whose only comment is
"Outa sight." Cool, very cool.

In short, the film should convince even the most dedicated
traditionalist that the members of the counter culture are
entirely recognizable in basic human terms, whatever their
verbal and sartorial eccentricities, even perhaps that with minimal effort they can be communicated with—no small accom-
plishment these days. And even if one suspects the movie of
somewhat softening the more abrasive qualities of the kids, it is
superb with their music. Wadleigh makes very effective use of
multiple images, the split screen and the freeze frame to

heighten the power of performances, and the sound recording is particularly good. One is focused in right on the music as one imagines the huge audience at Woodstock could not have been. The strength and artistry of individuals like Havens and Jimi Hendrix, the gently spaced out quality of John Sebastian are particularly impressive. And the split screen is very effective in revealing the inner dynamics of groups like The Who, Jefferson Airplane, Country Joe and the Fish.

But the biggest miracle of *Woodstock* is that it holds you, despite its great plotless length, despite the fact that you may not be part of the culture it celebrates. At Woodstock the line between art and experience, between artists and audience was erased. Apparently there was a rare kind of sharing there, a kind of sharing that the early visionaries of the screen envisioned their art helping to create. Seen in this perspective, Woodstock (and *Woodstock*) seem important steps in realizing a very old, very American dream. That it is always pleasant, often powerful—and endlessly stimulating to one's cultural imagination—is, of course, a blessing. But it is as a way of seeing what the kids are up to, without fawning all over them, that it may have its greatest merit.

4/24/70

THE FORBIN PROJECT

Science fiction has always lived in the bargain basement of the movies, generally the work of its least gifted creators and its most budget-conscious producers. Preoccupied, in almost child-like fashion, with mutants and monsters, it is held in special contempt even (perhaps one should say especially) by devotees of s-f literature. For as John Baxter puts it in his wise little book on the subject (*Science Fiction in the Cinema*), the sci fi writer typically believes "in order and the duty of human kind to observe it." His classic theme is to show prideful man care-lessly tampering with that order and the desperate efforts of reason to reassert itself before we are wiped out. At the flicks, on the other hand, they are preoccupied with ghoulies and ghosties, of intellectual interest to Jungian shrinks, if anyone.

Moreover, as science has marched on, right into the center of our consciousness, it has tended both to be more compellingly imaginative than the fiction about it, just as scary in its impli-cations. Perhaps more important, it has rendered us too sophis-ticated to regard the creature from the black lagoon, for ex-ample, as seriously spooky. As a result, our sci fi has tended to shift over to the social sciences and to mysticism for inspiration —*Planet of the Apes* being cultural anthropology run amuck, *2001* being either an exercise in transcendental meditation or a bloody bore, depending on your point of view.

In these circumstances it is pleasant to offer a modest salute to a modest little film called *The Forbin Project*, which stars no one you ever paid much attention to, is made with no more than routine competence, but which intelligently avoids the more common pitfalls of its genre while deploying its more engaging clichés in an attractive fashion—ah, there you are, girl scientist, very pretty when you shed that white coat.

Anyway, there's this Dr. Forbin (complete with a slight Germanic accent), who with the cheerful acquiescence of the military-industrial complex has concocted a real mother of a computer, into which he has plugged all our defensive hardware. Being very brainy and very quick off the mark, it can respond to any threat anywhere with just the right degree of force. Eliminates the possibility of human error, too.

Nice. We see the National Security Council sitting around congratulating itself on its own redundance when clang-clang-clang, Colossus, for that is its name, cries, "Tilt." The Russians, by God, have made a big machine, too. Well, sir, nothing will do but to arrange for the machines to have a tête-à-tête. And since their creators have thoughtfully given them the capacity for intellectual growth, they run through all of human knowledge in a matter of days and start winging it—inventing their own language, for example, which no human can understand. The next logical step is taking over the world.

Various paltry human efforts to daunt this scheme, though clever enough to interest you and me, scarcely bother the machines. For, you see, they either personally control all the weapons that could be used against them or they are capable of fighting them off. Which leaves one with the possibility of sending a troop of Boy Scouts armed with slingshots and BB guns against them. Not much use, since they are dug into mountains and reinforced with steel and concrete and who knows what all else.

None of this is any great shakes as screen art, since, as Baxter says, "characters have no functions except as symbols in the writer's development of his premise," and since the director is necessarily enslaved to the plot, which, as Kingsley Amis says, is the "hero" of most sci fi.

But it is crisply done, with nice touches of humor (as when the machine kindly interests itself in Forbin's sex life); it further develops the most interesting idea in 2001, which is that machines may be more quirky and amusing than the engineers who build them and run them; and it vivifies one of the omnipresent fantasies of our day, which is that the machines may possibly be on the brink of taking over. Finally, the picture takes leave of us in a nice shaky mood, under the impression that Old Colossus may be just as unbeatable as it thinks it is.

At the very least, *The Forbin Project* is solid entertainment, solving as it does the problem of presenting us with a believable monster at this late, sophisticated date. At most, it raises some issues that, if we cannot take them entirely seriously, we cannot dismiss too airily, either. Good show, chaps.

5/17/70

This is, obviously, a tribute to a genre and to the brave people who continue to try to keep it alive. The film received as good a set of notices as any in 1970, but not being a fancy item, the middle-brow audience skipped it, as it skipped The Ballad of Cable Hogue. They have reached that masochistic point where they will subject themselves to the pain of failed art rather than embrace the honest pleasure of good—and even instructive— entertainment. Really, I think this notion that movies must be art—or at least demonstrate aspirations in that direction—has reached lunatic levels. I accept my full share of the blame, for I've nattered on about the necessity for taking movies seriously, but sometimes I feel like cutting my tongue out.

GETTING STRAIGHT

Within the space of too few minutes at the end of *Getting Straight* a great deal happens to a decent, confused, liberal-minded graduate student named Harry Bailey: he blows his cool (and his chance for a degree) in his Master's orals, wins the beautiful girl he thought he had lost the night before and joins the student revolution that has, somewhat inexplicably, struck the second-rate campus where he has been trying with comical desperation to convert himself into a square peg of the sort that pinions society, currently fashionable opinion to the contrary notwithstanding.

If this sounds like someone flooded the movie's engine at a crucial moment, you should know that the mixture throughout what is always threatening to be a worthwhile film is exceedingly rich. There are, for example, two—count them, two—full-scale riots, a car that keeps falling apart in what the makers assume is a humorous fashion, a computer running amuck, a pothead freaking out, and a procession of academic archetypes as complete as you're ever likely to encounter—dumb jock, phony-liberal prexy, sold-out PR man, ed-school dean statistically quantifying students instead of relating to them, black militant, female militant, even a fuddy old Mr. Chips.

Now, one of the troubles with this mob is precisely that it is a mob—there is not enough time to sort it out, individuate its members by means of careful detail work. They all begin and end as cartoon creatures, which would be all right if farce was all that director Richard Rush and writer Robert Kaufman had in mind. But they are after different game as well—"relevant" social comment, for example, and in the case of Harry Bailey, sober multi-dimensional characterization as well. Indeed, it is because they occasionally succeed in the first of these goals and consistently succeed in the second (thanks largely to Elliott Gould's extraordinary gifts) that *Getting Straight* is such a frustrating, even angering, experience.

Quite often it reaches out toward a genuine understanding of the fears and blindnesses of the people who compose the establishment it (rightly) views with dismay, quite often it flashes signs of understanding those defects of intelligence and stability that afflict the youngsters with whom it (justifiably) sympathizes. But it will not remain tough-minded and even-handed for long, being intent on staying cozy with the romantic self-image of its intended audience—that "youth market" everyone in the movie game is now desperately wooing.

This is nowhere more clear than in the handling of Gould's character. He is a good man—he has been an activist in all the right causes and protests—and now, realizing that all that is a young man's game, he merely wants to get a degree. A sell-out is not his goal; he wants to teach kids whom others regard as unteachable, honorably engage himself in an honorable profession. That the world's turmoil is more than usually distracting in our epoch he understands; that the thrill of both political activism and big-spending consumerism will be denied him as a humble toiler in the desiccated vineyards of education he accepts. But he will follow the call of his talent, will define himself in his maturity, his own way.

Whereupon they start rigging the movie against him. His attempt to mediate between student militants and the administration fails, not so much because the issues between them are non-negotiable but because, it seems to me, they are non-existent, the sorts of problems you could solve by calling out the student council instead of the National Guard. Then Harry is denied his teaching certificate for no very good reason.

And as for that Master's exam, the final step in his radicalization, it is set up as no-win situation. In all three instances the script refuses Harry the use of his intelligence and his moral force—the very qualities that make him so appealing—when he really needs them. The idea is to make him a victim, make us believe that such a man would smile benignly on students laying waste to a building, would pick up a brick and heave it through a window in an act of symbolic solidarity.

This is worse than aesthetically unsatisfying and psychologically unpersuasive. It is, I think, immoral. For *Getting Straight* is telling us that we have reached so desperate a pass that there is no hope for the humane liberal values Harry represents, that he (and those of us who share his values) has no choice but violence. This is not so—not yet, anyway. The notion that the young have exhausted all hope of peacefully redressing their grievances is a dull-witted exaggeration, as, indeed, is the notion that they are really an oppressed class by any seriously applied historical standard. To frivolously encourage their present paranoia is irresponsible and superficial. In the context of a film that has thrown everything but the chemistry department's sink at us in an attempt to overwhelm our critical capacity, it is the final sign of commercial corruption. (The book on which it is based is, it might be noted, one of those rueful non-revolutionary college novels popular a decade and more ago.) Movie makers have fought for years to gain creative independence from the studios; it is dismaying to see them so quickly surrendering it to the presumed opinions of their audience! They should have called this one *Going Crooked*.

5/29/70

Let me make one brief blunt statement about this pile of garbage. It represented the nadir of Hollywood's drive to give the children what it thought they wanted. In a crowded field, it was the worst of them all.

MY NIGHT AT MAUD'S

"There is," says critic Andrew Sarris, "no greater spectacle in
the cinema than a man and a woman talking away their share
of eternity together." I happened to read that passage just
before seeing *My Night at Maud's,* and it seems to me that at
the very least its director, Eric Rohmer, brilliantly proves
Sarris's proposition. In so doing, he flies in the face of the
prevailing film aesthetic, which offers such warm comfort to all
those directors who have been gouging away at our eyeballs
with all the very latest instruments of visual torment.

Mr. Rohmer's idea of a really big eye trip is a glimpse in
black and white of some rather ordinary scenery passing by
outside a car window and his notion of a hot editing technique
is to use a reverse angle right where you'd expect to find a
reverse angle. Mostly his people just sit around and talk, un-
aided by Shavian or even Mankiewiczian wit. What they talk
around and about is a self-confessed mediocrity (Jean-Louis
Trintignant) who takes his minuscule adventures of mind and
spirit with desperate seriousness. An engineer working for a
large firm in a small town, he is deep into calculus and Pascal,
the remarkably dull sermons offered down at the local cathedral and, most important, Jansenism, the theological doctrine
that denies free will in favor of predestination. A friend, for
devious reasons, introduces him to the lady of the title, and
Trintignant passes a couple of ambivalent days with her, fearful that she will upset his conviction that he is predestined to

marry a blonde he has glimpsed (but not met) at the cathedral.

Turns out, by God (the phrase is used literally), that he *was* supposed to marry the blonde and that, indeed, she was more closely interwoven into his destiny than anyone suspected and that in the end things work out just as nicely as one hopes they will if Jansen was right. But the details of the story, if one can so dignify the skeleton over which Rohmer has stretched his movie, are of less consequence than the remarkable manner in which these ordinarily pretentious, faintly foolish, incredibly *verbal* people compel our attention—the shifting of a glance or of a position in a chair becomes an event as important as, say, a murder or a cavalry charge in an ordinary movie.

How soberly involved everyone is! How comic is the care with which they examine themselves and each other about their motives and the effect their small statements and actions are having! In particular, how moving it is to watch Trintignant prove himself one of the master screen actors of our time as he studies the life flowing past him to see if it proves or disproves the theories he has been toying with. Years ago D. W. Griffith perceived that one of the unique qualities of the movie camera was its ability to "photograph thought," a quality that has not been, by and large, adequately pursued in films of late but which is the principal aim of Rohmer, who is fortunate indeed to have found in Trintignant and friends (François Fabien, Marie-Christine Barrault, Antoine Vitez) actors who can give him some thoughts to shoot.

I doubt that any major American actors would risk such quiet roles in so quiet a picture, and I doubt that, in our present overheated climate, a man like Rohmer could obtain backing for a project containing so little action, so little "youth appeal." Is there, in fact, an American producer who understands that eroticism can be intellectual, may involve neither coupling nor stripping? Is there one who would risk a satire on the modern demi-intellectual's insistence on analyzing everything to death that you do not begin to laugh at until after you have left the theater and the lovely absurdity of the whole enterprise begins ticking like a time bomb in your brain? Is there one who would risk a dollar on a man whose style can only be described as classic formalism? I doubt it. Which means that if you value these virtues, you're going to have to read a lot of subtitles in order to rediscover them.

Still, *My Night at Maud's* has found a surprisingly large audience in New York among the thoughtfully silent minority, and I'm sure there exist elsewhere enough people of similar bent to give this dry, delicate, elegant novella of a film the audience it deserves.

6/19/70

I ended up voting for My Night at Maud's as the best film of 1970. The reason was simple—its exemplary simplicity of image combined with its exemplary complexity of thought. The movie had a purity, a wit, a sense of style that were, for me, breathtaking. It, along with The Rise of Louis XIV, The Passion of Anna, The Wild Child, and Tristana, made me think that possibly we are at the beginning of the end of baroque film making, that we are about to witness a return to a radical simplification of method. One need only compare it to something like Catch-22, the final (one hopes) effulgence, to see the virtues in this method. It has also the advantage of being inexpensive, and this may recommend it to cost-conscious producers. The trouble is that it requires genuine intelligence, a profound and disciplined austerity to make such films, and these are not qualities that are very highly developed among American directors.

CATCH-22

There are two basic ways we go crazy. One is existentially, that is, through the day-to-day accumulation of fragmentary evidence that the world is not quite the rational place we were brought up to believe it is. The other is traumatically, through some highly dramatic incident that breaks the mind instead of merely bending it once too often a little more than we can stand.

It can, of course, be argued that we come out at roughly the same place no matter which route we take there, but it seems to me the former method of freaking out is the more common and therefore the most instructive to study. So it must have seemed to Joseph Heller when he wrote *Catch-22*, which was an extensive but really quite delicate examination of the desperate stratagems individuals employ for purposes of survival when they are placed inside a huge hierarchical bureaucratic machine. His choice of subject—the U.S. Air Force bombing everything in sight during World War Two—naturally heightened our horror, provided the dramatic pressure a novel requires. But basically his business was to give us a paradigm of all the mad machines all of us can get caught up in, in peace as well as war. The great popular success of *Catch-22* was based on our recognition of this fact and, more important, I think, on our appreciation of the cool, even offhand, manner Heller used in tossing off the most outrageous characters and incidents, the reserved manner in which he suggested his point of view toward the terrible dehumanizing forces at work not only in modern war but in modern life in general.

Mike Nichols's movie version of the novel is, in tone, as hot and heavy as the original was cool and light. Indeed, I think it fair to say that he and writer Buck Henry have mislaid every bit of the humor that made the novel not only emotionally bearable but aesthetically memorable, replacing it with desperately earnest proof that they hate war. Part of their adaptive failure was probably inevitable. So much of the book's effectiveness stemmed from the rich matrix of relationships between its characters, the wide, in fact endless, range of their responses to the situation they shared. In the compressive process of screen adaptation a good deal was bound to be lost. Even so, these movie people seem to me only the ghosts of their former selves, more evidence of Nichols's desire to conspicuously consume acting talent than of a gift for skillfully employing it in larger numbers than he has heretofore attempted.

But the key to the film's almost total failure lies in its restructuring of the novel. It is shot as if it were a single hallucinatory flashback suffered by Yossarian, Heller's Everyman-turned-Bombardier. This gives Nichols several advantages. It conveniently focuses a sprawling book in which Yossarian, though central, was not really dominant. It allows him to jumble the time sequence, which in practical terms allows a director to throw in shockers—a nude here, a gush of blood there, a sight gag anywhere at all—whenever the pace lags. It also allows him to mix styles with some impunity—a bit of Bergman, a little filch from Fellini, some mocking references to the epic manner of our old war movies, a lot of theatrical expressionism, just plain pretty shooting when all else fails. It also excuses the lack of depth in all the characters that swim through his bad dream; after all, a man hallucinating doesn't see people in novelistic dimensions, does he?

Far from seeming wild and free, this dream structure struck me as both inhumanly and desperately manipulative, for it instantly imposes on both the material and the audience a single very simple point of view: I'm crazy, they're crazy, we're all crazy in this crazy world. The characters can never wriggle free of it and live for so much as a single wayward, truly human moment. We as an audience are never allowed to think, feel, respond as we will. We are as trapped at a single level of response as ever we were in those hack war movies to which Nichols affects superiority.

Worse, however, is the fact that Yossarian's hallucination circles back no less than three times to a single incident, the death in his arms of a stranger, a replacement gunner killed on his first mission in Yossarian's plane. This is the trauma that "explains" Yossarian, as Rosebud explained Citizen Kane, as childhood sexual alarms explained frigidity, nymphomania and God knows what all in a hundred forgotten movies of yesteryear. Yes, of course, the incident occurred in the book and it had its effect on Yossarian's eventual decision to desert and row to Sweden. But it was one of literally dozens of incidents, exchanges, imaginings that first made him mad and then made him run for his life. To simplify him in so radical a fashion is to betray him as a human being and to betray that complexity of vision, that vigorous and skillful art, which was responsible not only for his creation but for the powerful hold *Catch-22* has exercised on a generation.

                                        7/3/70

One could say it about many films, but one might as well say it about this one: in addition to its other defects, Catch-22 contains not one single character it is possible for us to care about as a human being, no one with whom we can identify. It is therefore without hope of giving us pleasure. The best we can do, the best its supporters could do, is to appreciate it—which is not the same thing. I should say, in fact, that the greatest defect of the American film in recent years—and one that is not shared generally by films from abroad—is this failure to remember that all fictive art requires our sympathetic engagement in the fate of one or more characters before we can attend to such other matters as may be on the artist's mind. No one can object to the general point of view presented by this film, but this agreement is not enough to sustain us. Neither is the feverish technique of the director. One understands that after all those years of dealing with sentimental archetypes a certain number of deliberate assaults on the audience's sensibility were necessary for our film makers as a kind of corrective, both for their talents and for our expectations about movies. But enough is enough. The theater of cruelty seems to me mostly self-romanticizing— the artist as rebel hero—and the pose is tiresome, finally. And self-defeating. Expecting the worst, most of us have learned to simply stay away from all movies. Which is what is now happening—unless the reviews guarantee (no matter what else they say) the bland, old-fashioned banalities of Airport. Those still regularly attending movies seem to do so dutifully, resolved to take their cultural medicine like little soldiers. It's no wonder television and the revival houses are doing so well.

We must also ask ourselves, I think, if a film like Catch-22 truly reflects the reality of our era. Is man really as vile as films like this insist he is? If so, how come it has happened overnight and only locally, as it were? How come, that is, that our movies have just discovered this remarkable fact and how come the rest of the world's film makers seem not to have noticed it? Does Mike Nichols really know something Ingmar Bergman doesn't? I think not. I think American show biz is in a swoon over its recent discovery of the tragic sense of life, preoccupied with it in an obsessive fashion and unable to place it in perspective as one of the facts of life, but not the only and not even, necessarily, the central one. It's possible that our movie makers will soon attain a certain perspective on this matter, cease screaming in pain and start showing us how some people have learned to live with it and still function as concerned and caring human beings. I hope so. Because, to tell the truth, I can't live much longer as a critic in this insane adolescent uproar and I'm entirely sympathetic with those non-combatants at home in front of their TV sets while I'm out being assaulted in the line of duty.

THE PASSION
OF ANNA

With *The Passion of Anna* the art of Ingmar Bergman reaches its pinnacle. Though it is one of his rare color films, it is in every important way his most austere and elliptical work, a thing of silences and enigmas that nevertheless makes very clear the tragic vision of life that possesses its author.

Gone at last are all traces of the baroque symbolism that marked—and often marred—his early work. Gone, too, is the yearning for evidence of the presence of God in the world. Bergman has, I think, accepted His death and, indeed, seems to find that event no longer worthy of comment. His absence is now simply one of the terms of our existence. Darkness is now settling over the island to which Bergman (and, of course, his characters) has retreated for four consecutive films, a darkness that is relieved by only the bleakest of winter lights.

That island is, of course, a psychological landscape as well as a physical one, and Bergman has gone there in the same spirit that his people have gone to that stark, spare place—out of revulsion at the meaningless cruelty of the world. There is no escape from it here, as *The Passion of Anna* makes abundantly clear, but it is at least somewhat reduced—to something like a manageable non-institutional human scale. Or so they permit themselves to hope.

This time those gathered here to await the end include the lady of the title, who yearns for a perfect transcendent love and probably, before the film began, accidentally-on-purpose killed her husband and child for failing to provide same; a financial failure, once jailed for forgery, who takes up with Anna mostly because she is there and may assuage the terrible emptiness he feels; an architect whose distinguished public career seems a mockery to him and who now takes (and endlessly catalogues) pictures which, one imagines, he intends to be a complete record of our increasing inhumanity; his wife, who has apparently not found even the transitory rewards that the others have savored in life.

Not a great deal "happens" to these people. The failure has an unsatisfactory sexual encounter with the architect's wife, a year-long "relationship" with Anna that always remains distant, cool. The architect (possibly a surrogate for Bergman) watches, his wife simply slips out of focus entirely. A madman, who might be any of the above (except the failure) or none of them, runs loose on the island, slaughtering animals. A man who may or may not have been falsely accused of this crime commits suicide. Anna tries to kill her lover, fails, drives off, and we are left with an image of him, an image that grows increasingly grainy until it looks like yet another modern horror photographed off a television screen, running first this way, then that, in an agony of indecision. Should he follow her or not?

We do not care. It is not important. Any action will, we know, turn out to be without resolving meaning. It will end only in the passage of more time. It is, in its quiet way, a shattering ending, brilliant both in its economy and its clarity. Bergman has, in that concluding sequence, as well as in the rest of the picture, stripped his art bare of all that is non-essential, all that offers any promise of warmth. Such hope as he extends stands outside the frame of the film. Periodically, we see a clapstick with one of the actor's names on it, after which he or she faces the camera in close-up and discusses (in what only seems an improvised manner) the motives, the possible future of his or her character. Actorlike, they entertain some optimism for them, implying art may be impossible without entertaining at least a shred of hope.

Maybe so. In any case, the art in this instance is of the highest order. The controlled brilliance of Bergman's favorite actors—Max von Sydow, Liv Ullmann, Bibi Andersson—must be mentioned. So must the psychological depth with which they—and Bergman—invest these people. They are never abstractions. They are, God help us, our brethren. To spend a couple of hours with them is to be in the presence of genius at its ripest, most mature moment. We may leave *The Passion of Anna* more dubious than ever about man's fate, but with our faith in the possibilities of screen art—much tested in recent months—miraculously restored.

7/24/70

THIS MAN MUST DIE

Respectable reviews, a few weeks' run in one of New York's less prominent art houses, a scattering of play dates across the country and goodbye with no discernible regrets—that has been the usual sequence for the films of Claude Chabrol, one of the founders of the New Wave, when they have arrived in the United States. Even *La Femme Infidèle*, more enthusiastically greeted by the critics than his previous works, did not significantly alter this depressing pattern, and I must confess that no one has been less enthusiastic than I have about Chabrol—admirable technique in the service of unpleasant themes has been my line. Indeed, I have been so dim about him that I have skipped screening some of his movies out of sheer reluctance to submit to a vision I was convinced I could never appreciate.

Now, however, we have *This Man Must Die*, and it strikes me as a movie of such elegance and profundity that I wish I could see his sixteen previous films over again in its light. Failing that, I hope my response to it proves typical and that others will enjoy the kind of conversion experience I did when they see it. Based on a novel by Nicholas Blake, it at first appears to be one of those routine stories of a man's obsession with revenge—in this case that of a widower (?) whose only child is killed by a hit-and-run driver. As is customary in stories of this kind, he succeeds where the police with all their manpower and technique fail, and I have read one review that, though favorable to the film as a whole, mentions this as a point on which we must will the suspension of disbelief.

Wrong. It is just here that Chabrol's artistry begins to come most forcefully into play. A less sophisticated artist might have been content to point out that a single man devoting all his energies to a single case may very believably do better than the overburdened cops. But Chabrol goes further than that. He makes the search for the killer a paradigm of the creative experience. There is the initial period of frantic and futile effort corresponding to that in which the artist seeks rational solutions to his problems. This has the effect of focusing his attention, shutting out distraction and, paradoxically, opening his mind so that it can respond to chance or "inspiration" when it offers aid. As so often happens, this comes when one has paid one's dues to the project in despair, when one has admitted helplessness and hopelessness.

After that, of course, everything seems to fall smoothly, inevitably into place. The searcher (who is, incidentally, a writer) is led without a hitch to his quarry, and he turns out to be a gratifyingly loutish, brutish fellow. It is quite clear that everyone who knows him would welcome his conveniently accidental demise. And, as if that were not satisfying enough, it develops that a good deal of what has seemed merely obsessive craziness by the avenger is, as he hoped, useful in the creation of false clues to mask a perfect crime. Why, it even looks as if he will be able to marry the girl, the murderer's sister-in-law, who has helped lead him to the desired climax.

But works of art have a way of surprising their creators, chastening their pride by taking on a life of their own that cannot be predicted or controlled. It would be unfair to say precisely what turns this plot insists on taking. Suffice it to say that the murderer is a father, too, and that a complete exchange of roles between him and his pursuer becomes impossible. Neither art nor life is an exercise in geometry.

One should speak of the way Chabrol uses his camera to sign his film with an unforgettable signature (there are two pans around the dead child's empty room that simply tear your heart out); his examination of the murderer's provincial bourgeois family that is near Balzacian; the performances of the whole cast in general and of Michel Duchaussoy as the stricken father in particular—a model of thoughtful control; the coda that lifts the film in one bold, simple stroke from melodrama to tragedy. Above all, it should be stressed that Chabrol has accomplished what many have attempted, the conversion of the murder mystery into a metaphysical mystery, using this popular form to probe at the silences and ambiguities of existence to reveal the nearly invisible strands that bind individual fates together in the web of life.

FIVE EASY PIECES

It is ironic, since the greatness (that word is carefully chosen) of *Five Easy Pieces* is essentially novelistic, that it is so difficult to capture its essence in written words. It is easy enough to say what must be said—that if you see nothing else this year, you must see this film—but to explain and justify that imperative coherently . . . that is a different matter.

Part of the critic's problem is that there are no convenient analogies between director Bob Rafelson's work and other movies. American film has almost no tradition of character study as it is practiced here. In fact, *Five Easy Pieces* (the reference is to piano music for beginners, incidentally) totally reverses our cinematic expectations. Typically, movies place their characters in some sort of emotional or physical peril, some forcing chamber, which compels them to reveal themselves as archetypes—as, secretly, we hoped they would be. Here, however, there is no crisis. It occurred before the movie began. There are only a series of incidents—moments of anger, comedy, nostalgia, passing sadness—that reveal the central character (consummately played by Jack Nicholson, who must now be regarded as one of the few truly gifted movie actors we have) to be neither what we thought he was in the beginning nor to be anything like an archetype. He is entirely an individual, and as such he remains to the end (and beyond it in the speculative reveries the movie inevitably induces) something of an enigma. Which is a way of saying that he refers us, refreshingly, to life—to those friends and loved ones whose behavior we can never quite predict or totally explain—instead of to other movies.

As a rule at this point it is convenient for both reviewer and reader to examine a film's story line, for in most instances the strength of a movie's pulse, even the quality of its character, can indeed be determined by this simple diagnostic procedure. But to say that *Five Easy Pieces* is about an oil-field hand who quits his job and journeys back into his past to visit his numerous family at the oppressive home he once left in an angry, desperate stab at survival through self-definition is to say almost nothing about the quality of the movie. Indeed, it implies a certain familiarity that may lessen your urgency to see the film. I mean, we have all seen *that* one before.

Perhaps it would be helpful to note that the journey is across class lines as well as into his personal history. For going back, Nicholson also moves up—from the beer, broads, bowling, brawling life of the boomers into a tight little world of piano duets, chitchat table talk, pitpat ping-pong games. Rarely is the contrast between two life styles—the one open and thoughtless and violent, the other tight and repressed and tense with intellectual effort—so vividly realized on film, and rarely is the emptiness to be found at the extremes of the low-brow, high-brow scales so poignantly explored.

But that, perhaps, makes the film seem lifelessly schematic, especially when you start numbering the careful oppositions it sets up: between the hot dry climate of the oil fields, the cold wet climate of the family home on an island in Puget Sound; between Rayette, the waitress he lives with in one life, and Catherine, the music student he scores with in the other; between the soul brother he works with on the rigs and the real brother he can scarcely speak to.

No, the life and the genius of the picture lies, as it so often does in fine fiction, in the digressions. Some of them are lengthy—the dialogue with a pair of lesbians Nicholson gives a lift to, one of whom is comically wigged out on cleanliness and ecology; an explosion of temper in a roadside diner where it is impossible to get a side order of toast. Some of them are momentary—a quick glance at his sister's face, puffy and neurotic as if she cried herself to sleep every night; the way his brother shuts a door in his face; the implication that the family derives a false measure of security from meaningless traditions, like *always* serving applesauce with gingerbread. From these, and from a hundred similar details—including the pictures on the walls—Rafelson, screenwriter Adrien Joyce and an exquisitely subtle group of actors create a richness of texture, a complex and ambiguous set of human relationships that will not, I think, ever fade from memory. The film of course ends with Nicholson taking off again into another anonymous, masculine world. But it offers no resolutions. We seem to sense as we leave the theater that these people are still alive somewhere in our world, the prodigal son still seeking the meaning of his life, the rest hiding from the meanings of theirs, all knowing that there are no answers or excuses above ground in the realm of ideas or ideology, where so many movies these days end up, but only in the hidden recesses of their silent hearts.

9/18/70

I was never happy with this review. It didn't seem to me to quite catch the spirit of this film. Now there has been a reaction against the film which is quite dismaying. What I want to stress here is its originality. There is simply no tradition in America for this kind of thing, and the attempt to understand it as a "road" picture betrays the inadequacy of our common critical metaphors. There has never been, to my knowledge, a film about the sort of genteel-artistic family that is portrayed here, never one about the young man whose revolt against the particular form of hypocrisy they embody causes him to deliberately embrace a rough, crude life. Yet one has known these people, known how desperate is the attempt to on the one hand shut out "reality," on the other to embrace it. Yet both attempts are, finally, fantasies. In both cases words—and there are many of them in Five Easy Pieces—are used as a defense against communication, not a means of effecting it. I think the movie is a paradigm of middle-class relationships between fathers and children and one of the few truly mature films in an era where there has been much talk but little evidence of maturity in our films. Quite frankly, the picky attitude of some critics about this movie sickens and infuriates me. What the hell do they want?

JOE

At the center of *Joe* there is a good cringy scene in which, for complicated and excessively melodramatic reasons, a $60,000-a-year ad man and his wife are forced to visit, and pretend to enjoy the company of, the movie's title character and his wife. Joe is a skilled laborer who does something mysterious involving a furnace, and he is afflicted with all the woes of his class that have become so tiresomely familiar in the last couple of years—inflation, fear of the blacks moving in down the block, paranoia about the youth culture, the love-it-or-leave-it syndrome in patriotic feeling.

Well, Mrs. Joe has ordered in Chinese food, which she serves right from the cardboard containers, and there are various dismal attempts to start a dialogue across the class lines—bargains at Macy's, kids, Joe's extensive gun collection. And though everyone tries hard, the evening does not, shall we say, quite come off. Dramatically this is true and right and even a little bit funny in a desperate sort of way. There is something touching about the awkwardness of these four people trying to find a common ground where they can meet in civility.

Moreover, it seems to me that American movies, which began as a kind of theater by and for workingmen in the days of the nickelodeon, have a long-neglected duty to return to their roots and observe what has been going on down there since the industry moved to Hollywood a half-century ago. I mean, it's been a long time since *Joe Smith, American* and *Whistle at*

Eaton Falls, the last pictures I can recall that had anything at all to do with the blue-collar world.

But excepting this sequence, and a few moments in another where Joe and Bill Compton, aforementioned ad man, go on a get-acquainted pub crawl, this film, despite its brave pretenses to gritty honesty, fails its opportunity. And though the producers are very proud of the fact that they did no studio work, the fact remains that the basic sensibility operating here is purely—and often laughably—commercial.

To begin with a small matter, *Joe* is lighted throughout as if it were, in fact, shot in a studio, all harsh and flat, and director John G. Avildsen handles his camera—and his actors—in the quickie style of days long gone. Worse, the script by Norman Wexler scarcely misses an opportunity to sell out his characters and, in the process, any hope he might have harbored that we would consistently believe in them.

He cannot conceive of any way to bring people together across the class lines except violence, so we have Bill killing this really fiendish dope peddler who was ruining his daughter and then, having registered extensive guilt and fear over that act, blabbing about it in a bar, where Joe decides he is (a) a hero of the silent majority and (b) a fellow he would like to blackmail into a pally relationship. It's a pretty thin premise for a movie.

And it gets skinnier. For in due course Bill's daughter once again disappears into the hippie subculture. Whereupon Bill and Joe, looking for her, set aside their cares long enough to participate, with every evidence of amazing self-abandon, in a pot and sex orgy, giving Avildsen a chance to show us some skin and some trippy camera work. Whereupon, quick as a wink, they torture out of one of their bedmates the location of a rural commune and proceed to gun down all the inmates thereof— including, by accident, Bill's daughter. Talk about your emotional roller-coaster rides! Talk about the imbecile inappropriateness of melodramatic imaginations attempting to cope with essentially serious material! Talk about disappointment!

Yeah, disappointment. For there is a certain crude vigor in

this film, some occasional glimmerings of honest sympathy for people driven half mad by incomprehensible social forces and resorting to violence in an attempt to simplify things radically. But it requires a complexity of view, an alertness to nuances of milieu and character, not to mention a rather finely honed ironic sense, to deal satisfactorily with this process. Still, it must be said that these people gave it a try, which is more than most of our fancier movie heads are doing. It may be that one day we can look back on *Joe* as the beginning of a new involvement with the lives of ordinary people, in which case we may forgive its vulgarity and stupidity as we do those of other pioneering works.

8/21/70

Joe was a travesty, of course. Its occasional moments of honesty were clearly accidental. And so was its success, since it happened to feature a hard-hat and was released at just the moment the construction workers were roaming around beating up students and, Heaven forfend, respectably dressed Wall Street junior executives. What was interesting to me was the horrid fascination it turned out to have for some of our more impressionable youth. I ran into a girl who claimed to have seen it a dozen or more times, she having allowed it to become a recurring nightmare. Poor dear, she was as deliciously thrilled by it as she must once have been by some favorite scary fairy tale. I gather that there were literally thousands of such repeaters among her age group. Indeed, one of the things that sets this youth audience apart from all previous ones (and movies have always essentially been the province of youth) is the way they latch on to just a handful of films each year, seeing them over and over again but showing little interest in venturing beyond those few films their peers have determined to be essential in forming the group's sensibility. Joe made it with them as a horror story—the first they ever made into a hit—and like more conventional horror stories, it succeeded not as realism but because it presented a group's worst fears in crudely archetypal form. They were so gripped by it, indeed, that they never seemed to notice—or mind—that just about every frame of this vulgar film stamped it as a crude attempt by the adult enemy to exploit them for commercial gain. But then, they never seem to notice that—as the success of Wild in the Streets or the career of Mick Jagger proves. In any event, I should not have taken quite so tolerant a tone as I did with this particular piece of junk.

THE WILD CHILD

It begins with a miracle of survival: a child left to die in the wilderness when he was two or three years old has somehow endured—mute, naked, unarmed—and when he is discovered by peasants from a nearby village some seven or eight years later, the fact that he is, to all intents and purposes, an animal overshadows his incredible achievement, which is simply that he exists.

It ends with another sort of miracle: clear evidence that love has grown between the boy, who does not know the meaning of the word, and his guardian-teacher, who, more out of scientific curiosity than humanitarianism, has agreed to try to educate him, though he has forgotten, if he ever knew, what it is to love.

Thus François Truffaut's *The Wild Child*, a film of exemplary austerity and endless fascination. The case of this child is a true one, and the dry scholarly notes of Jean Itard, the man who took him into his home, are the basis of Truffaut's story, the very stuff of his voice-over narration and, incidentally, one of the sources of Maria Montessori's educational theories. It is a historical incident (circa 1800) of such primal interest that it's hard to see how one could make a dull film of it. But it would have been possible to make one less finely tuned than Truffaut's, for, as we have reason to know from the many films that have treated the problem of educating the troubled or deficient child, the task is awesomely easy to sentimentalize and otherwise cheapen emotionally. I must also say that, good or bad, I have never been unmoved by one of these pictures. The small victories—the first word spoken, the first letter of the alphabet learned—are just enormously poignant. Similarly the small predictable defeats—the child running away or striking out blindly at the teacher, who is also perforce a tormentor —can be almost unbearable.

All of this is present in *The Wild Child*, but it is, I think, by far the richest film of its kind I have ever seen. First of all, Truffaut refuses to insist upon an emotional response, he invites us to make what we will of his movie and one could regard it almost as an instructional film if one wanted to. He keeps his camera quite distant from his principals and he has a way of cutting off big scenes before they make their way to the top of the emotional scale. The narration, flatly spoken and hurried through as one tends to do with scientific documents, is terribly useful in this regard. But it is even more useful in forming an ironic counterpoint to the deepening relationship we see developing before our eyes, and it takes great courage, control and insight to opt for irony when other modes would have been easier to use and, perhaps (given our expectations), more immediately appealing to us.

But then Truffaut has something more in mind than a Gallic *Miracle Worker*. Itard (whom the director plays, and nicely too) was a product of the Enlightenment. He believed that reason and its corollary, the scientific method, were man's highest achievements, noble and all-powerful tools the employment of which could only result in good. It is a view which, increasingly in our time, is discredited, every evil from the Bomb to the totalitarian state being the product of rationalism or a perversion of rationalism. What Truffaut is doing in his film is taking us back to the days before we lost our innocence about it, when reason could be clearly seen as the greatest of humane forces. Indeed, we see it operating in precisely that way on Itard. He takes in the wild child out of excessive zeal for science, in the hope of examining a noble savage of the sort so treasured by the *philosophes;* but intellectual curiosity leads him—as it should anyone—to an awakening of care, tenderness and concern for a fellow creature.

History tells us that "Victor," as Itard named his charge, was never able to function as a normal adult in civilized society, and several critics have faulted Truffaut for not making this point clear. They have implied that Itard's meddling destroyed Victor's ability to survive in the wild without granting him a compensatory ability to survive among men. But that is fatuous. Very likely he would have died eventually in the wilderness and he would have done so in silence, never having known the touch of a hand reaching out for him in love and never having contributed, however unconsciously, to the processes by which society struggles to civilize itself.

We know from *The 400 Blows* that Truffaut himself was a twentieth-century wild child. We know from him that he had his own Itard—the great critic André Bazin. We therefore may assume that he believes the important thing about Itard was not whether he failed or succeeded but that he tried. That is the only imperative of a movie that some have found cold, but which I find to be the great director's most personal and moving work since *The 400 Blows* and, by any standards, an ornament to the humane tradition in film art.

10/16/70

LITTLE FAUSS AND
BIG HALSY

It's customary to praise movies because they achieve a certain breadth and depth of vision, but *Little Fauss and Big Halsy* is good precisely because it is artfully thin and shallow, as determinedly lacking in the graces and amenities as the lives it examines. The title characters (played respectively by Michael J. Pollard and Robert Redford) are motorcycle racers of surpassing, if comical, incompetence, but the picture that director Sidney J. Furie drives pell-mell down a straightaway plot line is not a wheeler, for that genre is based on romanticizing primitive and violent losers, and there is scarcely a romantic note in this film. Indeed, the beginning of its appeal lies in the unblinking eye it casts upon the world of small-time racing, endurance runs and hill climbs. You always feel as if you're about to choke on the dust, the greasy hamburgers, the stench of small ambitions incessantly squelched.

But there is more to the film than a hard-edged portrayal of a curious demimonde. It is, thanks to Charles Eastman's good gritty script, a study of two quintessentially American characters, demonstrating the contrasting, near-archetypal ways we have of achieving an almost total lack of distinction. Fauss is a "tuner" (mechanic) who aspires to being a racer but lacks the capacity to assert himself competitively because he is a totally unformed human being—shy, inarticulate, childlike, dominated by parents who are cheerful morons. Halsy, on the other hand, is a "go-faster" in his own words, but he is also a petty thief, con man, liar (he offers at least five equally unconvincing explanations of how he acquired the picturesque scar that runs the length of his back) and congenital screw-up—perpetually losing races he might well have won had he only checked his temper or his bike's motor.

Together they add up to one more or less complete and functioning human being. The trouble is that they can't really stand each other, especially after a girl named Rita Nebraska joins their little caravan. We are never told why she was running around the starting line of a race stark naked or why she was on drugs or why now she's decided to go off them. All we know is that she is of a class or two above our heroes and a provoker of trouble between them, mostly because neither can find an adequate way of expressing love for her. It's Halsy, of course, who nearly wins her and then (also of course) loses her, just as it is he who, almost willfully, contrives to lose Little Fauss—not once but twice. That's the trouble with being a go-faster—a living parody of the success ethic, not to mention the old pioneer creed of avoiding roots, human entanglements.

For most of its length the movie never by word, deed or gesture suggests so bald a statement of its meaning, and only once does it slip and attempt to cop a plea for these goofs. That occurs at the very last moment, and I think it's worth mentioning as a minor mistake. Farrar Straus and Giroux has had the good taste to publish Eastman's beautifully written script and in it, in the last big race, he imagines Fauss and Halsy "lost in the crowd, for they are not winners but rather among those who make no significant mark and leave no permanent trace." The movie as shown, however, has Fauss emerging from the crowd, a winner at last, and the change seems dictated partly by the desire to have a character "develop" in the conventional sense, partly by the commercial need to give the kid audience some "soul" to identify with. I think it takes some of the sharp clean edge off the movie, and I'm sorry they did it.

Even so, it's a fine, tough, funny movie, distinguished by

Furie's extraordinary feel for empty spaces and the empty people that inhabit them, by strong acting (especially, in my prejudiced view, by Redford, who never succumbs to the star's temptation, which is to subtly dissociate himself from the character when asked to play a crud), most of all by the success with which it makes an unfamiliar milieu familiar—at least in part—by suggesting that wherever you find it the national obsession with winning and losing is never more elevated or elevating than its most absurd reduction, which just may be a bike race in the boondocks. We're all down there in the dust with Fauss and Halsy, and pretty damn foolish we look.

11/20/70

GIMME SHELTER

Ah, yes. The Counter Culture. Consciousness Three. The Greening of America. The Woodstock Nation. All that good stuff.

Of course, there's a dark side to it, symbolized by the inconvenient free concert at the Altamont Speedway near San Francisco a little over a year ago. It was arranged by Mick Jagger and the Rolling Stones as an attempt to have a little piece of the Woodstock action they could call their own, as a climax for their American tour and as something for the Maysles brothers to include in the documentary they were doing on the Stones' trip—with, one imagines, proceeds from film helping defray cost of concert, since even philosopher-kings like Jagger don't work for nothing, whatever their faithful followers like to think. In short, Altamont was one of those non-events that are so much a feature of the youth culture. But even non-events have a way of getting out of hand these days. Somebody—not Jagger, he now claims—hired the Hell's Angels to police Altamont, there was steadily mounting tension between them and the audience, and by the end of the concert four people were dead.

A real downer, perhaps the beginning of the depression that has since settled over the pop scene. And now we have *Gimme Shelter,* the movie that was at least part of the force motivating Altamont (although it never comes right out and says so). It includes sequences of Jagger and friends viewing footage exposed at the concert—making it perhaps the first actuality film that attempts to show its principals responding to the record of their own behavior in action, in crisis.

It is terribly interesting. For Jagger in particular appears to be nearly affectless, clinically a sign of profound alienation from self, work, world. Over his weak, unformed, almost premoral features almost no expression plays, and he makes no comment—except to ask for a rerun when the film makers show him the one killing they happened to catch. When he is satisfied that he has seen everything they have on that little matter, he simply gets up and leaves the screening session, bringing it—and the movie—to an end.

He could, of course, have refused to permit release of the film, but before we credit him with being a champion of free filmic expression I think we must at least consider the possibility that by permitting us to see him in so unflattering a light he is restating his alienation in yet another way. I think he is declaring that his hold on his cult is so powerful that it will accept anything he does or says and that the good opinion of the larger, more respectable audience is of no consequence to him. This is, of course, a heady and radical freedom for any performer to savor. And a terrible one.

For he has cast himself in a role not unlike that played in literature by Jean Genet, that of the outlaw saint. He makes no concessions to anyone. His music never charms, it only overwhelms. His personal style is deliberately unappetizing by conventional standards. And so to the undiscriminating he becomes something more than the most interesting musical figure to emerge from the pop ferment, something more than a phenomenon on the order of Presley or the Beatles. He becomes an existential hero.

He is at least dimly aware of this new and potentially dangerous factor in his celebrity. But, needless to say, he lacks the intelligence—social, philosophical, moral—to deal with it. He also—thank God—lacks the forcefulness of personality to really mobilize his followers in support of anything except adoration of Mick Jagger, as his rather pathetic attempts to control the crowd at Altamont demonstrate. And so, finally, he appears sometimes to be just another scared boy riding a tiger and hanging on for dear life, rather happy, it seemed, behind his wall of Hell's Angels, free as a result of their presence from all those feverishly clutching adolescent female hands. Finally, one imagines, he will withdraw physically, as he already has psychologically, from his public—just as the character he played in *Performance* did. Meantime, Jagger, the mess at Altamont and the movie about them are powerful reminders that the counter culture is, in large measure, the Hydra-headed creature of media manipulators and therefore part of the problem of corruption, not of its solution.

Indeed, the most comforting thing about *Gimme Shelter* is that we can see it. If the people behind it were at all serious about, let's say, creating a basis for political action out of Consciousness Three, they would have locked it in a vault. As it turns out, though, they will expose their outlaw saint as a sad little cretin merely to protect their modest investment in a piece of film.

1/29/71

I had intended the review of Gimme Shelter *to stand on its own as the conclusion to this book. The film itself seems to me a kind of culmination to this period in film making and maybe a portent of what is to come. Surely Jagger is the ultimate anti-hero for those of us who cannot see him as an outlaw saint. Surely this film, which admittedly has a kind of horrid fascination, is the ultimate "youth" film, the one in which most of the dangers and contradictions of a "youth" culture—most especially the fundamental one, in which the youths acquiesce in their own exploitation for commercial purposes—are exposed to plain sight. There is not a great deal to add on those matters* and, as a summary of my response to the film itself, I am content with the piece (which along with my review of Jagger's Performance and one of John Wayne's, The Green Berets, drew more crazy and sickening mail than any of my columns).

There is, however, one point to add, a point which began to impress itself upon me long before I saw Gimme Shelter and which has grown more and more significant in my thinking about movies ever since. It is this: the percentage of movies that are merely made, that are not thought out in all their implications and are not really felt or meant at all, keeps growing all the time. So many of our younger actors are, like Jagger, inhumanly cool—not to say stone(d) cold; so many of our films have about them an air of computerized calculation; so many are made without thought as to the cumulative social effect of dozens upon dozens of movies (and other cultural objects) that give us no decent guide to human behavior, no heroes worth talking about. One is not asking for empty cheerfulness or escape —there is plenty of that still available in popular culture, especially on television.

But what we do have a right to, if nothing else, is a sense of irony which is born of a profound knowledge of the world and of what one is doing in it, an awareness deeper than an awareness of what is, at the moment, selling. Beyond that, is it asking too much to expect with some frequency movies that go beyond the mere portrayal of the unquestionably ugly surface of our existence and illuminate it with a tragic sense of life? Buñuel does it in his way, Bergman in his, but it is hard to think of an American or an English director who consistently does it. In freeing film makers from the constraints of the studio system, the implicit hope was that this would begin to happen. But by and large it seems to me it has not. Our directors are free to show anything and everything—except, it would seem, their own deepest feelings about their material. Maybe these feelings do not exist; maybe the majority of directors are merely objective technicians; maybe the audience cannot stand movies that go beyond reportage of reality's surface, or emotions that

cut deeper than voyeuristic titillation. But, really, we must try—
if only to find out how badly off we are. As things now stand,
irony of ironies, the studio films of the thirties and forties come
in retrospect to look better and better to me. They may have
been full of romantic and idealistic bullshit, but one sees now
that the people who made these films (though not always the
men in the front offices) believed in this bullshit in approxi-
mately the same degree that their audience did. That is to say,
we shared with them certain unquestioned assumptions about
the nature of reality and, more significant, the potential of the
individual and of our institutions. This sharing energized their
films and our interest in them. Now, however, the most common response to American films is alienation; the most common
feeling about the people who make them is that they are profoundly different from the rest of us in the subjects that interest
them, in their aesthetics, in their political and social morality.
As a result, as I write this, production in this country is at a
virtual standstill, partly because of inflationary production costs,
but largely because of a failure of nerve. The people who make
movies now know so little about their dwindling audience that
they can't begin to guess what might interest—let alone move—
them. And the audience has lost confidence in the medium.
They really feel that the chances are they will be affronted or
bilked or otherwise set upon when they venture forth to a
movie. And they are right. The pictures, nowadays, that tend to
uphold the traditional humane values, that are likely to contain
recognizable human figures dealing with recognizable human
problems, are likely to eminate from abroad and, as noted at the
outset, are unlikely to be seen very widely here.

So we deal with this paradox: when Hollywood ceased to be a
factory town, as its artists gained greater freedom of speech, it
somehow lost the ability to consistently speak to us in a tongue
we can readily recognize as our own. It should have been otherwise. All our critical theories, all our conventional wisdom about
what was wrong out there all those years, indicated that this
should have been a golden age of film, not a period of decay that

looks mighty like terminal illness. It may just be a transitional phase that's taking an unconscionable time to pass, but as I look back over these notes, these hasty jottings in the dark, that represent five years of professional moviegoing, I'm inclined to borrow the most famous line from Easy Rider: "We blew it." And to add only this: that the judgment is not irrevocable; that there are, at least, a few good men still on the field, still trying to realize the promise that is implicit in the new artistic freedom of the American screen, quite explicit in the example of the personal films from abroad.

INDEX

341